D0929796

"Rooted Sorrow"

"Rooted Sorrow"

Dying in Early Modern England

Bettie Anne Doebler

Rutherford ● Madison ● Teaneck
Fairleigh Dickinson University Press
London and Toronto: Associated University Presses

© 1994 by Associated University Presses, Inc.

Associated University Presses
440 Forsgate Drive
Cranbury, NJ 08512

Associated University Presses
25 Sicilian Avenue
London WC1A 2QH, England

Associated University Presses
P.O. Box 338, Port Credit
Mississauga, Ontario
Canada L5G 4L8

The paper used in this publication meets the requirements of the American National Standard for Permanence of Paper for Printed Library Materials Z39.48-1984.

Library of Congress Cataloging-in-Publication Data

Doebler, Bettie Anne.
    Rooted sorrow : dying in early modern England / Bettie Anne Doebler.
        p. cm.
    Includes bibliographical references and index.
    ISBN 0-8386-3543-1 (alk. paper)
    1. English literature—Early modern, 1500–1700—History and criticism.   2. Death in literature.   3. Literature and society—England—History—17th century.   4. Death—Social aspects—England—History—17th century.   I. Title.
PR438.D44D63   1994
820.9'354—dc20

94-2935
CIP

To John and Mark,
for whom
I pursue the *artes vivendi*

Contents

List of Illustrations

Preface

Although it focuses upon themes of death, despair, and comfort in seventeenth-century literature, this book by necessity probes the interaction of culture and literature to sound the roots and variations of human thought and feeling upon such issues. The experience of death by seventeenth-century people (expressed by artists, thinkers, preachers, and literary characters) is the central focus of the study. To get at the variations played upon the theme, I approach the dying through an examination of the dynamic interaction of image, event, and word. I complicate that approach by speculating on the responses of audiences and readers. Inevitably there is a tradition here to be uncovered, but after nearly four hundred years, the many uses and modulations of that tradition are very much part of the expressive richness of seventeenth-century literature and thought. They require therefore an imaginative reconstruction of time and place as well as of literary intertextuality.

After trying to describe some of the major images that focus the tradition, I discuss the death of Essex at the hands of the state—a particular set of conventions on dying by execution of a particular person in a particular relationship with Elizabeth at the dying fall of her reign. I end the study with the lamentation of another Elizabeth, poetically rendered by a seeker of her patronage after the death of her eldest son. The book, framed in time and history, focuses on one level upon event and immediate reality. Both beginning and end argue the importance of social and historical context to theological, literary, and philosophic convention. There is, after all, no fixed human nature or response, in spite of continuing efforts to expose a common set of human responses. The anthropologists are right: culture shapes and completes with distinctions among peoples that become the focus of our greatest interest. I explore the third element of the "word" in a chapter on the popular devotional tradition. Within that chapter the art of dying is examined as it finds verbal expression in its most explicit forms.

The second section of the book deals with the temptation to despair within the tradition of preparation for death and primarily in terms of a frame of attitudes from Spenser and Milton and their

11

more mimetic expression in Shakespeare. According to this analysis of attitudes, the drama becomes a major cultural mode for integrating the image, event, and word of the prismatic approach that characterizes the period. Drama in some sense provides a bridge between the high art of the epic and more popular literary forms of devotion.

The third section, which focuses on a poetics of comfort, contains a long chapter on Donne, perhaps the best human example in the period of one who explicitly and artistically made death the center of his work, both in poetry and in the great body of his sermons. In Donne's work the man becomes a case study of the interaction among poetic image, life, and word in bringing together a poetics of comfort for seventeenth-century English people. The articulation of a life—the articulation of a process by which people came to a faith in the relationship between life and death—is embedded in the rich expressive forms of Donne's work. And yet the book ends with a section on lament, lest the comfort be understood as too simply reconciling. Milton, after all, thirty years later must still write his epic justification of the ways of God; and ordinary human beings must make a long day's journey through lament and grief to comfort.

Such a book as this is about the multiple expressions of death as a rite of passage and what that rite meant to the minds of many in seventeenth-century England from about 1590 to 1631. I do not mean to reduce that mind to a single pattern. Obviously, it takes many forms in the several social classes and the many sensibilities of the age. The ambivalences and ambiguities of drama make that point aptly. However, from the accumulation of expression brought together in this study, one can journey back into a time in which discourse concerning death was imaginative and varied, a time when exceptional flexibility and creativity of expressive language produced forms that contain mysterious fears and hopes for the assertion of a meaningful life.

In the completion of this work, my debts are many. They originate in my research under Allan H. Gilbert, Ruth Wallerstein, and Helen C. White, pioneers in seventeenth-century scholarship. In more recent years, Madeleine Doran gave me some badly needed encouragement for the project. I owe the most to librarians at the Huntington Library, who made their treasured materials accessible and available to a summer scholar. I am also grateful to Arizona State University for several faculty grants over the past ten years. To the Warburg Library, especially Joseph Trapp and Jennifer Montague, to the Bodleian Library, especially Julian Roberts, and to the

British Library, with its unnamed numerous helpers, I also extend much gratitude as well as to librarians at the Folger who started me in rare materials many years ago. My largest scholarly debts are owed to Phoebe Spinrad for a thorough critical reading of the manuscript, to my friend and colleague Elizabeth McCutcheon for her encouragement in difficult times for many years, and to my friend and colleague in history Retha Warnicke for particular help in historical research. I am especially grateful to Kathryn Harris for a stylistic reading of the manuscript. Needless to say, no one is responsible for the points at which I have stumbled. I am also grateful to several scholars in the field who read portions of the manuscript published elsewhere: particularly John Velz and Charles Forker, whose encouragement of my writing helped me to carry through on such a long-range and complex task. To Leah Marcus, I should like to express thanks for careful analysis of the Lamentations Chapter in another context. I am also grateful to Stephen J. Greenblatt for early bibliographical suggestions concerning the general project. The list could and perhaps should go on, certainly to include works published on death in recent years, but I shall mention only the Ariès encyclopedic survey as the most supportive of an idea I have long held: the way a culture faces death is at the core of its creativity and expression.

The people around me who have given me the most support are Laurence Cohen, a valued graduate student and research assistant, and of course my dear family: John, Mark, and my now-deceased mother, Ann. I thank as well my good friend and retired secretary Ruth Bardrick, who typed many versions of portions and the whole. To my present secretary Ann Evans I offer thanks for the many tasks she has performed in getting the manuscript ready for publication. And I owe much to James Dybdahl, who prepared the final version with care and expertise.

Acknowledgments

I am grateful to the publishers of *English Literary History, The George Herbert Journal, Hamlet Studies, Shakespeare Studies,* and *Texas Studies in Literature and Language: A Journal of the Humanities* for permission to reproduce material from the following published essays:

"Othello's Angels: The *Ars Moriendi*," *ELH: A Journal of English Literary History* 34, no. 2 (June 1967): 156–72;

"Magdalen Herbert Danvers and Donne's Vision of Comfort," *George Herbert Journal,* Memorial Volume for Amy Charles, 10, no. 1: 5–22. Co-authored with Retha M. Warnicke;

"*Hamlet:* A Grave Scene and Its Audience," *Hamlet Studies* 3, no. 2 (Winter 1981): 68–82;

"'Dispaire and Dye': The Ultimate Temptation of Richard III," *Shakespeare Studies* 7 (1974): 75–85;

"'Rooted Sorrow': Verbal and Visual Survivals of an *Ars* Commonplace (1590–1620)," *Texas Studies in Literature and Language: A Journal of the Humanities* 22, no. 3 (Fall 1980): 358–68.

"Inspiration against Despair." No. 4 in the *Ars moriendi*. Augsburg, 1465. Permission to reprint is from the Board of the Henry E. Huntington Library.

Introduction

Cultural Poetics: Notes on an Approach to Seventeenth-Century Literature

Yet your own Face at you shall grin,
Through the Black-bag of your skin. . . .

—Andrew Marvell

Prologue

This is a study of the ancient experience of summing up a life at its end, the personal last judgment of one's existence as culturally expressed and ritualized by English people of the early seventeenth century. The temptation to despair in the face of death and the comforts that counter it are expressed in a broad spectrum of human and literary response. The Renaissance documents on which the book is based do not speak, at least initially, to the general question of the value of life itself, although to some extent, all serious literature considers such a question—indeed forces such a consideration. *King Lear, Othello,* and numerous other works spring immediately to mind. But in an interpretation of those major tragedies, the immediate *focus* of the essays is on the literary experience of the central characters of Shakespeare's plays as they near death. Inevitably, literary texts are privileged by a literary scholar as shaping culture, but perhaps equally, the literary works are aptly regarded as instructive documents of cultural study and, indeed, are surrounded in this study by other texts and artifacts.

In the popular devotional and meditative materials of the latter sixteenth and first decades of the seventeenth centuries, the emphasis is much more limited and explicit; the instruction on dying well has to do with the most excruciatingly lonely experience of a lifetime—the moment of judgment when the quality of a life is weighed. The essay on Spenser and Milton is primarily limited to the theme of despair within the epic mode, the theme of despair as an allegori-

17

cal frame. Only the Donne essay and the essay on lamentation, with their typically personal contexts, probe fully the question of the value of life in the face of death viewed within the context of culturally accepted comfort.

If the weighing at the end were the total experience with which the book were concerned, I should probably be writing quite simply and literally about the temptation to despair. The testimony of Renaissance persons from More through Donne asserts that almost no one in the Renaissance summed up his life without an experience of shattering disquiet. This agonizing need for heroic faith has been condensed for the modern sensibility in Gerard Manley Hopkins's "Carrion-Comfort":

> No, I'll not carrion comfort, Despair,
> not feast on thee;
> Not untwist—slack they may be—
> these last strands of man
> In me or, most weary, cry, I can
> no more. I can;
> Can something, hope, wish day come,
> not choose not to be.

The "wisest ones" of Renaissance culture, as well as most English people of the period, recognized on their deathbed that they had not lived according to the Mosaic law. But the bulk of the psychomachia—in this shape primarily the tragicomedy of the battle between virtue and vice in the old *ars moriendi* tradition—reflects the interaction in Renaissance experience between the demonic forces of sin, through which one is tempted to relegate one's mistakes and oneself to eternal damnation, and the stronger forces, deeply embedded in that time and place, by means of which the *moriens* may see hope in the functioning of the guardian angel. For persons of that time, the dominance of hope was rooted in the redemptive power of a God that made up the difference between act and desire and reached out to take souls up into heavenly glory. For people in early modern England, the understanding of reality included the mysterious power of divine meaning.

Having put the matter in such large symbolic terms, I must emphasize that this is not a book about the mingling of hope and despair, or despair and comfort in the face of mortality for all times and all persons. There is in it, indeed, a universal dimension. But it is primarily a cultural study of a particular dynamic of hope and despair in English life as it related to the art of dying around the end of the sixteenth century and extended through the first three decades of the seventeenth century. It is of a particular time and place and comes out of a symbolic sensibility that responds deeply to drama and poetry, as well as to sermons and devotional treatises. Shakespeare's audience will be one of the specific communities the essay will look to; other seventeenth-century audiences include those present at Essex's execution, intelligent readers of poetry, readers within the devotional tradition, (more broadly) the various congregations of St. Paul's when Dr. Donne was Dean, and the small provincial congregation who heard (as well as read) the funeral sermon for Lady Clifton.

One might say that the book is a selective study of attitudes and associations of largely educated Londoners of that period in relation to death, and, even more narrowly, of the sort of literate, middle-and-upper-class Londoners who made up the bulk of Shakespeare's audience during that time. Among the plays considered, *Richard III* is earliest, produced in the nineties, partly for contrast to later, less formally allegorical materials; and the devotional literature stretches in appeal further down the English class structure. The major tragedies lie within the period from 1600 to 1610 and reflect (as well as shape, I believe) the attitudes of Londoners of the day toward dying. The study takes a risky leap into the imaginations (there were more than one) of another time, another place, in order to probe these mysterious and difficult issues.

It seems necessary to remind twentieth-century readers that this analysis of values depends upon a complex reading of a symbolic system at the root of the culture: what some critics label the "root metaphor," in this instance, an enormously influential version (or versions) of Christianity mingled with classical influences, mostly Roman, flowing into the culture through the European Renaissance. Such a statement may seem obvious as it applies to the literal symbols of the *ars moriendi* tradition, which come after all from the latter half of the fifteenth century. The *ars moriendi* tradition is an appropriate context for the orthodox Christian or the late medieval church before the turbulence of the Reformation. Even as late as the first half of the seventeenth century, when more secular texts were being privileged, my reading suggests that religious attitudes toward death remained conservative. Perhaps the comforts were even more intensely clung to in a period when the metaphysical roots of Christianity were being undermined by radical conflicts in institutional authority as well as by major changes in political and economic structures.

As to the personal and individual evaluation of a life, several assumptions about the nature of culture, human beings, and history come into play. Cultural anthropologist Clifford Geertz suggests that human beings are creatures completed—in part created—by their languages and their cultures. As a scholar of language and poetics, I must agree. In reading English literature of the early modern era, one must take into account as well the belief of Elizabethans that there is in them a *soul,* an individually created being—what the Hebrews, with their deeper understanding of the physiological relationships between body and mind, called *spirit.* Spirit implies some unique aptitude or ability to transcend body, time, place, culture under the impetus of a *created* or given aspect of human experience. When a belief in transcendence and transformation is alive in the culture, its conventions have virtually a life and power of their own.

This study assumes a dynamic interaction between the symbolic systems of a culture and its values and the unique qualities of the individual human imagination. Necessarily, the symbols of the culture are part of the imaginative life, conscious and unconscious, of both artists and audiences. The large shapes of the system appear in the language of Shakespeare's plays, the popular sources of devotional literature, religious art, cultural artifact, and in the theological allegories of Spenser that take a somewhat different shape in Milton but reflect many of the same attitudes. Such interactions create nuance and implication that made the experience of Shakespeare's genius fullest within the context of his own period—indeed, all the literature of the English Renaissance more richly understood within the dynamic intertextuality of its time.

Sometimes I wish I could really believe in the doctrine of the unchanging human heart. It would be simpler to read literature as universals than to exercise the complex judgments of history. Obviously, however, it is necessary and stimulating to recognize differences in time and place, even in the interaction between spirit and culture. Furthermore, for those who love history the differences made by place and circumstances as life unfolds under time are often the most interesting aspects of the study of humankind. Being able to see them feelingly as well as thoughtfully frees us from the prison of our own cultural perspective. The dichotomy of time's double function seen by the Renaissance both as destroyer and revealer of truth works for moderns as well as for Renaissance minds.

Against these large assumptions, this book is organized in three major sections. Part One deals with the audience/or readers of the period and their cultural associations with the *ars moriendi,* particularly the temptation to despair. The three chapters of Part One explore kinds of texts that fed into the commonplace associations of the English person of the early seventeenth century with the preparation for dying: visual images, historic events, and symbolic constructs, and the verbal tradition of popular devotion—all of which derive from a rich and continuous tradition of the art of dying well.

Interactive with the general attitudes of a culture are its major symbols and their most sophisticated verbal contexts. In Part Two, the material on despair in Spenser and Milton is intended to set up a perspective on theological allegories of the artistic imagination. It will function as a kind of frame for the popular associations surrounding drama in the first decade of the century. It is in the interstices between such symbolic metaphor and present experience that Shakespeare's audiences would have built reactions to specific plays and situations. In relation to the despair theme within the *ars moriendi,* the large allegorical types of Spenser and Milton and the more commonplace symbols from the popular tradition may be studied along a spectrum of responses to death. I have abstracted the particular passages from the epics as a kind of allegorical antidote to the more prosaic and looser treatment of the cultural context in the popular religious tradition. As we focus the light of scholarship upon the past, it is important to the sharpness of the image to assess within it a network of interactions that include both popular culture and high art.

Following the materials on the English epic are chapters that explore the use of the *ars moriendi* in scenes from several of Shakespeare's plays: *Richard III, Othello, King Lear,* and *Macbeth.* This section tries to assess the interaction between dramatic form—act, gesture, and language—and cultural associations of Shakespeare's audiences in relation to the overall theme. Here, again, the fundamental assumption is that the closer we come to both an empathetic and an intellectual point of view that reconstructs the culture of another time and place, the richer the experience that explores meanings of the works in art from that period.

At the same time, I am focusing primarily in this discussion not on the intellectual context as background but upon the dynamic difference culture makes to our understanding of specific scenes in Shakespeare. Although I am interweaving popular texts and images as a lively part of the associations of contemporary audiences, I am also trying to project the experience as it would have been articulated within the particular dramatic text. Inevitably, some repetition of ideas from Part I occurs, but I am hoping that the repetition will play against the context already explored to bring the modern reader into a fuller imaginative appreciation of literature as present to attitudes of the period.

What is intended to dominate the present reader's consciousness is Shakespeare's scene, illuminated and shaped by the set of ideas and values—perhaps commonplace but also more—by which a seventeenth-century audience organized its experiences of the relationships between life and death, time and eternity, the means of judging the worth of a soul, the fashioning of the true self. There is a circular movement to what the book is trying to do. As it brings cultural understanding to bear upon the literary experience, the literary text interacts with the other symbol systems of the culture and itself provides insights into cultural ideas and values. We learn, for instance, how Shakespeare projects Gloucester's temptation to despair in the Dover scene. At the same time we learn through the audience's experience of Edgar how people of another age were moved into a fuller sense of their own identity through recognition of the redemptive power of sacrificial love. Paradoxically, the unfolding of the dramatic narrative takes us inward into experience and outward into understanding.

In the third section the book moves into a discussion of comfort that includes an initial exploration of the psychology of mourning in the period. Although the drama focuses primarily on preparation for death, other expressive forms like the sermon or the devotional text concern themselves more explicitly with the comfort of the survivor. It is here in many instances that despair over the power of death finds, if not an answer, signs and strategies that restore hope.

Theory

When I articulate my own method of literary criticism as a student of seventeenth-century literature or, more specifically, as a literary historian, I am increasingly uneasy. If at one time art historian Svetlana Alpers squirmed when asked to corroborate stylistic norms for her field, I am even more unsure about norms for literature.[1] Categories of a general aesthetic, the right questions to ask, problems of intention—I remain consistently muddled about my aesthetic position on most of these issues. I cannot avoid the idea, furthermore, that a too consistent and elaborate theory imposes itself on the literary work and even the culture itself. Consequently, I cling to a general procedure instead: with characteristic English pragmatism, I start with the work of literature and read back and forth among surrounding texts, trying to establish an understanding of the work of art as embedded in its culture.

The clearest perspective that I can claim is my own peculiar brand of historical objectivism (or so my colleague who is an aesthetician assures me is the label); it is in some ways a misnomer, particularly as it asserts objectivity. Moderns cannot assert such a thing as objectivity within the current explosion of multiple interpretation, and so I grope for another term: one that designates the interaction between aesthetic analysis and historical scholarship. Such a process necessarily goes between the horns of subjectivism and objectivism. Obviously, my desire to assert such a position rests upon several assumptions, which have been largely hidden until challenged by published essays that might be included under the umbrella of the New Historicism.

Like many literary historians and like Northrop Frye a number of years ago, I have long ago rejected the basically Coleridgean notion of each poem as its own separate world. The current brand of poststructural criticism shares some of my assumptions. Among them is the assumption that semiotics brings us closer to culture than structuralism, certainly than *zeitgeist* or Coleridge, but modern practice remains either so chillingly abstract or so oblivious to the disjuncture between modern and Renaissance ideas that historical scholars often turn away. The "New History" perhaps leans too close to Marxism and modern sociological ideas to work well with the religious perspective of most of my writers. On the other hand, restatements of the old humanistic perspective often seem dull and cliché. The study of culture as a web of symbols is increasingly central to critical theory as notions of a fundamental human nature separate from culture and prior to it retreat tantalizingly into the past. Fortunately, we cannot get back to Swift's Yahoos, and human Houhynhmns seem more and more unlikely. One of my fundamental assumptions is that the meaning of English Renaissance art unfolds in an elaborate context of the rhetoric and society that gave it birth—not as a stylistic pattern of abstraction but in the dynamic interaction of political, social, economic, artistic, and intellectual conventions.

Recent anthropological studies, both from such distinguished scholars as the cultural anthropologist Clifford Geertz and the historian of religions Jonathan Z. Smith, remind us of the fundamental ways in which culture completes human nature.[2] Much earlier, Aristotle recognized this doubleness in human nature. Men and women both create their symbols and are themselves created by them. Artistic convention, then, both reflects and shapes other symbols in the culture. By convention, I mean historically defined metaphor and symbol—the language both expressive and revelatory of the power of belief. We find it both in popular forms and in the language of high art. In contrast to the New Critics, historical scholars have argued that language, though it reaches into the transcendent, is fundamentally historical and must be described within a historical context. This is so even when it forms an aesthetic construct that in some measure erects a barrier separating it from other "texts" in society.

My second assumption is that one approaches the historical context most fully (it is never possible to transport oneself wholly into another perspective) by a cultivation of empathy or what I prefer to think of as the historic imagination. That is to say, I consciously avoid trying to see into Shakespeare, Donne, or Milton through current twentieth-century ideological perspectives. Much as I may be concerned about the oppressed working woman of seventeenth-century England, I do not set out to examine how she may be stereotyped in Milton's Eve as gardener. Obviously, the examination of one's critical language may reveal unconscious modern biases, but it seems wise to avoid much modern diction or ideological categories when one approaches questions of Renaissance authority. Not that Shakespeare swallows the authoritative party line whole— careful readers have always seen that he does not. Only recently I caught myself alluding to *objectivity* in an effort to define the Renaissance attempt to portray essences in painting or poetry. Yet scholars are aware that the subject-object split is a post-Cartesian effect that peculiarly polarizes perennial classical and romantic impulses into unmanageable opposites of rationalism and subjectivism. English folk between 1590 and 1630 simply did not approach reality this way—even if we grant the beginnings of self-consciousness and role-playing that both Joan Webber and Stephen Greenblatt have described.[3]

A clear split between subject and object was not deeply felt or elaborately described by contemporary Renaissance persons. One reason for the continued feelings of wholeness or integration of experience among people in early modern England lies in the still vital religious sensibility, the continuity provided by the doctrine and experience of correspondence, the implications of acceptance of the old microcosm-macrocosm relationship that bound together the world of inner and outer. Sometimes I think that the power of paradox was what held it all together. More important for my argument here was the integration of ritual into drama and life, which encouraged the internalizing of external symbolic structures, especially at

points of passage, both for the individual and the culture, as Bevington has noted.[4] "I am flat map," says Donne, implying the microcosm, giving a metaphysical correlative to the correspondence.

In an effort to bring alive a whole milieu, I try to avoid most modern categories and language. However imperfectly, I am nevertheless trying to locate the nodal points (rituals, words, images, events,
and phrases) through which I can experience Elizabethan and Jacobean culture as if from the inside. Like C. S. Lewis, I want to think
and feel (and help the reader to share that feeling) as reasonably
educated readers or members (they were not all the same) of the
audience from the period felt, and I use not only empirical research
but also my imagination to do so. I might claim for myself a new
literary historicism such as that practiced by Dollimore and Goldberg, but I should have to qualify the label.[5] At the same time, I
should insist with my new historical colleagues that history is essential, that literature cannot be separated into an aesthetic world apart
from the dynamics of culture and power without flattening out its
rich implications and ambiguities.

Behind this exercise are both reading and intuition. I pore over
the primary texts, and I catch glimpses of the contexts, that is to
say, a network of relationships mirrored within the culture: as
Culler would say, *patterns* of structure and meaning; or from a more
fluid point of view, significant patterns such as relationships and
events emerge. In turn, then, I sketch contextual relationships between these internal verbal structures and other texts of the culture,
in a method that some of the new-new critics label *intertextuality*.
In a seminar on culture, Jonathan Z. Smith, historian of religions at
the University of Chicago, suggested that scholars are all on a
search for the significant *i.e.'s,* the few resonating symbols that provide the illuminating illustration of major cultural values.

In my study of the *ars moriendi* and its survival in the seventeenth
century, I keep coming back to the literary texts, the central symbolic structures, trying not to violate their internal integrity as
works of art even as I accept some of the possibilities of deconstruction, seeing them broken apart to extend within the network of their
culture. For example, my analysis of the patterns—explicit and submerged—of the temptation to despair in Shakespeare and other authors of the period must confront the internal dramatic structure
as dynamically related to devotional texts. The full text includes
interpretations that honor both the metaphorical structure of the
work and the implications for community audience, reader, or
viewer. I therefore also move outward from the work of art into the
culture and its values.

Because I aim in these essays to employ methods of historical criticism primarily with a focus on literature between 1590 and 1630 (with Milton a late summarizing exception), the study must also show familiarity with texts other than literary that probe shaping values of the period. Such values in the English verbal Renaissance are necessarily related to the major root metaphor that scholars have long recognized to be Christianity. In this instance, Christianity is further complicated by its lively conflation with particular attitudes: those of humanism, skepticism, empiricism, seventeenth-century Anglicanism, all in some measure modified by relationships with contemporary power. In verbal terms, Christian symbolism had by 1600 at least partially been submerged in its wedding to the texts of the Renaissance humanist tradition, with shifts in emphasis effected by that marriage. If the complex system of structure remains close to being the root metaphor of the literature of the period, the community of its readers had within it a theological orientation that is in the main humanistic rather than medieval: responsive to a primarily and increasingly mimetic image and at times using classical mythology for its apparent symbolic structure.[6]

Within this tradition the Christian and Neoplatonic idealism is modified, at times subverted, ever being brought closer to the mimetic surface we label *modern* and realistic. For example, knowing how the process of allegoresis works, we can see now that elaborate layering of metaphors is involved. In such a situation the descriptive and evaluative task of the critic becomes complex. Not only must one probe the primary text for emerging patterns of value, but in placing it contextually in surrounding texts, the critic must learn to read the conventions of those texts as they might have been perceived by the communities of educated readers. For instance, one must also take into account the context of church politics. Otherwise, he or she violates not so much the integrity of the so-called "separate work of art" but rather the central internal fiction or metaphor of the community or audience experience and its contemporary meaning.[7]

It has become increasingly clear that each major phase of western civilization has its own symbolic collection of related narratives, a metaphor of life and/or of history that itself embodies its major cultural values.[8] And within such an overarching metaphor are more fluid subcategories that bridge to several communities or readers. Such a metaphor is not, of course, representative of a simple homogeneous zeitgeist. Even the seventeenth century in England with its elaborate class system was far more pluralistic than scholars have generally recognized. The recognition of a *phase* or *period* is an artificial categorizing of flux for the sake of interpretation and understanding. But scholars can at least roughly identify a general body of assumptions and symbols that gives rise to several and various forms of themselves, not to mention smaller, less comprehensive narratives and images.

In the modern world, it is the evolution of history (in Darwinian, Hegelian, or Marxist categories) that is the dominant narrative to which our current symbolic interpretations of reality allude. It is no mistake, for example, that a relatively new discipline such as art history is built upon evolutionary assumptions about styles. Certainly art historians speak of the evolution of convention or style. Such a process or relationship is not, however, a static one in which the root narrative remains constant. At times, the most current representation of values changes the original overarching metaphor, or at least enlarges the possibilities for multiple interpretation. Within the continuing dialectic between the overarching value structure and current events, symbols, and theories, only a few key assumptions and symbols remain reasonably constant until finally, as they are eroded or are replaced, one sees the change in the root metaphor (or, in other terms, the web of symbolic structure) and the probability that one is confronting another social "period" with different values. The seventeenth century is an important period for discovering such transitions.

The following essay will explore the interaction in such a context with several plays of Shakespeare, with some poems and sermons of Donne, and with other nondramatic texts at the center of other cultural texts. It will concern itself with the way in which audience and reader associations mingle and interact. These fundamental Christian metaphors by which the late sixteenth, early seventeenth century experienced dying illuminate modern experience of the plays and other forms. So different are the modern contexts of death and dying (and yet so *like* is the modern need to evaluate at the end) that such a reconstruction of the commonplaces and surrounding texts becomes necessary to understanding.

Most scholars agree that death is an experience that focuses one of the nodal points or major symbols through which one might interpret the values of the culture during the sixteenth and early seventeenth centuries in England. There is less agreement about the mingling of Roman Catholic, Anglican, and Puritan elements. Literature often softens theological distinctions as it focuses upon the ambiguities of experience. The analytic quality of scholarly discourse is sometimes inadequate to the discussion of iconography and neoplatonic thought patterns in which fusion and connection are the driving forces. More specifically, manifestations of major symbols in event, image, and art (popular and fine) that encompass the range of attitudes toward death provide texts for the study of an overarching pattern of Christian life as a brief moment of culture integrated into the greatest drama of the period.

Originally, I had intended a broad study of the survival of the *ars moriendi* in Shakespeare, but as I worked more closely with the materials I found a natural focus, particularly within the tragedies, upon the most dramatic episode within the great series: the temptation to despair. At the same time I realized that other materials from the art of dying as they emerged in nondramatic literature were integrally related to the drama and the interactions of culture. The essays that follow probe scenes from Shakespeare and other literary sources as they may be more fully experienced through an understanding of cultural associations with those closely related aspects of life and death: hope and despair or despair and comfort. The section on Donne and a literature of grief emphasizes a life of dying into life and the emergence of a poetics of comfort.

It is the peculiar nature of the symbolic and figurative language of Renaissance literature to provide a marriage bed for sense experience and the transcendent, but so delicate are the intimate relationships between these dimensions that treating literary texts just like all other surrounding texts may well rule out those moments when the two worlds meet. For example, the text of *Othello* involves a concentration of meanings much deeper and more resonant than that of a contemporary Renaissance sermon on matrimony. At any rate, the foci of my essay remain the literary works. They include a probing of context that enriches and interprets the literary structure, but I do not treat all symbolic structures as equal. I locate my symbolic focus within the literary text and then try to analyze its relationship to the commonplace symbolic tradition of the culture and the associations of Shakespeare's audience.[9] Hence the essay emphasizes Shakespeare's temptation to despair and the *ars moriendi*. Around the beginning of the seventeenth century a cultural-literary dynamic operates in the relationship between the old popular narrative of the *ars moriendi* and its sophisticated and often submerged or displaced expression, especially in such a play as *King Lear*.

Self-Fashioning Again

In the survival of the *ars moriendi* the deathbed confrontation of the character or dying person with the stubborn facts of his life (its inevitable recapitulation of the personal narrative of existence) was for the Renaissance person the final assessment of self. What Steven Greenblatt refers to in his book *Renaissance Self-Fashioning* as "self-fashioning" was for the serious Christian the *agon* by which the soul completed or restored its merger with the original creation of the Word, thereby becoming ready for death.[10] The *I* of Donne's poem "Hymne to God my God in My Sicknesse," who lies tuning his soul in preparation for joining the Choir of Saints, is a striking example.

Greenblatt's appealing definition of self-fashioning as an emergent cultural impulse throughout the sixteenth and seventeenth centuries is predominantly secular, perhaps partly the result of looking backward to early modern England as a transformation from a medieval communal perspective to an individualism of the sort so valued in the twentieth century. There are, of course, winds of change that support such a position. It is always exciting to recognize in the literature that provides the human story the foreshadowings of modern experience, the relevance that students have always found most interesting. The New Historicism allows us this latitude with the past, accepting assumptions from a historical dialectic that links past with present. In fact, it is the very interaction between those emergent concepts and the inherited structures of value in the late sixteenth and early seventeenth centuries that creates the rich dichotomous relationship with such masters of vividly dramatic fiction as Shakespeare himself. From an anthropological point of view, Victor Turner's concept of liminality can be seen as representative of the seventeenth century hovering on the threshold of modernity. But emerging individualism is in tension with historical determinism.

In sum, it seems to me undeniable that the freedom of play that Elizabethans and Jacobeans found for role-playing in their culture was something—if not new—newly stimulated by cultural developments such as nationalism, reformation, and developing capitalism. From a political point of view, the changes inherent in the shift from the Tudor to the Stuart dynasty after 1603 in England built up to the major radical event of the first half of the century: The Civil War in the forties and the subsequent Puritan Commonwealth, including the execution of a king. Although he privileges change over continuity, Jonathan Dollimore correctly asserts the need for literary scholars to examine more closely the ways in which the Jacobean period heralds modifications in popular attitudes of respect for the authority of crown and aristocracy.

To some extent the execution of Charles I in 1649 is a great emblematic pivot for such changes. The conception of place and function within a changing society must be seen against powerful inherited realities of Augustinian and even Athanasian notions of selfhood in the England of the Renaissance. It is not enough to pay lip service to the religious ideas of the period as they found expression in changing institutions. Underlying even the lively influences of newly emerging churches was the root metaphor of the Christian self as the image of God. The typical representation of Adam and Eve, the engravings of Dürer in the North, and the paintings of Michelangelo on the Sistine ceiling show the prelapsarian self as a beautiful image of the perfection of God Himself. Only after the Fall does the self take on human sin and fallibility as in the grieving and less than godlike figures of Masaccio's *Expulsion from the Garden*.

A theological reading of self-fashioning consistent with most Renaissance thinking would recognize that within the Augustinian pattern fallen man and woman are throughout their lives on earth pilgrims (albeit often tragic) in quest of the holy grail. According to Augustinian thinking in *The City of God,* those who live according to the will of God belong to the city that will emerge at the end of time as the great kingdom. Because human beings live in a fallen world, that city is mysteriously interpenetrated by the City of Man and its fallen image. In their sense of the corrupt and fallen cities of immediate reality, the New Historicists come together with the Christian humanists as modified by Calvinism in early seventeenth-century Anglicanism.

As creatures of the Fall, even if they should wish to live according to God's will, human beings may fail to recognize it, mainly because their own wills are distorted. The will and capacity for love that human beings inherit from the God whose name is love are intertwined. But as Dante's *Inferno* engraved on the minds of western civilization, human fallen nature causes everyone to love the wrong objects in the wrong measure or the wrong way. As the children of God, English people of the seventeenth century (instructed by preachers and devotional texts) still thought that it was incumbent upon human beings to love God and the eternal things of his creation that belong to his city, and that included themselves. As people slip away from his will for them into loving those transient things that only seem to be the proper objects of their love—things that according to the great metaphors of Spenser look beautiful to frail human eyes but hide within them the poison of sin—they find themselves farther away from their created selves.

According to the Augustinian thinking that developed from these basic ideas, people in the course of their lives become progressively unable to see into their hearts until in the depths of their anguish, they find themselves, like Dante's fictional self, off the true path of pilgrimage, disoriented by sin, unable to find their way back to the pathway to God and thus to their true selves. As the new Puritanism and the Old Testament told Renaissance believers, it is when they recognize their lostness that God's loving grace draws them with adamantine magnetism back to him. It may be through a Beatrice or some other instance of genuine love in their lives, or the instrument of grace may be less clearly identifiable; but for English men and women the major cultural ideas in religion supported the hope that the Creator would always metaphorically and literally search out the lost sheep.

A Herbert or a Donne puts the recovery of self in terms of internal metaphors that echo the Augustinian personality of *The Confessions. Burn off the rust,* says Donne, or *Break the stone of the hard heart,* prays Herbert. The fashioning of self thus conceived is not really self-fashioning in the modern sense but individual openness to God's grace that mysteriously transforms the sinful life, uncovering his law written upon the human heart. Those selves that the world knows—the selves fashioned in the fiery smithy of the heart and presented to the world—ultimately come under even their own judgment, said Renaissance devotional writers, if Christians follow the instructions to make all of life a dying—a dying to self in order to be reborn. The tradition from Paul through centuries of Christian writers that was such a strong line in Renaissance thinking asserted that only in the preparation for death might the Christian lose the old selves in order to find the one self. Many writers thereby recognized the great rhythm accepted in the period between life in the City of the Plain and life in the City of God. Of course, neither the secular interpretation of self-fashioning nor that of gracious self-fashioning can be understood as absolute. Rather, the richness of this period of English literature derives from the power of metaphor to reflect the paradoxical in human experience, the pull between ideal and the insistent demands of particular reality.

Such a lyric phase of the experience merely subsumes, however, the more detailed and dramatic breakdown into scene of the old *ars moriendi.* In the late medieval version of the *ars,* the Devil's last five temptations contain both a testing and an assessment of the worth of the life of the *moriens* through the five temptations: against faith, to despair, to impatience, to vainglory, and to avarice. The most dramatic text of the *ars* marries the visual and the verbal. As we shall see, visual "texts" are very often as revealing as verbal texts; more interestingly, the emblematic interaction of the two points meaning and feeling. In the tradition of the *ars* especially, the popular iconography provides the scholar with an underlining of important points of value. Both visual and verbal texts record both a personal and communal Last Judgment preceding what Renaissance theologians believed to be the irrevocable event before Christ the judge.

The strongest dramatic allusion emerges in the old temptation to despair, when the dying one probes his inability to live by the law through the images of the sins he has committed.[11] To raise the hope of salvation for the sinner the inspirations of the Good Angel allude to such sacred stories as those of the great saints. Here, for example, typology itself encourages the practice of role-playing that Greenblatt calls *improvisation.* Such stories assure salvation and suggest the centrality of the revealed Word at the end of the sixteenth century. The Bible that many moderns know: stripped of folklore, medieval legend, and tradition has not yet emerged out of the Protestant tradition. Even the Authorized Version of 1611 remains for many seventeenth-century readers or hearers an elaborate network of narratives and images inherited from the Scriptural tradition of the Middle Ages. That tradition, still linked to the People's Bibles and legends of the saints, can either be alluded to or integrated into the dynamics of particular artistic or experiential contexts. By the early seventeenth century biblical figures, patriarchs, and New Testament saints have in England replaced most of the Roman Catholic ones, but they function still as intermediary for many. In the instance of the *ars moriendi* the "good news" of Christianity is displaced into the somewhat frightening drama by which the dying individual seeks the answer to the question of salvation, but it is a "good news" in which the fears aroused are countered by a nearly endless typology of redemption. At the end of the tragicomedy of dying is the "fashioning," recovery of the created self.

"Rooted Sorrow"

Part 1
Image, Event, and Word:
A Cultural Interaction

1

The Visual Text as Mirror of Feeling: Skull, Skeleton, and Deathbed

> When the Painter Timanthes having portrayed Iphigenia before the Altar reedie to perish, while hee had drawne the portrature of manie mourning about her, and had spent all his cunning in setting foorth their grief at last hee came to Agamemnon the Damosels Father and cast a vaile over the face of his portrature, he not being able by anie arte to expresse so great a sorrow. . . .[1]
>
> —Zachary Boyd

In the second volume of his *ars* book, Zachary Boyd describes a classical painting of Agamemnon at the sacrifice of Iphigenia in order to communicate the agony of Agamemnon's grief at having to sacrifice his own daughter. Through the allusion to the painting of a father's loss, he assures Elizabeth, Queen of Bohemia and daughter of James I, that he has no words to express her sorrow as a mother over the death of her son: "I have none Eloquence Madame which sufficientlie express your Magesties grief." This is the old paradox: denial in language itself of the efficacy of both word and art to express the most powerful feelings of life. Throughout history artists have tried different ways of coping with such moments—the high points of joy as well as grief. Writers, for example, may deny the power of words while using the very denial to comfort. Those who love music have become accustomed to the ways in which the use of silence can be such a technique of expression. Perhaps to a less dramatic degree in literature, particularly in poetry, radical use of pause can express the inadequacy of words; or, more frequently perhaps, a kind of stripping away of language to bare simplicity, as in the anguished Lear's "Never, never, never, never, never."

The paradoxical effort to find expression for the inexpressible heights and depths of human experience emerges in Boyd's description of the Greek painter Timanthes (Pliny XXXV.64) putting a veil—perhaps a shadow in the painting—over the face of Agamemnon as he sacrificed his daughter. Boyd recognizes that through such a symbolic technique of restraint the visual artist communicates intensity of feeling. What may seem on the surface the simple narrative reproduction of an incident carries within its aesthetic composition an interpretation of the story, an emotional concentration. I would argue further that the visual in most forms of popular art that focuses on death or grief is predominantly structured to communicate affective points of value and feeling, often where they seem most difficult to express, just as in many great metaphors within the iconography of death in the Renaissance. In his introductory essays (including the Dedicatory Epistle) to Holbein's *Simulachres et Historiées Faces de la Mort,* Jean Vauzelles seemed aware of the possible accusation that he was lending credence to Protestantism by his association with pictures accompanied by paraphrased quotations from the Bible. He justified the pictures by the argument that they impress the mind more vividly than any rhetoric—a position that many twentieth-century scholars as well as sixteenth could accept.

If the conventions of actual (albeit ritual) event, literal deathbeds and executions, are crucial sources of the commonplace associations with death, texts are also important sources. Both essentially embody emotion in concrete and incarnate forms. As Allan H. Gilbert suggests in *The Symbolic Persons in the Masques of Ben Jonson,* in the early seventeenth century the lines between the mythological and allegorical were blurred; the visual associated with various personifications must have given point and vividness to abstract ideas. For an imagination so strongly verbal in its understanding of metaphor as that of the English between 1550 and 1650, the visual was surely as essential to understanding as it is to critics and scholars of a later time when the very pictorial language of metaphor seems threatened. Certainly, however, the popularity of the emblem and of dramatic form in the seventeenth century argues such a position. The illusion of drama itself is sustained by a vibrant interaction between image and word, image and event, history and aesthetic construct. In some major sense, drama inherits the power of ritual from ancient civilization, the acting out of major rites and values. Although Aristotle emphasizes the importance of logical structure in dramatic articulation, his seemingly simple "imitation of an action" was also a recognition of the essentially visual appeal of "acting out" a story.[2]

Several forms of visual convention help to locate for scholars focal points for communal values in assessing the period's complex attitudes toward death. Major symbols such as the skeleton, the skull, and the deathbed appear in various visual contexts that point guides through the rich and detailed maze of seventeenth-century words and historical detail and provide the context for dramatic images on stage. For Shakespeare's audience a few popular images, often simple, function as resonating symbols in both visual and verbal forms of the human experience of death. The shaping of these symbols in emblems, woodcuts, tombs, paintings, and even designs on plate and armor often gives intellectual clues to more meaningful interpretations of historical moment than verbal text, but more important to drama, to the feelings of Shakespeare's audience.[3] Particularly important for the twentieth-century student of audience response is to identify key symbols such as the skull, skeleton, and deathbed in the great web of cultural tradition in the period and to trace the delicate lines between those popular emblematic constructs and Shakespeare's text. It is in the crackling dynamic between the inner world of art and the worldview of his audience that drama lives, that the full meanings implied by the work of art may be teased out.[4] In the later essays on the place of the *ars moriendi* in Shakespeare's plays I allude to several images and visual constructs of the temptations and inspirations that illustrate subtly changing contexts within which Shakespeare's audience experienced stage dying and that provide a basis of experience for later development in the poetics of comfort.[5]

The major sources of both narrative and symbol for Renaissance visual iconography are two traditions: the *danse macabre* and the *ars moriendi*. The earlier was the *danse macabre,* which developed as part of the response to the Black Death as early as 1345 and continued to provide one major line, particularly in Northern art, for visual symbolism throughout the fifteenth and sixteenth centuries. The *danse* itself was a very old tradition, possibly originating much earlier but appearing as a painting on the wall of the Churchyard of the Innocents in Paris and as an image spreading throughout Europe during the height of the Black Death (1345–60).[6] The major English example was painted on the north cloister of St. Paul's. All such images emphasized that one must prepare for death lest he or she be caught unawares. The figure of Death as a grinning skeleton that seized people of all ranks and types in the very midst of life is a powerful visual conception that engaged the imagination of Europeans for at least three hundred years. Of the cruel presence of death as experienced by those people during the great plague and its later visitations, current scholarly opinion supports the devastating reality. That the Black Death killed approximately one third to one half the population of Europe and Asia in twenty years is enough to stimulate the modern imagination to empathize with people who were terrified by the pervasiveness of sudden death.

Although later recurrences of bubonic plague throughout the fifteenth, sixteenth, and early seventeenth centuries were not as widely or massively destructive, the frequency of recurrence and the horrors of the disease provided a solemn reminder that death remained for many the master of life. In London between 1602 and 1604 parish christenings were recorded at 4,789 and burials at 38,244.[7] Of the latter, 30,578 were attributed to the plague. An even worse recurrence of the dread epidemic has been recorded in 1625 when Donne for a time took refuge at the country home of his old friend, Lady Danvers, formerly Magdalen Herbert and mother of George, in order to escape the city.

The most vivid example of a fully elaborated dance of death in English sixteenth-century sources surrounds the presentation of the popular ballad "The Daunce and Song of Death," published in 1568–69 and collected in the *Huth Manuscripts* in the British Library. The central image of the "Daunce" has the Old Man, the Beggar, the King, the Child, the Wise Man, and the Foole in lively dance with its numerous variations.[8] The most frequent appearance of the dance of death found visual expression in the simple *memento-mori* convention, particularly in poems and graphics as they appeared in England with Holbein's great series. In the sixteenth century the grinning figure of sudden death emerged in the midst of life. The woodcuts for Petrarch's *Triumph of Death* were a frequently reprinted image of the pervasiveness and place of death within the imagination of European culture, particularly in the South. The number of Renaissance translations of Petrarch's "Triumphs," including one by the Countess of Pembroke, sister to Sir Philip Sidney, suggests the popularity of these ideas and images in the England of the sixteenth century. One double-paged illustration published in Venice includes the image of triumph on one side with the chariot of death crushing a number of people who represented the leveling of various representatives of society: king, pope, bishop, knight, and so on; on the facing page four others (with some variation in size and arrangement) appeared in several widely popular books at the end of the fifteenth century and beginning of the sixteenth.[9]

Among other English popular materials in the British Library one of the most arresting is a "dance-triumph" that probably conflates the dance of death and the themes of Petrarch's *Triumph of Death*.[10] The watercolored woodcut image accompanies a ballad that begins, "The bishop vaunts to pray for thother fower": the king, the harlot, the lawyer, and the country clown. Speaking within the text of the

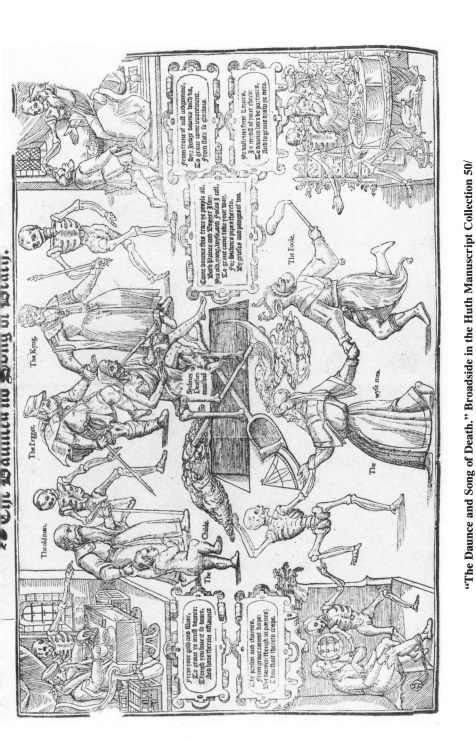

"The Daunce and Song of Death." Broadside in the Huth Manuscript Collection 50/32. Permission to reprint is from the Board of the British Library.

"I praye for you fower," (Dance of Death). Broadside in the Huth Manuscript Collec—

ballad, each of the "actors" claims the supreme power of his function. In the visual image, each figure has his statement of claim in a box at his feet: "I praye for you fower," says the bishop; "I defend you fower," says the king; "I vanques you fower," the harlot; "I help you to your right," the lawyer; "I feede you fower," says the country clown. At the far right the large figure of death has one hand on the countryman's shoulder and one hand holding the spear poised over his head. Death's own triumphal statement appears not beneath his feet but over his head and just under the spear: "I kill you all." Beneath the woodcut and before the full text of the ballad is an eight-line broken stanza that ends, "Ech to their cause, for gard of their degree, and yet death is the conqueror you see." In the background at the top of the woodcut is a small image of the four feasting under a bower with the clown on all fours, virtually holding the table on his back. The text of the ballad explains that image: "And thus the cause I cary on my backe, This table here of plenty not of dearthe. I feaste them all, their hunger I appease." Approaching the company is a small figure of death, a shroud over one shoulder and his spear in the other hand.

The religious aspect of the Triumph is suggested virtually by the images of birds: on the right a covey of geese finding its way home and on the left a falling sparrow. More explicitly, the "Authors Apostrophe to the Reader," which follows the ballad, sounds the moral point of the whole:

> Here may you see, what as the world might be,
> The rich, the poore, Earl, Cesar, Duke and King,
> Death spareth not the chiefest high degree,
> He triumphes still, on every earthly thing,
> While then we live let us endevor still,
> That all our works agree with Gods good will.[11]

As with the various forms of the visual variations upon the popular dance of death theme, this image uses fear to instigate moral action. The overwhelmingly affective message of the whole is the sweeping and terrifying conquest of death over the proud claims of those representing various functions within society. In short, the feelings that such a presentation must have left with the vast majority of those who saw it must have been associated more with somber warning of the pervasiveness and power of death than with the inspiration to do good.[12]

Even more pervasive than such elaborate images as these in the English tradition during the sixteenth century were separate *me-*

mento-moris. An essay by Roland M. Frye in *The Shakespeare Quarterly* and also his later book on *Hamlet* survey a number of the more sophisticated versions that occurred in paintings, but a tremendous number of engravings and woodcuts was even more widely disseminated.[13] For instance, in addition to the Holbein *Imagines Mortis,* the *memento-mori* series appeared often as single engravings (and as late as the nineteenth century in the Psalter of an edition of the Book of Common Prayer).[14]

All the *memento-moris* were designed on initial presentation to frighten, to make the point that "That night thy soul shall be required of thee," whereas the *ars moriendi* tradition, the second important source of symbolism, although it may have begun with warning, was a humane and consolatory answer to such a stimulus, as both O'Connor and Beaty have pointed out.[15]

More recently, David Atkinson affirms that consolatory emphasis in his discussion of the Protestant transformation of the *ars moriendi* in England.[16] The skull and the skeleton, vivid and shocking reminders of the presence of death in Elizabethan life, were countered by the more complete narrative (or drama) of the "good death," summed up within the *ars moriendi* tradition and focused for many in the image of the dying one on his deathbed.

The fifteenth-century examples make the symbols most explicit, whereas later there is a kind of telescoping. In the beautiful Grimani Breviary manuscript, acquired by Cardinal Grimani in 1520 but executed between 1480 and 1490, one of the handsomest and most comprehensive expressions of the seminal symbolic material, virtually all the conventions of the good death are summed up in one image. In this representation the sequential and complex narrative of the battle between temptation and inspiration is only generalized by the presence of two figures over the head of the *moriens:* that of the good angel and the bad.[17] In the Commemoration of All Souls in the *Golden Legend* we learn that these images represent in the people's Bible the continuing battle between good and evil.[18]

Most of the images within the central circle in the Grimani Breviary, however, are displaced images of the conflict between the good and bad angels with the frail and human image of the *moriens* at the center of the drama. He receives extreme unction from the figure at the bedside, and somewhat to the rear of the bed on the right the doctors continue their discussion of his condition. In the doorway family and onlookers hover. On the right, further forward, as we view the painting, two figures kneel beside a table; on the tabel is a pyx containing the eucharist. Near the foreground of the representation one priest reads from a devotional text, while another anoints the cold feet of him who is dying. The central object of comfort is, of course, the crucifix at the right of the moriens's head. At the foot of the bed on the right are women mourners. On the left, several men at a table count money and write accounts or a will. This activity has been seen as the division of the fortune of the *moriens* by the greedy heirs, but more consonant with what is obviously a good death is the recognition of the conventional need for the good man to put his earthly house in order before his death.

As the manuals of dying tell us throughout the sixteenth and seventeenth centuries, the art of dying well includes the making of a will and the disposition of one's worldly goods.[19] Such an accounting includes the paying of one's debts and the full reconciliation with one's fellows and family.

This largely mimetic image of death is recognizably a good dying for several reasons. In addition to the details that suggest the presence of all the conventional elements for salvation, several allegorical structures foreshadow the ultimately happy outcome.[20] At the bottom of the page is a chaotic and brutal *memento-mori*, emphasizing the suddenness with which several figures of death attack a group of hunters. Sudden death may be seen as set against the elaborate preparation of the scene in the circle, and the viewer is reminded of the old opposition.[21] The *memento-mori* warning against death in the midst of life is built into the miniature, but clearly subordinated. The visual emphasis is upon the image of the good death with its hope and faith in salvation.

The argument for daily dying was to some degree a protection against being caught unawares. But fundamental to the tradition was a strong sense of preference for the orderly dying at home as a culmination to a lifetime of devotional preparation. Not only the sense of death as the dramatic culmination to earthly life figures in this preference but also two other factors: the great eschatological question of salvation and the more practical concern for mustering all the salutary defenses against the last assault of Satan. Persons in the fifteenth and sixteenth centuries seem to have been uneasily aware of the craft of Lucifer in obtaining souls at the last minute and the consequent need for the instruments of grace. In the Grimani manuscript from the Roman Catholic tradition, the focus is upon the Office of the Dead and the power of the sacrament. More common in England a hundred years later are scenes in which family and friends are portrayed as spiritual comforters to reassure the dying of the possibility of a good death even without benefit of clergy.[22] This emphasis made it possible for the *ars* to be absorbed naturally into the Reformation devotional tradition in England.[23]

Although the Grimani manuscript derives from an earlier and southern European sacramental tradition, it is useful in the study of seventeenth-century English attitudes because the visual text includes all the aids to a good dying within the iconographical circular structure surrounding the dying man. In addition to the contrast between the carefully prepared death in the circle and the frightening sudden death at the bottom of the page, several other structural comparisons inform the symbolism. In the upper right of the miniature outside the circle, good and bad angels do battle for the souls of the saved and damned and thereby suggest the judgment that lies beyond the earthly preparation. At the upper left-hand corner, however, is the circular structure of heaven itself with God dimly visible at the center. The correspondence between the central circle of the deathbed scene and that of the City of God reminds the viewer of the circle of eternity, commonplace in English symbolism as well.[24] The earthly dying is, of course, the moment of life most in touch with the realm of eternity. A more complex theological view suggests that the two spheres are linked by the operation of redemptive mercy upon the so-called good death. In spite of hints of the terrifying in the painting, including the *memento-mori* at the bottom border and the suggestion of possible damnation at the upper right, the image of the whole is one of comfort and reassurance.

Popular *ars* woodcuts, however, that we shall examine in detail a little later, were the major visual source of associations for Shakespeare's audience and Donne's congregation. Such a valuable manuscript painting as the Grimani was obviously prepared for the aristocracy, and this provenance might explain its comprehensive and detailed symbolism, even to the reproduction of symbolic colors. The richly human mimeticism of the central death scene may have some relation to its Italian origin, but Bosch's "Death of the Miser," now in the Mellon Gallery in Washington, suggests that by the early 1500s the same combination of naturalism and allegory functioned in the conventions of the North. Another example of a good death among family and friends from the same tradition of the illustrated manuscript occurs in the English translation of *Le Livre de bien vivre,* 1503.[25]

A woodcut from the popular ballad tradition at the end of the sixteenth century (1596) reassures us, however, that the iconography of painting and woodcuts cross-fertilized each other for at least a hundred years. As one might expect, woodcuts are simpler and less well executed than manuscript painting. The one accompanying the ballad entitled "The crie of the poore for the death of the Right Honorable Earle of Huntington" belongs with the many

The crie of the poore for the death of the Right Honourable Earle of Huntington.
To the tune of the Earle of Bedford.

O God of thy mercie remember the poore,
And graunt vs thy blessings thy plenty & store:
For dead is Lord Hastinges, the more is our griefe,
And now vp to heauen we cry for relicfe.   (one.
Then waile we, then weepe we, then mourne we ech
The good Earle of Huntington from vs is gone.

To poore and to needie, to high and to low,
Lord Hastinges was friendly, all people doth know:
His gates were still open the straunger to feede,
And comfort the succourles alwaies in neede.
Then waile we, &c.

The husbandles Widdow he euer did cherrish,
And fatherles Infants he likewise would nourish:
To weake and to sicke, to lame and to blinde,
Our good Earle of Huntington euer was kinde.
Then waile we, &c.

The naked he clothed with garments from cold,
And frankely bestowed his siluer and gold:
His purse was still open in giuing the poore,
That alwaies came flocking to Huntingtons doore.
Then waile we, &c.

His tennants that daylie repairde to his house,
Was fed with his bacon, his biefe and his souse:
Their rents were not raised, their fines were but small
And manie poore Tennants paide nothing at all.
Then waile we, &c.

Such Landlordes in England we seldome shall finde,
That to their poore Tennants wil beare the like minde,
Lord Hastinges therefore is ioyfully crownde,
With Angels in heauen where peace doth abound.
Then waile we, &c.

His wisedome so pleased the Queene of this land,
The sword of true Iustice, she put in his hand:
Of Yorke he was President, made by her Grace,
Her lawes to maintaine and rule in her place.
Then waile we, &c.

Such mercifull pittie remainde in his brest,
That all men had Iustice, and none were oprest:
His Office in vertue, so godly he spent,
That Prince and his countrie, his losse may lament.
Then waile we, &c.

And likewise Lord Hastings S. Georges true knight,
Did weare the gold garter of England so bright:
The gift of a Prince, king Edward first gaue,
A Gem for a Souldier and Counceller graue.
Then waile we, &c.

His coyne was not whoorded, to flourish in pride,
His Rings and his Iewels, and Chaines to prouide:
But gaue it to Souldiers, wounded in warres,
That pike and the bullet, hath lamed with scarres.
Then waile we, &c.

He built vp no Pallace, nor purchase no Towne,
But gaue it to Schollers to get him renowne:
As Oxford and Cambridge can rightly declare,
how many poore Schollers maintained are there.
Then waile we, &c.

No groues he inclosed, nor felled no woodes,
No pastures he paled to doe himselfe good:
To Commons and Countrie, he liude a good friend,
And gaue to the needie what God did him send.
Then waile we, &c.

He likewise prouided in time of great neede:
If England were forced with warres to proceede:
Both men and munition, with horses of warre,
The proude foes of England, at all times to scarre.
Then waile we, &c.

Our Queene and our Countrie, hath cause to complaine,
That death in his furie this Noble hath slaine:
Yet England reioyce we, reioyce without feare,
Lord Hastinges hath left a most Noble heire.
Then waile we, &c.

A thousand poore Widdowes for Huntingtons sake,
As manie poore children, their prayers will make:
That God may long prosper his heire left behinde,
And graunt him old Huntingtons true noble minde.
Then waile we, &c.

Then pray we for Countrie, for Prince and for Peares,
That God may indew them with most happie peares:
Lord blesse vs with vertue, with plentie and peace,
And manie moe subiects like him to increase.   (one.
Then waile we, then weepe we, then mourne we ech
Our good Earle of Huntington from vs is gone.

FINIS.

Printed at London for VVilliam Blackvvall,
and are to be sold at his shoppe nere
Guild-Hall gate. 1 5 9 6.

"The Crie of the poore for the death of . . . Huntington." Ballad in the Huth Ms.
Collection (1596). Permission to reprint is from the Board of the British Library.

popular elegies that are extant. The date of the ballad is misleading as far as the woodcut is concerned because the usual practice was to use old woodblocks that were available.[26]

The style of the illustrative woodcut for the ballad is crude; gone are skeletons, angels, and demons, but the essential mimetic elements of the "good death" remain. A clergyman holds open a devotional book and gestures instructively, possibly making the sign of the cross. The hands of the *moriens* clasp in prayer, and the woman at the other side of the bed pulls up the covers. A gentleman, possibly a physician, stands at the right of the bed, and throughout the room family members kneel in prayer. At a table, front right, a clerk writes the will.

As time goes on, it takes less and less visual detail for the popular tradition to indicate the conventions of the good death. It may be well to remember that this principle would translate to more sophisticated art; the symbolism becomes increasingly understated. When we turn to the ballad itself, we learn that the Earl of Huntington died a good death because he lived a virtuous and nonavaricious life:

> He built up no Pallace, nor purchased
> no Towne,
> But gave it to Schollers to get him
> renowne. . . .

Attitudes from popular social criticism shape the praise of the Earl. He enclosed no groves and felled no woods. Commons and country alike will mourn him. He fulfilled his function as a landlord, a warrior, and a servant of the queen. As a result, he will dwell with the angels. It is interesting to note, however, that there is little concern for the spiritual details of his dying.[27] The treatment is externalized—focused on the virtuous acts that make up the good life.

At the end of the sixteenth century a body of religious feelings and ideas operating as associations with the deathbed for Europeans can be illustrated visually from the sturdy survival of the *ars moriendi* both in series and in single illustration. The *ars moriendi*, really the source of the more contemporary English versions mentioned above, appeared originally in the second half of the fifteenth century in two major textual forms: one the great xylographic books printed at Cologne (ca. 1450), Augsburg, and elsewhere (1470); and the other the unillustrated version that appeared in several manifestations between 1465 and 1475, mostly in northern European countries. Ariès argues that a French version of this was the original *ars* book. Sister Mary Catharine O'Connor thinks that the unillustrated text is the earlier, probably a German version, but more recently Nancy Lee Beaty has spoken persuasively for the seminal nature of the woodblock book that combines illustration and instruction. Although the unillustrated version translated by Caxton in 1491 became the more influential on the English devotional tradition, both texts are essentially the same in instruction and in their focus upon the drama of dying as a great climatic moment of evaluation of the self: the final moment of "self-fashioning" in which the Christian ideally loses the self to find it.

Both versions base the drama upon the assumption of an ongoing battle between good and evil. In this instance, the struggle is expressed in the medieval legend that Satan makes a mighty last-ditch attack upon the soul that involves five legendary temptations of the Christian: against faith, to despair, to impatience, to vainglory, and to avarice. The legend also asserts the opposing presence of redemptive power in the universe, in this particular instance in the guise of the Good Angel who counters the Satanic temptations alternately with appropriate inspirations. The inspirations remind the dying one that God's redemptive power manifests itself not only in guardian angels but also in the great human types in the Communion of Saints, in the mysterious atonement of the crucifixion, and finally in the possibility of a happy death for the individual. After all, as a culmination of the drama the soul of the dying is received into angelic hands. The crucial transition between death and life eternal finds a symbolic structure in this elaborate sequence of temptations and inspirations that climax in a happy ending when the transformed soul issues from the mouth of the dying into the hands of an angel.

The illustrations that provide the most vividly dramatized fifteenth-century text of this version of the psychomachia appear in an undated version of twelve printed leaves that was reproduced in facsimile by the Holbein Society in the nineteenth century. The original fifteenth-century copy is in the British Library. The publication is suggested as ca. 1450, but more recent biographical information suggests that ca. 1460 is a more likely date. There is no evidence of a xylographic book or an *ars moriendi* text until after the completion of the Gutenberg Bible in 1455; and the Huntington Library dates its copy of the Augsburg edition as ca. 1470. The *Biblia pauperum* appeared probably in the Netherlands ca. 1465, just a few years earlier. It is most likely that only a few dozen of the *ars* books were made in each printing, since the woodblocks tended to be soft and to deteriorate after a few printings. The Huntington copy of fourteen printed leaves, for example, shows deterioration

"The Happy Death." No. 11 *Ars moriendi* (facsimile edition). Permission to reprint is from the Board of the British Library.

in certain sections of the prints, for instance, in the figure of Paul's being struck down on the road to Damascus in the representation of the Inspiration against Despair (and toward hope). The British Library copy is the only perfect copy and was the most important treasure acquired by the British Museum at the Weigel Sale at Leipsig in 1872.

The woodcut illustrations articulate a set of expectations and implied instruction for the dying that the text elaborates in a clear and rational (if somewhat simplistic) explanation. It is, however, from the illustrative scenes that one is most struck by the symbolic vision of the artist. The mingling of the allegorical and the experiential in the drawings suggests the intermingling of the profound with the ordinary that creates for many modern readers the charm of the medieval period. One sees in the portrayal of the emaciated *moriens,* naked, but with covers to his breast, an everyman, of course; there is no attempt at particularization, but there is a simplicity that universalizes the experience and probably reassured the original readers and viewers of the reality of a created order in the universe that countered the macabre terror of the Dance of Death.

The series of illustrations do not, however, present a sentimental view of comforts alone, as some writers in the late sixteenth century tend to do in devotional texts. The struggle between good and evil is clearly an heroic one, but the greater strength and power of the good are clearly in control of the universe, whatever the powers of illness and death that mark the human transition into eternity. The conventions of the symbolism alone provide a kind of comic treatment of evil that ultimately trivializes it in the face of the dignity of the good. I do not wish, however, to overstress this point, as even the good is at times brought down to human level; the ordinary and the comic are difficult to separate.

The temptations, however, are particularly lively. The canvas is crowded with demons that surround the bedside of *moriens* and conjure up dangerous and destructive images in an effort to ensnare his soul. Although it portrays the Virgin, Christ, and God the Father, from left to right, the first temptation, against faith, is dominated by demons. Two demons stretch out between them a scroll bearing the legend: *"Infernus factus est."* Below the scroll are figures of three doctors: one fat, in dramatic contrast to the sick man. On the next right is a demon with a scroll telling the dying one in Latin to "Do as the Pagans." An illustrative image of such advice appears in the form of a king and queen kneeling before an idolatrous image on a pedestal. On the extreme right, another demon touches the dying man's shoulder with his right hand and displays a banderolle in his left: *"Interficias te ipsum"*—"Kill even thyself." Below in the crowded composition are two figures. The one on the left is female and mostly naked; she holds rods in her right hand and a scourge in her left. The last figure illustrates the temptation to suicide that the artist here associates with loss of faith: a man cuts his own throat with a knife.

The second temptation, to despair, also presents a lively dance of demons. Six hideous creatures posture as they attempt to ensnare the soul of the dying one. This particular temptation, which becomes the dominant one from 1550 on and the central study of dramatic dying, is particularly effective in its power to bring into focus the painful memories of the failures of a lifetime. The semicomic imagery of the demons is subordinated to the moralized content that confronts the dying one with his failure to have lived according to God's law. One demon holds a banderolle with *Ecce peccata tua* on it ("Behold thy sins"); another one with a list of sins; others with individual sins: *"Perjurus es"; "Fornicatus es";* even *Occidisti,* "Thou has killed." At the foot of the bed is the man he has killed. Another man holds a dagger to accuse the *moriens* of murder; later in the tradition this image becomes an encouragement to suicide. Others appear in the composition as images of those whom he has wronged.

The third temptation, to impatience, takes the most comic form of the five. Although the medieval view of patience included humility and a deeply Christian acceptance of suffering, the artist of the original *ars* series maintained enough distance from the indignities of dying to take advantage of comic possibilities. In this representation, the emphasis is not upon the passive suffering of the *moriens* but upon an explosion of impatience. The dying one, softened perhaps by the assault upon his old failures in the temptation to despair, is depicted in the midst of kicking out in impatience. He has broken out of the covers, his right leg kicking a male figure, doctor or servant, who looks resentful of the treatment. The composition focuses on the overturned table that must have resulted from the impatient kick of the *moriens.* Perhaps the most interesting aspect of this woodcut is that it clearly shows the temptation having been yielded to, while the other temptations in the series seem to have been portrayed at an earlier point in the narrative.

The fourth temptation, for instance, to vainglory, shows five hideous demons assailing the *moriens.* One urges him to boast with a banderolle that says *Gloriare;* a second saying in Latin: "Thou has been firm in faith"; a third with a crown and scroll and a banderolle with the Latin of "Thou hast deserved a crown." To the right of the

"The Temptation to Despair." No. 3, *Ars Moriendi* (facsimile edition). Permission to reprint is from the Board of the British Library.

dying one a fourth demon tries to thrust upon him a crown as he is saying: "Thou has persevered in patience." The fifth demon in this crowded canvas bears a scroll, also: "Exalt thyself." Above the *moriens,* attendant figures, and demons are the Father, the Son, and the Virgin, hovering over figures of innocent children in prayer. The letterpress description is translated the "Temptation of the Devil to Vainglory."

The final temptation, to avarice, understood to be the last great temptation and one to which the old are particularly vulnerable, shows three demons actively attacking the *moriens.* Like the Temptation to Vainglory, this one takes place at the high point of the demons' temptation. Avarice is presented not only as greed for material possessions but in the larger medieval sense of attachment to the world. The woodcut demon points to relations or friends of the dying: a male, three females, and a child. Another of the demons gestures toward a wealthy house in the cellar of which are four casks of wine. A servant fills a jug from each to indicate the appeal of worldly enjoyment. The letterpress page is headed, *Temptacio dyaboli de avaricia."*

The woodcuts of the temptations are more lively as drawings than the interspersed inspirations. The artist's imagination is clearly more satiric than inspirational. In spite of that, however, some of the symbolic aspects of the inspirations provide interesting insights into the redemptive resources that the late medieval mind saw in the universe. The Good Angel is, of course, the dominant figure in the visual landscape of all the inspiration woodcuts. In each, he or she holds a scroll that sums up the theme of the inspiration, as, for example, in the first inspiration (the second woodcut): *"Sis firmus infide"* or "Be thou firm in faith". The first inspiration has within it other persistent symbols of the Christian redemptive power in the universe: Above the bed, left to right, are the Virgin, Jesus, God the Father, and Moses (portrayed with the horns that represent a iconographical mistranslation). And above these are also saints and angels. Below the central image of the *moriens,* the vanquished demons somewhat comically squirm. One says "Let us flee"; another "We are overcome"; another "We struggle in vain." The text on the opposing page is headed *"Bon inspiracio."*

The fourth woodcut and the second inspiration "against desperation" is the most interesting of all in regard to its influence on literature in the latter sixteenth century. It shows a crowded but well-composed image of the Guardian Angel and the *moriens,* pointed inspirationally with a banner: *"Nequaquam desperes"* [never despair]. The penitent thief on the cross provides a visually dominant

"The Inspiration against Despair." No. 4, *Ars moriendi* (facsimile edition). Permission to reprint is from the British Library.

image of the comforting type of "last-minute" penitence and salvation. Because of his posture we recognize him as distinct from the figure of Christ. Figures of other great sinners who were saved after genuine repentance stand beside the thief: Mary Magdalene with her attribute the pot of spikenard and St. Peter with a large key to the kingdom in his right hand. He is accompanied by the cock that crew after he had denied Jesus three times. At the foot of the bed are the somewhat distorted figures of Saul of Tarsus and his horse, cast to the ground on the road to Damascus. All are then sinners who were saved—a composite call to hope for *moriens*. As in the first temptation (and others), demons have been routed, one in the lower corner with a banderolle of submission; another demon escapes under the bedstead.

The third of the inspirations—crucial to the drama of temptation—is the inspiration by the good angel to patience. The angel is at the center of the composition with wings outspread, and one senses the way in which patience is a covering virtue for the whole experience of the drama. If the *moriens* can respond in this instance to patience, the happy ending will be assured, and the drawing points to that assurance. The *moriens* folds his hands in prayer, perhaps indicating a reversal of his mood in the temptation to impatience and a reaffirmation of his desire to associate himself with the patience of the several saints pictured—all of whom underwent great suffering—St. Barbara, with her attribute of the tower surmounted by a steeple; St. Catherine, with wheel and sword; St. Lawrence, with a gridiron. On the right are God the Father and Jesus. The demons seem to have been totally overcome by this phalanx of redemptive power. On the right one demon tumbles headlong; on the left are hindparts of a demon escaping comically under the bed with a scroll translating "I have been overcome."

The fourth inspiration follows the subtlest of all the temptations: to vainglory. After all, the *moriens* has managed to persevere in patience, having also overcome loss of faith and despair over the sins of the past, and it is no wonder that Satan should have tried at this stage to arouse the pride of the *moriens*. Three angels appear to deliver the inspiration that will counter the temptation. The main angel in the center points with its right hand to a scroll: *"Superbos punio"*: "I punish the proud." Under this the artist has placed a hellmouth, embellished by flames, in which three figures writhe. One of the figures is a priest, as if to suggest that even the most seemingly virtuous cannot avoid vainglory.

Above this angel is another with a scroll in his left hand: *"Sis humilis"* or "Be humble." On the left the third angel holds up its right hand. Above is St. Anthony with bell and crozier. At the top of the drawing is the Trinity accompanied by the Virgin Mary. The dominant demon on the right is probably Satan, whose two huge teeth almost close on the neck of the victim who has indulged in pride. At the foot of the picture, a characteristically overcome demon has the scroll *"Victus sum"* ("I have been overcome"). Another escapes under the bedspread.

The last temptation (to avarice) is, of course, followed by the inspiration against it. It is appropriate to this culminating inspiration that the two greatest types of mercy appear above on either side of the canopy: on the right is the Virgin Mary and on the left a full-length picture of Christ on the cross. Next on the left are three heads of sheep, then a man and two women. Below one of the women is a maiden and above her the head of a man. It is not entirely clear who these are, but the angel's scroll that translates into "Don't concern yourself for your friends" implies that they are friends, or possibly friends and family, of the dying. The angel who holds the scroll also holds a curtain to conceal from the *moriens* a woman and a man. Critics have speculated on the identity of these two, but it seems clear that they represent those from whom the *moriens* is being helped to detach himself. At the foot of the picture a demon bears a scroll with a variation on the usual routed demon's comment: "Quid faciam" or "What shall I do?"

The last and eleventh woodcut resolves the opposition of temptation and inspiration, evil and good. In this woodcut, the artist seems to rise to the seriousness of the final moment. The *moriens* is portrayed in his last agony. On the right, a monk helps him hold a lighted candle. The *moriens,* however, has just breathed his last, and the artist shows the breath—leaving his mouth in the shape of a child, symbolic of his soul that is being received by the angelic host. To the right of this group, just above the Monk, are three figures: St. Peter, with sword; Mary Magdalene, with spikenard; and the Virgin Mary. Behind these are nimbuses of eight other saints (heads are shown of two). To the right is the full-length figure of Christ on the cross, and to his right is John, the beloved disciple, in prayer. Above him, there are (probably) two apostles with nimbuses. In the lower picture—in this climactic scene six demons rage with disappointment.

This analysis of the most elaborately articulated visual tradition of comfort for the dying shows how carefully and imaginatively the artist has followed the homilectic framework. The drawing is vigorous, the simple symbolism clear and powerful. It is no wonder that this series became a focal point for attitudes toward dying for at least two hundred years.

As late as 1623, the whole series (copied from a fifteenth-century series) appeared in an edition of the *ars moriendi* illustrated text with thirteen copper engravings. The artist is thought to be Matthew Zink or Zabel who worked in the sixteenth century following the design of the block-books of the fifteenth century, copied from the Master of 1466. The series of eleven copper engravings were, according to Passavant, published in Munich.[28]

After the early sixteenth century the survival of the *ars* woodcuts is less easy to document. *The Boke Named the Royal,* translated and published by Caxton in 1488 and republished by Wynkyn de Worde in 1507, has a woodcut of the temptation to impatience on the cover (frontispiece) and contains the temptation to avarice and the scene of the happy dying but not the temptation to despair. In Wynkyn de Worde's *Doctrynall of deth* (1532), the temptation to impatience woodcut is again the frontispiece, and the temptation to avarice appears inside. The woodcut at the front is appropriate to the double theme that illness tempts one to "grutch against God" and that he who would obtain salvation must fight for it, "Specyally agaynst theyr body in tyme of temptacyon and sekenes."[29] Among the woodcuts in the series the temptation to impatience most vividly expresses the trials of illness. Otherwise, I can find in the English tradition only single instances of the woodcuts. Beaty points out that it is the earlier fifteenth-century text, the unillustrated text of the *ars,* that found its way whole into the English tradition.[30]

The great series of temptations and inspirations may have existed for English persons more clearly in verbal terms than in visual terms, although it is difficult to believe that the enormous wealth of explicit verbal variations upon the five temptations, five inspirations, and happy death lacked visual counterparts in the imagination. Perhaps the presence in England of continental books that did contain the series and also single instances in English books in stained glass or in stone were enough to stimulate the visual associations of a Shakespearean audience that has been shown to be more highly educated than Harbage thought.[31] Certainly, many verbal allusions suggest that the image of the deathbed carried associations with the *ars* allegory throughout the sixteenth and seventeenth centuries. English practice at actual deathbeds may well have reinforced this awareness.

The very infrequency of the appearance of the entire woodcut series may have made more possible the conflation of certain elements—for example, the shifting of the temptation to suicide from the temptation against faith to the temptation to despair. A more speculative possibility is that the lack of frequent contact with the woodcut series as a whole may have actually contributed to the way in which the temptation to despair loomed large both in the latter part of the sixteenth century and in the early seventeenth, when the genre of tragedy focused that temptation as central, but I suspect that such an idea is only a single strand within the historical web of possibilities.

Whatever the problems in tracing a direct and powerful visual influence of the whole fifteenth-century *ars* series on English culture (as distinguished from continental), the elaboration of the conventions in numerous verbal texts makes it useful for scholars of Shakespeare and other writers on early modern England to study them against the visual background. Since the *ars* woodcut series is itself a dramatic narrative of the happy death, it shapes the more expository elements of the devotional tradition toward drama.

According to O'Connor, the whole tradition of instruction for a happy death, or a happy issue out of the final combat of good and bad angels for the possession of the soul, was a late fourteenth- (possibly early fifteenth-) century response to some of the more frightening images of death associated with the dance motif during the great plague. The tradition brought comfort to the dying in two ways: It provided assurance of the presence of redemptive powers and it offered careful instruction in what to expect at that crucial moment of existence. It lies behind the frequent sixteenth-century images of deathbeds, actually also a genre of painting (and graphics) that included the categories of the death of the Virgin and the death of saints. The medieval audience was frequently presented with allusions to the temptation to despair. For Shakespeare's audience, a fully mimetic death scene must have brought forth, even through the first half of the seventeenth century, intensely felt associations with demons and angels, types of saints and types of sinners, as well as the more simply mimetic preparations. I have analyzed such associations in my discussions of *Othello* and *Richard III,* and there are numerous other allusions in Shakespeare to associations of the audience with the deathbed. One cannot read Donne's "Hymne to God my God, in my sicknesse" without envisioning him upon his deathbed, tuning that great soul of his for the long journey. That the deathbed also hovers over historical dyings that take place out of bed becomes a paradox in the discussion of the execution of Essex that follows.

2

Execution and Ritual Dying: Lord Essex as Cultural Event

For all which I humblie beseech my Saviour Christ to be a Mediatour to the eternall Majestie for my pardon: especially for this my last sinne, this *great,* this *bloudy,* this *crying,* this *infectious* sinne, whereby so many have for love to me been drawne to offend God, to offend their Soveraign, to offend the world.

—Essex (William Barlow)

Robert Devereux, the Earl of Essex, flamboyant and treacherous favorite of Elizabeth I, was beheaded for treason at eight o'clock in the morning on 24 February 1601. In that year, 24 February was Ash Wednesday, the first day of Lent, and the day may be seen as symbolic for the English of the time of the turmoil and sorrow of Elizabeth's last years as queen. It was a private execution in the courtyard of the Tower, rather than a public one.[1] Essex had requested privacy ostensibly because of his bitter sense of the fickleness of popular favor; he said that he wished it in order to avoid any temptation to crowd pleasing. The terrible sentence appropriate to treason—hanging, drawing, and quartering—had been commuted to beheading by a merciful and prudent queen. Essex had remained impenitent until the last week before the execution. Like most of the great figures accused of treason who had died under the Tudors, however, Lord Essex came at last through the anticipation of his last moments to kiss the hand that killed him.

Historians have wondered and theorized over the many incongruities between characters and their dying that surfaced in the executions of the sixteenth century. Were the penitent statements sincere? If so, how can the change at the end be explained? What is the relationship between the spiritual idealism embedded in the attitudes of the day toward dying and the brutal facts of execution and near-absolute power? Whatever the complex answers, Essex's final repudiation of the sin of revolt, infectious offense against his Sovereign and the world, has the ring of sincere penitence within the drama of his death.[2]

This chapter explores the death of Essex within the ritual of execution as it embodies a particular form of the *ars moriendi* and as it provides a concrete instance of the avoidance of despair. The death also provides an illustration of the way in which actual historical events both reflected and shaped English attitudes toward death, providing an immediate interplay of image and word from the tradition played out in a temporal drama. Instead of the usual deathbed setting for reconciliation between the *moriens* and God, the place of execution becomes the stage on which the political rebel was brought to full contrition and penitence toward his sovereign and God. The radical change in state of mind from rebellion to penitence finds expression in fictionalized dramatic scenes of execution that Shakespeare and other dramatists draw upon in their plays. In most cases, however, historical instances shaped the fictions. The death of Essex is informational background for such stage executions and provides material for speculation on the ways in which ritual modes actually influenced spiritual transformation. Perhaps more importantly from a literary point of view, it was an event that clarifies a number of implications for the reader or audience response of the period.

The details of Essex's death reflect both his own imperfect character and the power of the social and religious conventions of the day. The reconciliation of man and convention provides an evocative historical text for those who wish to probe the associations of Renaissance people at the turn of the century with the rituals of dying. Although Essex is not representative of ordinary "dyings," he does belong to the subgenre of public execution to which Englishmen had thrilled for a hundred years and which they had invested with numerous symbolic meanings. One can see accounts of his death as offering both historical text and significant context for drama in their mingling of event, image, and word. Such an interaction had long evoked commonplace associations in a crowd of English people. The attitudes and values that cluster around such an occasion form associations with death that the community of Shakespeare's audience brought with them to the theater when they were confronted with dramatic executions. Whether the accounts of such deaths are literally true is less important than the suggestions of conventions expressed within these accounts concerning the values of the culture.

It is impossible to project an entirely valid collage of current attitudes toward death in English society in the early seventeenth century, even in a period with a sense of the strong continuity of religious values. After a period of audience-centered criticism modern scholars are particularly sensitive to the charge that the Shakespearean audience cannot be reduced to a single "like" mind or some statistical average of it. At the same time, however, our own attempts to improvise the possible interpretations of a particular time and place lead us to attempt a loose construct—that is, to provide some guidelines for attitudes held by Shakespeare's audiences, with appropriate allowance for various levels of Shakespeare's stage and language.[3] Such associations are deeply rooted in the symbolic rituals of the period, however displaced and particularized by historical event.

We are both aided and troubled by the knowledge that executions were among the most popular and dramatically ritualized events of the Elizabethan and Jacobean periods. Before Essex's execution in 1601, many executions in the sixteenth century must have had powerful associations, even as in a distant memory: particularly those of Mary Queen of Scots, and, earlier, the wives of Henry VIII. But women, although perhaps the most pathetic, were probably less powerful as images of revolt and repentance than men. More's execution was a counterexample of the powerfully exceptional refusal, but even he died "the King's good servant." It is said, for example, that Elizabethans had a real taste for violence and enjoyed the spectacle of drawing and quartering that accompanied the death of Catholic Norfolk in the reign of Henry. The martyrdom of hundreds chronicled in Foxe represents the most remembered event of Mary Tudor's reign. Even under Burleigh and the more lenient Elizabeth, those implicated in plotting against the queen represented an important group of executions, especially after her excommunication by the pope in 1570.

That all these people dramatized their dying in a public way makes visible the conventions and moralized attitudes toward death that are woven into Tudor England's tapestry of values. At the same time every death of a famous "traitor" is an instance of the major effects of national and sovereign power to use the traitor to reinforce the strength and authority of the crown. The simplest explanation for the final penitence and submission of each of those executed is fear: both of suffering the full agony of torture and a traitor's death and of causing their families to suffer economically.[4] Power in such circumstances was hardly absolute, whether the individual was guilty or largely innocent (as was the case in many Tudor executions). It is, of course, particularly difficult for moderns to see why the innocent died so submissively, in many cases admitting their guilt, as Lacey Baldwin Smith catalogs in his definitive article "English Treason Trials and Confessions in the Sixteenth-Century."[5]

Smith and I agree that the submission of each was part of a larger political and religious perspective that has become virtually inaccessible to modern culture: It involved "obedience to the law, to the desire of the King, and to the mandate of the nation that had willed his death."[6] Further, of course, and crucial to the acceptance of these earthly powers by the dying was the sense that in facing death one must also accept a kind of providential fatalism: that God himself had ordained the "going forth" as the "coming hither." *Obedience* is one of the words that has little or no positive connotation for modern scholars since the overwhelming power of romantic individualism has made itself felt. Because "obedience" tends to exist only in the modern lexicon as the response to tyrannous and absolute power, the process by which obedience is internalized before the rightful authorities of the universe stretches all our powers of historical empathy to assess. But the elaborate anthropological conventions—even rituals—by which such transformation took place are the subject of this essay.

If Philippe Ariès in his large study of death is even generally correct, death in general still stalks the seventeenth century in a somewhat tame guise, as "a natural and respectable end to life that the theologians and devotional writers saw as the bridge to eternal joy."[7] In one of his sermons, Donne tolls the still popular *contemptus mundi* theme:

> This world then is but an Occasionall world, a world only to be us'd; and that but so, *as though we us'd it not;* The next world is the world to be enjoy'd, and that so, as that we may joy in nothing by the way, but as it directs and conduces to that end; Nay, though we have no Joy at all, though God deny us all conveniences here, *Etiamsi occiderit,* though he end a weary life, with a painfull death, as there is no other hope, but in him, so there needs no other, for that alone is both abundant, and infallible in the selfe.[8]

Within this context the moment of death becomes the climactic moment of a life. However mixed the emotions, probably the popular mind of the seventeenth century held it so, and Shakespeare played upon that assumption and gave it dramatic power, especially in his tragedies and also in portrayals of executions in other kinds of plays, as with that of Buckingham in *Henry VIII.*

It would be a mistake, however, to take the conventions voiced by Donne as too literal or too comprehensive expressions of early seventeenth-century attitudes. Most seventeenth-century people experienced life primarily in terms of worldly desires and satisfactions. Too much nonsense written about the Middle Ages accepts the well-tried conventional themes of homily as if they represented the full range of human feeling in the time. As Huizinga and others have pointed out, persons in the Middle Ages surely experienced the human and "secular" concerns of all of us.[9] It is equally simplistic, of course, to assume something like the reverse for early modern England, that Christianity was a worn-out set of attitudes by the seventeenth century and that Donne was merely paying lip service to the authority of the church and conventions of popular preaching. Ariès is still making a much needed correction to scholarship when he emphasizes the continuity between the late Middle Ages and the Renaissance rather than the reductive contrast between the former as a period when "earthly life is a mere antechamber to eternity" and the latter when death has ceased to be the beginning of a new life.[10] Certainly the number of meditations on the *contemptus mundi* theme in the first years of the seventeenth century proclaim the continuity of the tradition. The more balanced approach assesses the complex interaction between the still-perceived life *sub-specie aeternitatis* as envisioned in the Christian tradition and the increasingly secular pressures of a developing nonagrarian, nationalistic, and embryonically technological society. We are most concerned, after all, with the responses of a city population— Shakespeare's London audiences, who would be likely to respond to themes and attitudes toward death with a mixture of associations.

At the same time that one recognizes a limited modernity in an urban population, one must remember that the old correspondence between this world and the still vital heavenly city of Augustine provided a tremendous check upon just emergent "modern values." Donne's *contemptus mundi* was still part of an elaborate web of continuing religious symbolism, particularly in the difficult political context of the transition from the old glory of Elizabeth to the less congenial and optimistic world of the Stuarts in the early seventeenth century. In the first thirty years of the seventeenth century the number of devotional works urging preparation for death remained high.[11]

Against this effort to reaffirm the ultimate supremacy of heavenly glory over the fleeting pleasures of a world ruled by fickle *Occasio,* we can understand the continuing importance of the moment of death for Elizabethans and Jacobeans. Death scenes of well-known persons for the past hundred years illustrate that death as rite of passage became for the public figure a dramatic summation of the displacement of the old *ars moriendi* temptations and inspirations to appeal to current attitudes toward death. In the imagination of the English people *how* a prominent person met the last assault of Satan upon his soul was the key to understanding the quality of his past life and the future of his soul.[12]

And for public figures who died in a private situation there was enormous public interest in accounts of the manner of their deaths. For example, the later descriptions of the melancholy and stoical death of Elizabeth, for example, were eagerly sought by everyone. The fact and manner of her death were an important episode in Dekker's *The Wonderful Year 1603* (not wonderful in our sense of the word, but a year of natural and supernatural wonders).[13] Such details as her sad comment on the fleeting nature of affection, her melancholy statement to Lord Willoughby, "How little faith there is in Israel" shortly before her death, or even her reported abandonment of political concerns for spiritual ones under the guidance of her chaplain became matters of great public interest, both during and after her death.[14] The "spiritualizing" of the account naturally became more prominent as the time after the literal event lengthened and the cult of Elizabeth as Virgin Queen became associated with a type of Virgin Mary. She became in the minds of many the emblem of a comforting set of popular English attitudes when James I failed to capture the affection of the English people. One visual illustration of this kind of mythologizing occurs in the posthumous portrait of Elizabeth with Time and Death. Instead of the usual civic symbolism of her reign, this portrait shows her seated in a meditative posture, a book of devotion open before her and Father Time and a skeletal figure of Death in the dark and somber background.

If the natural death of Elizabeth provided a mythic basis for current attitudes, the category of death scenes to which Essex belongs was an even more popular kind of dying. The drama of execution had long furnished the most vivid death scenes within the historical genre. Roper's account of More's death a century earlier reveals, of course, an instance of a great and noble man dying under the executioner's ax—a death viewed by many as the death of a martyr. Fisher was another noble figure to die in such a manner during Henry's reign. Indeed, one might write a history of political and religious change throughout the sixteenth century by focusing solely upon executions, including those of the Protestant martyrs under Mary Tudor and under Elizabeth the death of Mary Stuart herself. What made these deaths so memorable, of course, was what they shared with drama: an audience, a player, and, to a lesser degree, a stage. They also embody the play of image, event, and language that sustains the lively art of dying in the culture.

The conventions of these public deaths were essentially the same. For one, there was tremendous interest in the last words of the dying. The obvious pressures to recant a political position in opposition to current authority were brought to bear during the imprisonment and especially by the attendant clergy sent to the prisoners to help them prepare for the end. An additional convention was part of the widely understood preparation inherited from the *ars moriendi* tradition. At the moment of death, the devotional literature urged the dying one to have settled all his accounts, including payment of debts (for instance, the important one of paying the executioner and the arrangement of property and business affairs), and reconciliation of all old quarrels or misunderstandings. In a culture that still looked to the queen or king as the divinely ordained head of state and the duly accepted representative of the whole nation—the old liege lord to whom the subject owed his full loyalty—it is not surprising that a good death by execution must include the confession of fault toward the sovereign as well as toward God. The confession of sins was extended to a whole process of confession, contrition, and penance designed to put one right with the corresponding powers of one's existence, earthly sovereign and divine one.

After the one condemned to die had made his peace with earthly powers, the ritual order of his words and actions was designed to move to a higher spiritual plane, in short, to show the speaker ready for death in such a way that heaven would seem his natural destination. That public figures did this in full consciousness of an audience is perfectly clear. However *private* Essex's execution was said to be, it was only comparatively so. From a modern perspective one might be tempted to say that the very pressures of convention encouraged theatricality and hypocrisy rather than genuine penitence and spiritual growth, yet this attitude ignores English distinctions between public and private obligation. Such a man as Ralegh, however flamboyant and egotistical, makes such skillful use of the tradition, as Greenblatt shows us in his book on Ralegh, that one feels he has used the tradition to get at James in a last subversive gesture of self-dramatization rather than as a preparation for his own judgment before the throne of God.[15]

All Renaissance executions had something of the theatrical in them. Certainly Robert Devereux in his egotism was similar in personality to Ralegh, though more winning and popular.[16] Yet certain features in the way in which Englishmen felt about public occasion and ritual separate them from us in the modern, intensely private, sense of what the religious life is. In his short *Preface to Paradise Lost,* Lewis reminds the reader that the Renaissance was still a time when a king could wear cloth-of-gold in a procession without insisting upon his personal glory, that in fact when he put on gold he was most fully submitting self to the office of kingship.[17] It is difficult, nevertheless, for moderns to believe easily in the conversion of Essex at the end, coming as it does under political pressure. Essex's request for private rather than public execution, however, suggests that he was sincere in his penitence, especially in his desire to follow the ritual of a "good death" without playing to the gallery.

There was still somehow deeply embedded in the sense of role-playing of the period a perspective upon ritual by which one might play a part without what moderns think of as *ego.* Within the objective grandeur of the liturgy of the church, for a prime example, the priest took the part of Christ himself: "This is my body, broken for you," and there was no personal pride or theatricality in a self-conscious sense; there was only professional humility in the submersion of the self in the role. No one would argue, of course, that every instance of ritual behavior reached the ideal, but the general pattern was paradoxical, designed to exclude personal vanity while glorifying the role.

In the case of those executed, a set of conventions within which the person likewise submerged himself constituted the general pattern of a noble death. The end of the experience for the one about to die suggested his oneness with the type of all suffering death: that of Christ himself. Some of the devotional books expounded the idea that the last illness was itself a kind of crucifixion of suffering that unites one with Christ.[18] Certainly a beheading was even closer to the violent suffering of the Passion.[19] The oneness with Christ was suggested in the old *ars moriendi* woodcuts in the presence of the crucifix as the image of redemption, but by the early seventeenth century, the more fully developed devotional tradition of walking humbly in the footsteps of Christ had been popularized not only in England by the many translations of Thomas à Kempis's *Imitation of Christ* but also by numerous historical and devotional elaborations upon the simple theme. What might seem to moderns the grossest egotism—speaking the last words of Christ, for example—was for many Englishmen at the beginning of the seventeenth century the final ritual act of humble submission before death.

It is in interaction with this powerful devotional tradition with its pressures to turn the major events of life into liturgical articulation that the Essex rebellion and his execution took place. Recently, scholars have noticed the shaping of civic pageantry by a strong religious and liturgical tradition. One might say that in the death of a traitor, however attractive to the fickle populace, two kinds of pageantry met: the whole political and civil pageant in the execution itself, the mighty arm of power and moment, and the religious and liturgical, the overarching power of the spiritual and eternal in the preparation of a soul.[20]

On the Sunday after the beheading, William Barlow, chaplain to the queen and at one time a close friend of Lord Essex, preached at Paul's Cross on the execution. It is to him that we are indebted both for an understanding of the official position toward Essex and also for the detailed account of Essex's own dying, including a transcription of his prayers and last words.[21] Obviously, Barlow represented the power of the monarchy; authority was concerned about the mood of London. Even though the crowd at the sermon cheered Barlow when he mentioned her majesty, the executioner (sheriff) had almost been killed by the crowd as he returned from his grim task. The crowd loved both Elizabeth and Essex.

Barlow reports that Essex had been adamant in his rebelliousness until nearly the end, when he became the emblem of the kind of deathbed conversion that the English people found the most moving example of the mercy of God.[22] The might of Essex's resistance even in prison made the change dramatic and underlined the power of the monarchy as aligned with divine authority. However Barlow exaggerated certain elements in the account, it is clearly designed to appeal to commonplace values. The conventional way to die well had sounded again and again throughout the long devotional tradition as to *live well,* and still the ideal death was believed to be a quiet death after a good life, a death at home surrounded by family and friends, with some time for the last orderly ritual of dying.[23] But Elizabethans were well aware that few historical personages, if any, lived fully according to God's law. What was by the end of the sixteenth century the most inherently dramatic death was one that required a full confrontation with one's sins at the end and a humble throwing of oneself upon the mercy of God. Reformation attitudes toward grace were operative in making this kind of death the ideal although such an ideal was by no means limited to Protestants. In terms of Renaissance typology in 1600, the thief on the cross became the frequent emblem of such a death, and executions of public figures allowed for the fullest dramatization of such conversion.[24] One would recall that in the Inspiration against Despair in the old *ars moriendi* woodcuts, the thief on the cross is shown in the midst of manna raining from heaven.

For many the death of Essex was a literal and present configuration of the type. As political event, the execution was the culmination of a long and fierce love-hate conflict between the equally strong wills of the young man and his monarch. In spite of the good advice to be submissive, which Francis Bacon gave him a number of times in relation to a number of situations, Essex often asserted his will over Elizabeth and often won her over, but he lost her confidence during the process.[25] His boldness as a military leader and his popularity with his men were admirable qualities for Elizabeth as long as she could rely upon his loyalty to herself and her policies: and he was deeply attractive to her; she valued him highly for his bravery and boldness.

There were, of course, many times when Elizabeth grew angry with her favorite. She expected clear recognition of her authority. She never wished to bear the expenses of war, and she often found his excursions inexcusably expensive. For example, the expedition to France in 1591 justified her worst fears. According to Neale, a hundred miles away from his infantry Essex entered Compiègne to visit the king. He came on horseback preceded by six pages in orange velvet embroidered with gold. While there with his elaborate entourage, he won a leaping match against the French. In order to return safely, he was forced to send for his infantry and in a foolish skirmish lost the life of his brother. In the meantime, he had spent a month in France and accomplished nothing. And Elizabeth was well aware that soldiers must be paid. Later, having made peace with her after having extravagantly knighted twenty-four of his followers, he returned to France for the siege of Rouen, another foolish and expensive expedition.

The story of Cádiz in 1596 was, however, not a failure but an example of the kind of bold exploit at which Essex was most successful. Nevertheless, it represented the kind of expedition the queen feared during the last years of her reign. In 1596, the year in which Howard and Essex planned the expedition against Cádiz, it was the third year of drought, crop failure, and misery for the English people. Elizabeth anticipated famine, and despite the efforts of the government, the poor were dying in the streets. When Essex free-handedly gave the plunder from his expedition to his men instead of returning it to the crown as promised, Elizabeth was rightly angered even while she was proud of his success.

Essex's fundamental lack of respect for the "old woman," as he spoke of her (according to a letter to Francis Bacon), had always been a problem and showed itself in numerous instances. Essex believed that she must be brought to agreement by a "kind of necessity and authority." After a series of disagreements, including his failure to get his friend Sir Robert Sidney appointed to a coveted post and, soon after, the misfortunes of the Islands Voyage, Essex, sulking over a slight from Howard, refused to attend Parliament. Elizabeth coaxed him back to happiness by making him earl marshal, just as earlier in 1597 she had appeased him with the office of master of ordnance. In 1598, just before Burleigh died, there were heated debates over peace negotiations with Spain, when Essex led the contingent in the English Council for war. In the same year in July the conflict exploded over the appointment of a lord deputy.[26]

It was, however, in the Irish rebellion that Essex's own rebellious nature was most fully revealed. He managed somehow to back himself into a corner by his criticism of all his predecessors so that he had no excuse for failure in a difficult situation. Apparently, after a very long and strange campaign, reports reached the queen that Essex had met with Tyrone alone (backed by a small army) at a ford and revealed there some of his wild plans to become king of England. At any rate, the two had concluded a peace, almost wholly to the benefit of the Irish, and the tremendous effort of the campaign (£300,000 for paying the soldiers) seemed wasted. Elizabeth said later that she had no intention of pardoning the Irish rebels, and Essex returned to England in clear opposition to Elizabeth's commands.[27]

Elaborate plotting had occupied Essex's circle for some time, and word had reached the queen of it. With her customary shrewdness, she remained silent. There was even a time in which Essex bounced between imprisonment and near-forgiveness. Finally, at the end of September 1599 she had him confined over the Irish fiasco under the custody of Lord Keeper Egerton. She undoubtedly remained fond of him almost to the end, as she showed when illness brought him near death in December 1599. His scurrilous attack upon Cecil, however, hardened her heart and she decided at one point to bring him to trial. However, in February, both Bacon and Cecil himself prevailed upon her to cancel it. In March, Essex was allowed to go to his house, although with a keeper. For several months, the queen vacillated between anger and favor. One of Essex's friends published the *Apology,* written in 1598, which brought back an earlier conflict.[28]

In July, however, the keeper was removed, and by August Essex was free to go anywhere but court. He continued to write letters to the queen, and she was softening. Still fixed in opposition, however, Essex on the sly continued to seek to extend his power. Through his friend Mountjoy, the New Lord Deputy of Ireland, he sent word to James VI of Scotland, negotiating to declare him heir to the throne. The returning messengers were, however, captured by the government. By the end of July, Essex was planning to seize the court by force. Probably by August the court was aware of the conspiracy, but Elizabeth was silent.[29]

Elizabeth showed, however, her distrust of him by failing to renew the farm or lease of customs on sweet wines that fell due in the fall of 1600. The last humble letter from Essex that historians have was written to Bacon on 17 November 1600, Accession Day, but curiously wild remarks for the context revealed a rebellious heart, accusing the queen of a distorted mind as well as body, "her mind as crooked as her carcass."[30] It was not, however, until Tuesday, 3 February 1601, that the boil came to a head. Essex called five leaders to meet to consider his proposals for rebellion. Specifically, they discussed elaborate plans for taking over the court, even possibly, to harmfully seizing the body of the queen.

That night the Council took action and summoned Essex. He refused to come and decided to ride to rally the city, blaming Bacon and Cecil and pretending there was a plot to murder him. On 8 February several leaders came to Essex House in the name of the queen and were taken hostage. Essex and about two hundred men then rode into the city claiming that he was the queen's true man. Behind him came the mayor's herald proclaiming him traitor. The voice of authority intimidated people who saw treason as the most heinous crime. Many slipped away, and the sheriff failed to produce men to help. Seeing his own weakness, Essex tried to return home. He finally arrived at his house, but the hostages were gone, and he found himself besieged. He surrendered to the lord admiral after burning some treasonous documents, including a letter from James he wore around his neck.[31]

The city was placed under close guard, and Essex was imprisoned in the Tower. When he was brought to trial a week later, he was dressed grandly in black and seemed "utterly proud," says Barlow. "I owe God a death," he said.[32] He cast bitter aspersions on Ralegh and Cecil and showed himself both brave and without contrition. The trial took place 15 February and revealed him near the end seemingly set in pride and rebelliousness. During the next ten days, however, his chaplain, Mr. Ashton, it was reported, brought the proud soul to humility and Christian readiness for death.[33] Therein lies a tale of political pressure and deception.

The stubborn details of Essex's life and character were largely visible to the people in his highly public life as military leader and court favorite. Given Renaissance assumptions that equated rebellion against the crown with mortal sin, the only way to a good death lay in a preparation that included full confrontation with one's sins, full contrition and penance, and a mighty effort to throw oneself upon the mercy of Christ. Such a radical change was indeed allowed for in the *ars moriendi* tradition. Scripture was marshalled to warn people to prepare throughout life: "The hour of death will quickly overtake thee, and therefore looke how thou livest. . . . If thou has a good conscience, thou wouldest not much feare death." Luke 12. Or "Watch therefore, for ye know neither the day nor the hour wherein the Son of man cometh." Matt. 25:13. "Blessed is hee, that hath alwayes before his eyes the houre of his death, and disposeth himselfe daily thereunto." Eccles. 7.

Nevertheless, such pious warnings usually appeared at the beginning of treatises. The substance of the *ars* drama had to do with helping people with the immediate problems of dying: at the very end or on their deathbeds facing an imperfect life and changing their minds so that their souls might be freed from their bodies with some hope of that promise of the last woodcut—reception of the souls out of the mouths of the dying into the Communion of Saints. The chaplain to the queen, William Barlow, reported at Paul's Cross such a preparation, made both at the execution at Paul's Cross and also earlier during Essex's last hours under the tutelage of Ashton, his personal chaplain, and two other clergymen representing the crown (Barlow himself and Dr. Montford). Barlow reports the scene with Essex in prison:

> I am become another man [Essex said], the cause thereof as ascribed to the worke of Gods spirite within him; and the meanes to his chaplain Maister *Ashton* who was there present with us, for he, as he said to the honourable the Lord Keeper and the rest, hath plowed vp my hart, as he said to us, hath brought me down and humbled me.[34]

Clearly, Ashton's part in the recognition was that of catalyst. But after reporting Essex's change of heart, indicated in the wonderful metaphoric "he . . . hath plowed up my hart," Barlow describes the subsequent fine grinding of the legal consequences. Essex had written a complete four-page confession, then sent for Cecil, who had come accompanied by the lord keeper, the lord treasurer, and the lord admiral, and then had asked forgiveness for calumny.[35] All of this was part of the tradition of the good death by which the *moriens* sought reconciliation with all he had offended. The lengthy process was part of the "acting out" that allowed transformation—

the historical transformation that ultimately informs its reflection in drama.

Barlow attached to his sermon a more detailed account of the actual drama: the immediate end, "The true copy, in substance, of the late Earle of Essex, his behavior, speech, and prayer, at the time of his execution." Such an account was necessary perhaps because the execution was private. Attendant, however, were "the earls of Cumberland and Hertford, Lord Viscount Bendon, Lord Thomas Haward, the Lord Darcie, and the Lord Compton, as well as sixteen members of the guard, three divines, and the executioner."[36]

In this time and place the costume was part of the cultural demands of the convention.[37] Motivated by a clear sense of ritual propriety, and possible ego, Essex was dressed for the most important event of his life. He wore a gown of wrought velvet, a black satin suit underneath, a black felt hat, and a ruff. He addressed the witnesses with a confession of sin and asked forgiveness of the queen. Reminded by Montford to pray for his enemies, he did so; encouraged against the fear of death by Dr. Barlow himself, he asked God to strengthen him. Barlow reports his formal prayer, which was clearly in the tradition of the soul's last combat:

> O God, Creator of all things,
> and judge of all men, thou
> has let me knowe by warrant
> out of thye worde, that Sathan
> is the most busie when our end
> is neerest, and that Sathan
> being resisted will flee.
> I humbly beseech thee to assist
> me in this last combat. . . .[38]

In the spirit of the *ars moriendi,* including the imagery of the last woodcut, Essex asserted his faith in the happy outcome of the battle.

> Graunt me the inward comfort of thy spirit
> . . . and when my life and body
> shall part, send thy blessed
> Angels which may receive
> my soule, and convaye it
> to the joyes in heaven.[39]

It would have been difficult for anyone familiar with the many woodcuts and engravings of the final scene of the deathbed to avoid seeing in the words the small body of the soul issuing from the mouth of the dying into the hands of an angel. Just before his dying Essex had announced, "In humility and obedience I prostrate myself to my deserved punishment."[40]

Having confessed himself fully, he rehearsed the Lord's prayer; paid the executioner and gave his forgiveness to him; said the Creed and two verses of Psalm 51. At the end, he spoke another short prayer as he prepared to prostrate himself. His final words, echoing Christ and again sounding the conventions of the good death, were "Lord into thy hands I commend my spirite." The little drama was complete, a dignified and humble liturgical submission to death. Barlow tells us that his head was severed in three blows, but the first was "deadly, and absolutely."[41]

This deceptively simple ritual contained the essential themes and attitudes of Renaissance dying. Whatever internal reservations may have remained, it is no wonder that Essex's death profoundly moved those who watched, calling forth as it did those associations. His prayer framed him before those present as one who was setting his soul in order for eternity. The final act of Essex's life redeems the image of his life in some fundamentally dramatic way from the randomness and disorder that emerge in his history. The Christian pilgrimage asserts its pattern by which the self created by God is restored to its purified selfhood by the encounter with dying. The audience was obviously convinced.

My reading of such a transformation (whatever questions one may have about its literal truth), or perhaps, more modestly, of the effects of a somewhat messy, inconsistent, willful, and charming man's ritualized and public dying, suggests the narrative and dramatic power of such rituals to integrate and order a life. Anthropologists have seen in drama itself considerable analogous power. Similarly, the completed story of Essex provided an actual historical representation of human dying that Shakespeare's audience would have brought to tragic viewing in the storehouse of their imaginations.[42] One remembers that *Hamlet* appeared in the same year.

In other words, something happens in the *playing* of the scene itself. The powerful cultural elements of setting one's life in order for death did, even in the highly charged political atmosphere of the early seventeenth century, *effect* a change in Essex. *Cultural* script and improvisation—almost in direct opposition to the particular character of Essex—seem to bring about the actual reconciliation of rebel and authority. That it happened only after undoubted brutal manipulation of power and pressure while he was imprisoned nevertheless does not negate the change. It could happen only perhaps in a culture where civic progress, tournament, and rhetoric all provide a near-constant interplay between idea and mimesis, thus reminding the audience and the player of values that can raise ordinary life into a ceremony of innocence.

3

The Popular Word:
Two Case Studies in Devotion

> Life (saith the Philosopher) is but a borrowed dreame of pleasure, a vision of delight, a pageant of transitory happinesse, and Death is a Harbinger of eternitie, a bringer of felicitie, a Messenger of glory & it is a pyrat of life, and yet a pilot to life, a conductor to the heavenly haven of blisse, the Angell to keepe Paradise, wherein none enters but by the entrance of his fatall sword. Sith therefore (Death) thou art the Groomeporter to let out life, and let in life, the remouer (as Aeschilus calleth thee) of worldly sorrows. . . . I hereby welcome thee to the loathsome banquet of my body. . . . that I may say my Grace at this last supper, and then sit down upon my dying bed.—Samuel Garey, *Deaths Welcome*[1]

The *Word* not only suggests what moderns would call the "verbal tradition" but also asserts the continuity between the Bible as Logos, the ultimate source of the Judeo-Christian tradition whose concepts conflate to form the root metaphor of Renaissance language, and the various expressions of biblical symbolism in contemporary verbal texts of early modern England. The seventeenth-century reader of literature and Shakespeare's audiences, whatever class, age, or condition, shared in this symbolic system. Scholars have noticed that Roman Catholic and Protestant alike at the end of the sixteenth century quote freely from Scripture and at the same time allude to Bible stories and images that become part of the symbolic folk scripture inherited from the Middle Ages.[2] With the increasing loss of the saints as familiar emblems of sacred story, renewed interest in prophets and patriarchs produced another category of popular biblical symbols.[3] Certainly the humanist tradition and the tremendous interest in biblical translation stimulated by the invention of moveable type and by Reformation impulses gave new life to the typological scheme by which theological commentary and illustration had during the Middle Ages knit together Old and New Testament into a veritable code of commonplace theology.[4] And the Word as related to death—the binding together of life and death in a great system of paradoxical fear and welcome—distilled those typological relationships.

Even in the midst of the theological controversies that buzzed around other aspects of life, books of devotion, comparatively conservative, continued through the seventeenth century to incorporate variations upon the typological system, including selected wisdom from the classics. Samuel Garey in the quotation at the head of this chapter includes Angels, Paradise, and Aeschylus in a completely easy combination. It is almost as if encroaching changes intensified the desire to link aspects of historical experience with a central Christian message that found its real focus in the context of dying. Frequently, it becomes tedious reading to have all the biblical types of some act or aspect of Christ's nature listed, as the preacher Perkins in a tract lists the last words of virtually every person who dies in the Bible (and some in later history), including a few classical figures, in order to illustrate his Cambridge humanistic education.[5]

At the center of typology, of course—the point of reference for all other examples—is the figure of Christ himself. Scholars have noticed that the late sixteenth and the early seventeenth century saw in the words or acts of virtually any figure in the Old Testament (or historical figures in ancient or in modern times) some parallel to the words and life of Christ. Erasmus gave impetus to this habit of mind by emphasizing the simplicity of following the steps or the way of Christ. Thomas à Kempis's *Imitatio Christi*, first translated into English in the early sixteenth century, went through numerous editions during the next hundred years. Although the editions slowed down in the latter half of the century, there is still a translation by B. F. in 1615 listed in the STC.[6]

The third edition of a popular devotional work, Jerome's *Seaven Helpes to Heaven*, was published in 1620. It contains not only Simeon's "dying Song, directing one to live holly and dye happily," but also an account of the dying words of the martyrs, said to be like "Apples of Gold in Pictures of Silver."[7] The emphasis upon the welcoming aspects of death was an important strain in the seventeenth-century devotional efforts to stress comfort over fear. Most important for the *ars* tradition was the idea that the death of Christ was the supreme example of the type to which the Christian's own death should in crucial aspects conform. One of the major links of this idea with drama was the way in which the tradition of sacred kingship provided a historical type of Christ.

The verbal tradition that shapes these themes is too complex to treat comprehensively as a unit within this chapter. To assess its richness in providing a web of association with death for seventeenth-century readers and for Shakespeare's audience, full coverage would demand inclusion of many kinds of verbal texts: survivals of the *ars* and other traditions within the iconography of death in ballads, devotional treatises, lyric and epic poems, sermons, epitaphs, liturgical services, and so on, perhaps even to smaller subcategories.[8] In this chapter, however, rather than a systematic history of works or even theological ideas, I have selected two devotional texts (to be considered along with earlier allusions to event and image) to establish the large outlines of popular convention. In representative works, popular convention often touches off powerful subliminal responses in the audience of the period; perhaps more crucial for modern readers is the hope of seeing a single text as an illuminated window into the experience of the past.

Two popular texts, then, represent the art of dying for this chapter, although I shall allude to other devotional works in the historic context. Both were published in the period between 1590 and 1610, the years that appear to be most crucial for the study of commonplace associations for Shakespeare's audience as it reacted to the tragedies. We shall see that even in the 1620s Donne's congregation responds to most of the same themes. Although in most of the *ars* books and their heirs, Catholic and Protestant, the major themes and issues are similar, a few differences in assumption and emphasis have caused me to select two popular examples—one from each major tradition, Roman Catholic and Protestant: Don Peter of Luca's *A Dialogue of Dying Wel*, translated from Italian into French and finally in 1602 into English by Richard Verstegan and William Perkins's *A Salue for a Sicke Man*, published in 1595 by the printer for Cambridge University (republished in Perkins's works in 1612).[9] Although clearly by our period the Anglican Church is well established, devotional books include both Catholic and Protestant examples, as Martz has shown.

Both texts must be seen against their generic heritage. They are descendants of the old *ars* blockbooks, with many of the same characteristics. They derive from Caxton's unillustrated *ars The Craft for to deye* (1491) and therefore bear no woodcuts.[10] At the same time, they reiterate most of the old themes, obviously elaborated, as those of a hundred years earlier. The call to the continual remembrance of death echoes across the centuries in *A Dialogue of Dying Wel:* "Nothing truly is more apt and profitable than the continual remembrance of death, and the meditation thereof used and practiced as it ought to be."[11] Perkins opens his essay with the gloomy verse from Ecclesiasticus (and the classics) that sounds the related *contemptus mundi* theme: "The day of death is better than the day

that one is bourne."[12] The extreme popularity of such books in England indicates the widespread interest in common devotional
themes. Religious books represent well over three quarters of the
books published in England between 1560 and 1640, as one sees
easily from the STC.

Although there are constant reminders in both books, as in all
such books, that living well is dying well, the emphasis in these as
in all the best examples of the *ars* books, remains on the deathbed
experience. The late medieval attitudes toward dying are remarkably hardy as mediated through the Christian humanists and even
within the later Puritan tradition. For English persons of the time
the immediate question concerned survival of the soul in the last
combat with Satan and the pains of death. Underlying that concern
is the great psychomachic struggle to overcome evil with good. All
the great family of the *ars* books is centrally concerned with overcoming sin: the complex confrontation of the individual with the
sins of a lifetime and the necessarily accompanying reassurance
that he can be given of the salvation of his soul.[13] Traditional Roman
Catholics were more concerned with the means of salvation; Calvinist Protestants with election; Anglicans with a more broadly pervasive doctrine of grace.[14] But all persuasions (in our period mostly
within Anglicanism) accented the means of overcoming sin as they
lay dying. In an age that still believed eternity hung upon the tuning
of the soul on the deathbed, clear instruction for such a process was
in great demand, and the texts by Peter de Luca and Perkins are
only two of many in the period. Such a concern may seem to moderns obsessive and morbid, but—to oversimplify—it may be seen
as parallel to the modern desire to achieve success, to fulfill one's
potentiality, or to restore self-esteem.

Zachary Boyd's *The Last Battel of the Soule in Death* is a late
Scottish (1629) example of the *ars* tradition that spells out in two
volumes nearly all the issues that devotional writers had explored
for nearly two hundred years. An earlier and less extended work
is the popular Thomas Becon's *The Sicke Mans Salue,* which was
published by the great printer John Day in 1582 and which (although
still in one volume) also tried to cover all the relevant devotional
themes, particularly through the then-current form of the dialogue,
in this instance between the sick man Epaphroditus and his friends
Philemon, Eusebius, Theophilus, and Christopher. This book is an
amalgamation of Christian-Stoic-Calvinist ideas and begins appropriately enough by setting forth Job as a type of perfect patience.[15]
As in the two later texts, the fundamental assumption is that this
life is transitory and of much less importance than the one to come:

"Man that is bourne of a woman hath but a short tyme that he liveth, he is replenished with many miseries. He cometh and withereth away agayne like a flower."[16]

Although secular concerns in early modern England must have moderated the *contemptus mundi* theme, it remains a familiar staple in the devotional tradition as well as the sermons of the period. From the beginning of the sixteenth century to the end of the first third of the seventeenth virtually all the English *ars* books sound the ancient and melancholy theme of mortality from the Bible and other religious writings. First the reader is told to confront the necessity of death, and then he is told that he must prepare himself for it. The typology referred to includes both the Bible and the great figures of classical learning. By the end of the sixteenth century, Socrates with his dictum of "daily dying" seems virtually as authoritative as Job.[17] "Pray for me, Socrates," says the great humanist Erasmus.

The preparation for death includes a body of basic instruction: Once the necessity of death is accepted, what is essential to a happy outcome is to confront the "sting" of death, the sin by which Satan brought death into the world, the possibility of spiritual death. There are in the devotional books various means of confronting such sin, but the characteristic symbolic mode of the *ars moriendi* books has at its center the metaphor of the last combat with the devil, and some form of that combat becomes a defining aspect of the *ars*. In other words, as we saw in the visual images, the *moriens* in the text of these books is described as facing the series of five temptations and five inspirations that was the central structure of both the earliest fifteenth-century *ars* texts: the nonillustrated Caxton mentioned above and the great woodblock series of eleven scenes accompanied by text.[18] These temptations and variations upon comforts and strengths that will help the dying to overcome the former become the sign of the *ars* tradition and herald the expected way by which English men and women came to confront the sins of a lifetime.

By the end of the sixteenth century and the turn of the seventeenth, devotional works began to displace the narrative forms of both temptations and inspirations. The clarity of the metaphor and the drama of the confrontation largely gave way to homily and theologizing, and the books elaborate upon, and allude to, the structure of the combat, without, after all, making the narrative metaphor apply to the work. Sometimes not all of the temptations are mentioned. Frequently the inspirations are cast in terms of comforts as the balance seems to shift away from fear. As a student pointed out some years ago in a dissertation on Donne's use of the *ars*, the popular texts still present or allude to the combat—such representative devotional works that extend well into the seventeenth century, including, in addition to the several already mentioned, *The Doctrine of Dying-Well;* Nicholas Byfield's *The Cure of the Fear of Death;* Robert Hill's *The Path-way to Prayer and Pietie;* Cardinal Bellarmine's *Art of Dying Well;* James Cole's *Of Death a True Description;* Christopher Sutton's *Disce Mori;* and Lewis Bayley's little jewel, *The Practice of Piety.*[19] In the best of these, a simple piety transcends the moralizing and creates a voice of innocence and devotion, but the medieval legend of the combat does not provide the organizational metaphor.

From these seventeenth-century examples of the English *ars* we might speculate that the old medieval structure of the psychomachia surfaces with its opposition between virtues and vices. But it has been so fully integrated into the seventeenth-century English Pauline attitudes toward death that interest has shifted to some of the more displaced elements, i.e., particular situations, as we see in Perkins's little book designed especially for sailors who might die at sea, soldiers going into battle, and women about to suffer the considerable dangers of childbirth.[20] Practical instructions for setting one's house in order and writing one's will also tended to be more greatly elaborated in the later Puritan seventeenth-century books. But we would be mistaken to assume from the shift in structure that the spiritual combat between temptations and inspirations is no longer underlying the tradition. Certainly it survives at a deep level, as we shall see later. Shakespeare, for example, like other artists, pares away some of the theologizing in order to refocus the tradition in earlier metaphorical and dramatic terms.

In the *ars* books I have chosen as representative at the end of the century, there seems to be little theological justification for the necessity for death; the emphasis is experiential or psychological rather than theological. It is in the more sophisticated, and more intellectual, theological tracts, such as Hooker's "Laws of Ecclesiastical Policy," that sin is explored in detail as the consequence of the Fall or that a philosophic or semimedical argument is presented for sin and death as necessary to the nature of human beings.[21] Such a necessity is largely assumed in the more popular devotional tracts, where the emphasis remains on how to combat death. That man fell by Adam and rose by Christ is the balance upon which the Old and New Testaments hang in the popular imagination. And death came into the world with Adam. Yet the sternness of death as terrifying warning does not set the tone of most books in the devotional tradition. As we might gather from the earlier section on the image, the *memento mori* theme sounds most insistently in the ballads, where sometimes the visual images of the *danse macabre* are also stunning warnings to prepare. In most of the late sixteenth-century examples of the verbal tradition the emphasis emerges clearly as upon the comforts, the assurances that can see one through the valley of the shadow of death. Inevitably fear is a strong impetus, but in most of the treatises, it is quickly channeled into instruction designed to help the individual combat his sense of helplessness before mortality.

Many of these brief (sometimes only 10–17 pages) devotional books focus on the theme of overcoming the fear of death. An early example is Erasmus's A *Comfortable Exhortation Agaynste the Feare of Death,* dedicated to a friend who is grieving.[22] Probably most of these books are designed to comfort those who are grieving over the loss of family and friends. Even in a random sampling of *ars* books (in addition to the Erasmus *Exhortation*) there are several others explicitly dedicated to the grieving: one to the Countess of Pembroke and one to Elizabeth, daughter of Charles I and the Queen of Bohemia (volume II of Boyd's *The Last Battell*). The latter, which contains a powerfully dramatic statement of the queen's own lamentation over the loss of her son, is couched in images of grief (mostly biblical) that echo David's lamentation for Absalom: "Would that I had died for thee."[23] The lamentation appears at the beginning of the volume, and the comforts seem to follow in a natural sequence from that recognition of grief. Inevitably, a personal loss presents a stimulus to the meditation on death—the loss itself a particularized *memento mori,* but we shall pursue this in the third section of this book.

Since the desire to comfort the grieving as well as the sick is frequently the immediate stimulus for such tracts, one need not be surprised at the number of such works that strongly focus the comforts of the tradition, sounding the *contemptus mundi* in moving and poetic terms. Foxe in *An Exhortation to the Sicke* is both homely and poetic as he comforts not the grieving but those who are themselves in danger of death:

> So also it [death] taketh us away from the sharpe
> winter and al bitter stormes: it taketh a man
> from hys frendes and kinfolkes. So also it doth
> from all his enemies and slaundering tongues;
> plucketh you from wife and children; adde also
> from all the griefes and sorrowes that happen by wyfe and
> children.[24]

Death here loses its macabre personification and emerges as an agent of release, a change that attracts to the image some of the qualities of popular stoicism. Later Milton records that change. Similarly, the titles themselves of some of the works reveal such an emphasis, as for example, in the little book by Baynes, *Comfort and Instruction in Affliction: A Letter full of divine comforts and instructions unto all, in the time of sicknesse, or any other chastisements of the Lord* or, earlier, Becon's *The Solace of the Sovle agaynst the bytter stormes of sycknes and death, greatly encouragynge the faythfull, paciently to suffer the good pleasure of God in all kynde of aduersitiee.*[25] Obviously, great funeral sermons of the period tended also to focus comfort and patience for the mourners as well as praise for the dead. By the end of the sixteenth century there seem to be few (as one might expect) within the devotional category that gave free play to the awesome and macabre power of Death. Samuel Rowland's *A Terrible Battell between the two consumers of the whole world: time and death* (1606) is one of the few exceptions that suggest the somber melancholy that pervades Donne's *Deaths Duell.*[26]

The two main representations of the popular devotional tradition of the late sixteenth and early seventeenth centuries show a "tame" death, one that devotional writers tried to portray as the instrument of a merciful God in his elaborate articulation of a fallen nature softened by redemption.[27] One might remember, however, that so strong a reiteration of comfort would be but one side of the cultural dialectic: it is surely a response to a historic situation, the growing sense in the early seventeenth century of a world in which both the body politic and the ancient institution of the church were either corrupt or beset and fragmented. In England specifically, even in the greatest period of preaching and power in the Word as it came through the Book of Common Prayer and the King James Version of the Bible, there were tensions and conflicts within Anglicanism that would in the forties erupt in the Puritan Revolution.

In the body politic, there was a general disappointment in the ability of James to project the image of a great prince that Elizabeth had provided for the English during the period of the Armada. Economic and political factors inevitably played against religious ones, and scholars have seen the drama of the first thirty years of the century as reflecting a growing sense of melancholy and loss of optimism. Writers of all kinds of devotional literature sought to reassert hope and order, but they in some measure pulled against the stream. The growth of the Cult of Elizabeth, with its nostalgia for the great days of Elizabeth's reign, suggests the growing disillusionment during the early years of the Stuarts.[28] Literary and worldly men like Ralegh and Donne believed the world was in its last age, and the drama—more sensitive than other forms of literature to the mood of the time—moved through tragedy to a sense of "problem" and finally to the Shakespearean reconcilements of the romances, only to become in the hands of the Jacobean playwrights a body of literature that was a bellwether for corruption.

Our two representative texts stand as examples of the popular efforts to shore up hope and to reassert the ancient, powerful theme of Christian redemption against the building insecurity of a civilization whose institutions had been weakened at the foundations. For ordinary people, however, the great new ideas of science or the secular implications of Reformation theology were surely as remote as the shifting moon herself. Uneasiness and pessimism were contagious, but these were largely feelings, not philosophy. The devotional tracts did not have to answer complex arguments. They merely had to sound again the familiar themes that asserted eternal values in a world that people knew uneasily was always shifting with the moontides but which seemed especially unstable with the changing of the Elizabethan political order to that of the Stuarts.[29] *A Dialogue of Dying Well* reasserts the seeds of the tradition: the inexorability of death, the unreliability of the world, and the concern for personal salvation, all part of a unified tradition from the Christian past but shaped and intensified by current political and religious forces. The tradition articulates itself as representative of a unity of disparate attitudes or historical perspectives:

> Wyse Salomon, Diuyne Plato, moral Seneca, yea and all our holy men of tyme past, as well learned as unlearned, have of one accord confirmed & approved this doctrine of death both with words and deeds. (sig. C–C2)

Hebraic, Platonic, Roman philosophies all fuse with the holy voices of the Christian tradition. This little book, like such widely different works as the earlier More's *Utopia* and later Becon's *Salue for a Sicke Manne,* is written in the popular form of the dialogue, but the dialogue between Merchant and Hermit is mainly a frame for the Hermit's instruction for the good death, which begins with an interpretation of what the "remembrance" of death consists (sig. C2). According to the Hermit, the conventional channel for such a remembrance is

> Willinglie to heare speaking and preaching of the terrible conditions & paynes of death, and willinglie to read spiritual books, where that matter

is handled, and where the stories and examples bee written of many persons, which by feare of death have been converted. For such examples help much, and not a little more sinners to repentance. (sig. C2)

In a fundamental sense, the Hermit follows the Ignatian meditative "psychology," whose first stage is an appeal to the senses by which the mind may be channeled into the full meditative concentration. According to St. Bernard, the memory is awakened by such an appeal.[30] In meditation on the passion, for example, one must first read the gospel and image forth the sensory details of the scene. Meditation upon death, however, has a second phase that may more effectively stimulate the memory than either the sacred texts of the Scriptures or spiritual books based upon it: And that, says the Hermit, is the practice of visiting the dying, as well as graveyards, monuments, and sepulchers of the dead (sig. C2).

The second phase of remembrance urged by the Hermit includes a section devoted to the conventional meditation upon the skull and mortality. With its *ubi sunt* theme and its questions of the owner, the meditation on the skull may seem unusually extended to the modern reader, who may well ask why the visiting of the sick and dying should not have allowed a similar elaboration. The popularity and power of the skull as an emblem of meditation produced and reproduced in graphics, paintings, design, and even jewelry are keys to the answer. It is this popularity that Shakespeare plays with in the graveyard scene in *Hamlet*. The major theme of the skull's imagined answer is that the owner was unprepared for death, and the meditation becomes a further stimulation to the living to die daily (sig. C3–C5).

The third and most important instruction by the Hermit, however, is one in which the pains of death are felt, as the Hermit puts it, "in our selves" (sig. C5). The first we have seen with our eyes, the second heard with our ears, and the third goes inward, where the Merchant is warned to prepare the soul to be strong and constant against its own death (sig. C5). The structure of the preparation is one that, like the Ignation pattern, appeals to the memory through the eyes, stimulates discursive reason through hearing what goes on at the actual deaths of others, and finally moves the affections through the facing of one's own death.

Such a remembrance is, of course, in great measure, a somber warning and intended to arouse fear. A sophisticated devotional tradition had developed over many centuries that struggled with the fact of mortality within the paradox of Christian fear and hope. Within that rhetorical tradition, even in the hands of popular writers and preachers, a subtle articulation of human fears and longings had been built into the conventions—just enough fear and warning to draw the reader or listener into full openness to the instruction for dying. Writers of such treatises were aware that too much fear could lead to despair, and so they struggled with the necessity to structure the rhetoric to articulate emotions to end in hope.

In the instruction concerning the actual moments of dying, the author marshals the comforts and practical means to assure salvation. As we might expect, this little Roman Catholic manual is both more elaborate in its instruction and more sacramental in its emphasis than Perkins's treatise. It is more conservative than the main line of devotion or even the main line of humanist culture that McClure in his important essay on humanist mourning describes as having moved from the comfort of ritual to the more rhetorical comforts of language. Although the fifteenth-century *ars* texts were designed originally for those who died without benefit of attending clergy, almost simultaneously books appeared that urged the importance and comfort of extreme unction.[31]

The ideal death, after all, in the Roman Catholic tradition pictured in the Books of Hours and often illustrated by the death scenes of saints or the Virgin, showed the *moriens* receiving the last sacrament. Anglicanism picks up this theme in the 1609 Book of Common Prayer:

> But if any man, either by reason of extremitie of sickenesse, or for want of warning in due time to the Curate, or for lacke of company to receive with him, or by any other just impediment, doe not receive the Sacrament of Christes body and blood: then the Curate shall instruct him, that if he doe truely repent him of his sinnes, and stedfastly believe that Jesus Christ hath suffered death upon the Crosse for him, and shed his blood for his redemption, earnestly remembering the benefits hee hath thereby, and giving him hearty thanks therefore, hee doeth eate and drinke the body and blood of our saviour Christ profitably to his soules health although he doe not receive the Sacrament with his mouth.

In spite of the origin of the *ars* in a plague situation that often prohibited the presence of clergy at the deathbed, most of the Roman Catholic texts make it clear that the presence of clergy at the death is highly desirable.[32] Likewise, by the early seventeenth century Anglican funeral sermons also indicate that ministers were often present at the dying.

In *A Dialogue*, the Roman author urges the availability of the Eucharist and Unction. Verstegan advises further that the reader take advantage of the sacraments of the church throughout a lifetime. At the dying itself, the author asks friends to be present who will take upon themselves the responsibility to have the sacrament available, as well as images of the crucifix and of "our Ladie." The text points to the crucifix as the crucial image from the woodcuts to serve both as an amulet against demons and as the central symbol of the mercy of God. The image of "our Ladie," however, is included only in frankly Roman texts such as this one.

In the description of the last temptations of the devil the writer of the *Dialogue* or the persona of the Hermit generalizes more broadly. That is, with the exception of a reference or two to the Virgin, the instruction is what one would find in either Catholic or Protestant treatises of this kind, including the advice to avoid either vainglory or desperation as one assesses the possibility of his own salvation. The emphasis again is on reassurance: if one takes the occasion of every small sickness to arm himself against the devil—if he bears in mind always the mercy of Christ—he will have a happy issue out of the trials of death. On the level of his earthly relationships and responsibilities, the *moriens* is advised to have a friend or friends present who will help set in order his earthly possessions. He must discharge debts, pass on belongings, and be sure that he is reconciled to everyone. The friends also have the responsibility to encourage him, once these practical matters are taken care of, to continue the full preparation of his soul.

The last chapter deals, then, with this final stage of preparation, in which the Hermit sets forth a fourfold rule for dying according to the pattern set forth in the death of Christ:

> for wee ought to know, that as the lyfe of our Saviour hath bene geuen vs for a rule, and for the instruction of our lyfe: so also his death hath bene set before vs to teach vs how to dy. (35)

This passage implies a predominantly Roman approach. Though Protestant instructions emphasize also the mercy of Christ as central and refer to his life and last words as a pattern to be followed, the suffering and Passion as such do not become such an elaborated focus. For example, the third rule mentioned above refers to Christ's leavetaking of his mother and his friends (sig. F). The application of the four rules is explained with great care, again in the Roman tradition with emphasis upon a ritual set of acts. Conventionally, however, the four acts of preparation by Christ were the following: first, that he ascended the cross poor, as R. V. puts it, "reserving no worldly thing for himself"; second, that he prayed for himself and for his enemies; third, that he took leave of his mother and friends and commended his mother to the care of his beloved friend John; and fourth, that with cries, tears, and prayers, he commended his spirit to the Father. These four acts become the basis for four rules in the last stage of dying, and the Hermit urges their application:

> all these things ought the sick man to do, that is vpon his last passage, and in the agonie of death. So that after he hath caused his parents and frendes to retyre; having taken his leaue of them, hee shal first think vpon the state of his conscience, and then call vpon almighty God, not with a loud voyce but with deep and profound sighes from the bottome of his hart, . . . let him repent himself of eurie sinne he hath committed . . . of ten tymes let him say. *In manus tuas Domine commendo spiritum meum.* (38)

One would think that this meditation upon the last stage of dying would end *A Dialogue,* but after the peroration the young Merchant turns to the Hermit to ask questions that have raised doubts for him: (1) whether we are bound to desire death; (2) whether we should have ill opinion of those who die unwillingly; (3) whether we should also have a bad opinion of those who die mad or with blasphemies on their tongues; and (4) whether we should think ill of those who die suddenly or violently; (5) whether it is lawful to wish to communicate with the dead; (6) whether deathbed repentance is possible to those who have lived ill; (7) whether the devil appears to all who die; (8) whether Christ will descend corporally to judge everyone particularly; (9) whether Christ appears generally to all at the hour of death; (10) whether judgment takes place immediately after death; (11) whether, if particular judgment takes place, the soul is carried to the appointed place; (12) if everyone suffers equally in death (pp. 39–49).

Such questions remind us that the *ars* tradition is old and well developed. At one time or another, all the important questions have been asked, and these late versions from Becon to Boyd suggest increasing efforts to be comprehensive. The Hermit's answers are largely the expected ones that bring comfort. One does not necessarily desire death, but one must not cling to life. Because we cannot tell whether the wild words of the deathbed are the natural end of a wicked life or the result of sickness, we should not necessarily think ill of one who dies in such a state. However sudden or violent a person's end, it is a good death if the life has been good. The continuing tradition of the folklore behind the *ars* is supported by the Hermit's answer that "ordinarily the devils appear to all" (44–45);

the Hermit cites the testimony of holy men, particularly Ecclesiasticus, St. Vincent, and St. Gregory:

> The same S. Gregorie also wryteth that the devil in the end of lyfe appeereth aswel to the good as the evil; yea and that hee durst appear to Christe himself beeing on the crosse. (45)

The redemptive message of the *ars* tradition is summarized in the Hermit's answer as to whether Christ appears corporally to make personal judgment at each death:

> . . . it is not conuenable that Christes humanitie in one instant should bee to this end in so many places, and therefore they say, our blessed Saviour doth not discend personally to give this particular judgment, but rather committeth that office to the good Angel that is given vs four our gard, . . . and the Angel, so made iudge, condemneth or absolueth the soule according to iustice: and after guideth it to the place assinged, eyther in heauen, in hell, or in purgatorie, according as it hath deserued. But to the vniuersal judgment, our blessed Saviour will discend and judge the quick and the dead. (46)

Notice that the function of the Guardian Angel underlines the way in which the deathbed has become an individual "Last Judgment," consolingly reassuring for those who were not entirely sure what delays might keep them from heavenly bliss. After the Hermit has satisfied the questions and doubts of the young man, he leaves with the Hermit's blessing and in order to learn to die well (we are told) gives all his riches to the poor, to churches, and to hospitals; enters into religion; and observes all the rules set forth by the wise old Hermit, until at least "having liued long and vertuously, hee happely rendred his sould into the handes of this creator, to whome bee all honour and glorie world withoutend, Amen" (50–51). Thus ends the little treatise made up of the narrative frame that includes the Hermit and Merchant and that contained three chapters of instruction and twelve rules (four in each chapter)—all an elaborate preparation for dying in the Roman Catholic tradition.

The emerging Protestant version of the tradition can be seen in numerous guises. William Perkins was one of the most popular of the "new men." Perkins, an Anglican preacher, published his little manual, *A Salve for a Sicke Man*, in 1595, a few years before the English translation of *A Dialogue*. Its alternate title suggests more explicitly its interest in regard to our current subject: *A Treatise Containing the Nature, Differences, and Kindes of Death; As Also the Right Manner of Dying Well.* The title page informs us that it is not intended, however, to be a simple restructuring of the old *ars* manuals for those who die a peaceful death with friends about them. Rather, as mentioned earlier, it is intended for those who might die suddenly violently, or out of season: for mariners, soldiers, or women in childbirth. These three types of persons might be more in need of comfort and instruction than the usual English person of the period because they would be unlikely to die under the same leisurely circumstances as those who died in season.[33]

There is modernity in Perkins that is missing in Peter de Luca, and even though, as Martz has told us, Protestants read Catholic books of devotion, the more Protestant attitudes that allowed more particularizing of situations and class were gaining popularity. The little book suggests the greater awareness of differences in social circumstances among the new Anglican clergy, the more highly developed rhetoric aimed at different audiences by the end of the sixteenth century, and the increasing sensitivity to the varied circumstances of ordinary English people. At any rate, one notices that many of the devotional manuals by the early seventeenth century are more particularized as to audience, whether they are aiming at a new broader audience that buys devotional books on the streets of London or at the patronage of the gentry or the aristocracy. For example, Boyd's *Last Battell of the Soule*, volume I, is dedicated to Charles I; volume II is dedicated to Elizabeth, Queen of Bohemia and daughter of James I, as a book of comfort for the death of her child and shows in its form its royal patronage.[34]

Perkins's devotional book, however, aimed at a popular, predominantly bourgeois audience, is (like Anglicanism in the period) deeply imbued with the Calvinist model of reality and reflects that influence in its practical focus upon an orderly, sober, but not mystical, preparation for death. On a more theological plane, it emphasizes the necessity of being "redeemed, justified, sanctified by Christ."[35] Like *A Dialogue for Dying Wel*, *A Salve* begins with the *contemptus mundi* theme. For aristocrat and ordinary Englishmen alike at the turn of the century there was the radical necessity to establish that special perspective through which death might seem welcome. As Perkins puts it—and here he is in touch with the harsh realities of life's struggle for the English person of the nineties—

Furthermore, when God will send his own servants to heaven, he sends them a contrary way, even by the gates of hell: and when it is his pleasure to make men depend on his favor and providence, he makes feele his anger and to be nothing in themselves, that they may wholly depend upon him, and be whatsoever they are in him. (p. 15)

"To be nothing in themselves, that they may wholly depend vpon him"—as Lewalski and William Halewood, among others, have established—in the English church of the end of the century the imprint of Calvinism was strong.[36] Perkins's attitude toward dying is part and parcel of his view of a world largely determined by God's fore-ordination. Such a world is one in which joy comes only to those who live life in full submission to providence, who accept suffering as the way by which the elect come to belong ultimately to Christ, "rescued" by a radical grace, justified by an utterly submissive faith.

Perkins's powerful image of the love of God sums up the appeal to the imagination of a faith that demands an absolute letting go of the individual will; he begins in what is his most moving metaphor:

> The love of God is like a sea, into which when a man is cast, he neither feeles bottome nor sees banke. . . . (15)

The simple metaphor of the swimmer suggests Perkins's gift for reaching a broad audience. In sum, Perkins says that the love of God is mysterious and wonderful and terrible—beyond the human ability to see boundaries, bottoms, or limits. So risky is such a life of commitment to God, says Perkins, that one may likely at times be subject to despair; he goes on, however, to comfort his reader with the doctrine of election:

> therefore . . . despaire, wither it arise of weaknesses of nature or of conscience of sinne; though it fall out about the time of death, can not prejudice the salvation of them that are effectually called. (15)

This Calvinist statement differs from the Roman attitude expressed in the Dialogue in its greater sympathy for the depths of fear and the greater recognition that the darkness of human experience can overwhelm the individual consciousness. At the same time, this statement also asserts the absolute certainty of the love that controls the fate of those "effectually called," the elect, whose salvation is assured. In an important sense, this paradox of helplessness and assurance becomes widely felt in England in the early seventeenth-century. It becomes a popular assumption for many Anglicans who are not strictly Calvinist but who experience the influence of Calvinism within the Anglican church. Perkins thought of himself as mainline Anglican, not Puritan.

In spite of the apparent severity and simplicity of the doctrine of election, scholars are aware that election worked on the human personality in sophisticated ways. On a fundamental level, it

brought about a kind of self-fashioning whereby the Christian tried
to create himself in his image of the elect.[37] For one thing, it allowed
its advocates to notice and to tolerate more openly the many variations on human responses among the dying. From this perspective,
it was not necessary to prove salvation through works and in so
doing to distort human behavior in order to convince both others
and oneself of merit. As Perkins admits in his treatise,

> And first of all touching despaire, it is true that not only wicked and
> loose persons despaire in death, but also repentant sinners, who often-
> times in their sicknesse, testify of themselues as it were to be in hell,
> and to apprehend the very pangs and torments thereof. (14)

English people of the period had noticed themselves that the good
did not always die peacefully as one expected them to, and the devotional literature developed a compassionate view of the variations
caused by illness and other circumstances. Once Perkins has established through the conventions of the *contemptus mundi* his dark
vision of life under time, he moves swiftly into the subject of death
as a welcome release from the misery of life and the pangs of death:

> Thus much of freedom from misery, which is the first benefit that comes
> by death, and the first step to life: now follows the second, which is, that
> death gives an entrance to the soule, that it may come into the presence
> of the everliving God, of Christ, of all the angels and saints in heaven.
> (23)

According to most of the devotional writers, this release from
suffering is what makes the horrifying fact of death bearable, even
joyful: "The worthiness of this benefit makes the death of the righteous to be no death, but rather a blessing to be wished of all men"
(p. 23). Out of the *contemptus mundi* assumption springs the rigorist
view by which all mourning for the dead was thought by some zeal-
ous Puritans to be sinful.[38]

For all his practical common sense and his careful attention to
the ordering of life as preparation for death, Perkins transforms the
hope of eternal felicity into a poetic vision of the interval of sleep in
death from which the elect ultimately wake in joy:

> Even so the bodies of men have their winter also, in which they are
> turned to dust, and so remain for the space of many thousand yeres,
> yet in the day of judgement by means of that mysticall conjunction with
> Christ, shall divine and quickning vertue stream thence to all the bodies

of the elect to cause them to live againe, and that to life eternall . . . . (35)

It is within this transforming vision of the relationship between life and death that Perkins moves into establishing the preparation for death. Out of this assumption one comes to prepare daily for death; as Perkins adopts the familiar Socratic and humanist attitude within his context, "the life of a Christian is nothing but a meditation of death" (35). He urges the reader to accept life as weariness, and pain and death as a bridge to felicity. The general preparation then for dying includes a kind of alertness and sensitivity to all the types of death within life:

> So likewise he that would be able to bear the crosse of all crosses, namely death it self, must first of all learne to beare small crosses, as sicknesses in body, troubles in mind, with losses of goods and of friends, and of good name: which I may fitly tearme little deaths. (47)

Perkins continues to point out, as preachers had been doing for hundreds of years, that afflictions are the "harbingers and purveiors [purveyors] of death" (p. 47). The passage in the treatise rises then to a crescendo of rhetoric that justifies the ongoing preparation as essential to the good death:

> We are first to learn how to intertain these messengers, that when death the lord himselfe shall come, we may in better manner intertain him. (47)

In the next section, Perkins clarifies the major differences between the "papist instruction" and his own. He points out that the Romans insist upon the sacramental approach to dying: (1) sacramental confession; (2) receiving the host; (3) "annoiling" or receiving extreme unction (48–54). According to Perkins, these are all superficial and comparatively useless. As we might expect, he identifies his Protestant instruction with the affective and genuinely heartfelt preparation that he organizes under the general category of seeking reconciliation with God. In his instruction, the dying person must first root out sin by a new examination of heart and life. Then he or she must move to a new confession made directly to God (not through an intermediary). Finally the dying one must make a new prayer of dedication (54–57).

If he cannot do it alone, says Perkins, recognizing the frequent practical limitations of illness—the *moriens* should seek help, confess sins, call others in to pray (58–62). Although this bow to the necessity for intermediary help may seem inconsistent with Perkins's attack upon the papist's reliance upon priestly and sacramental help, it is not really so, since he makes it clear that this is only in case of dire need.

Lest pain and suffering cause the dying to despair, he is advised by Perkins to fix all his thoughts on the blessed afterlife as a means of staying close to God's presence (63–64). In the *ars* books of the period the heavenly afterlife is the obvious comfort. The *moriens* is thus assured and reassured by Perkins of the presence and help of God during this difficult time (70). Perhaps even more strongly comforting than the existence of heaven are the continuities and interpenetrations between heaven and earth in the iconography. The reader is reminded of the rich tradition of comfort out of which all the *ars* books emerge, especially the woodcut series with the consistent reassurance of the presence of the Guardian Angel in the inspirations. In this medium, the universe is a repository of the power of the creator. Perkins emphasizes God's presence through what some critics might label the maternal aspect of his care:

> the ministery of his good Angels, whom the Lord hath appointed as keepers and nources unto his seruants to hold them up and beare them in their armes as a gard unto them against the devil & his angels. And al this is verified specially in sicknes, at which time the holy angels are not only present with such as feare God, but ready also to receive & to carry their souls into heauen, as appears by the example of Lazarus. (70)

Once Perkins has moved his instruction beyond the daily dying into the deathbed itself, he places his manual in the category of the late *ars moriendi* books by including various kinds of practical instruction. He speaks of many kinds of Christian "physicke," making it clear that he affirms the new, more assertive Renaissance attitudes toward the hope of cure through healing (75–77). At the same time, however, he indicates that there comes a point where it is the solemn obligation of the physician to let the patient know that he is dying (79). At this point, then, the patient must turn toward the last major stages of preparation: the setting of his house in order and the final ordering of his soul for the journey.

The first stage is, of course, very concrete: writing a will and fulfilling one's obligations as a steward of God's material gifts to man. In this section, Perkins addresses the practical responsibilities of the dying Christian. For example, he deals with the rules of inheritance and the English legal doctrine of primogeniture (83–87). Although the title pages indicates that the treatise was intended for, among others, women who might die in childbirth, the author actually has in mind, at least in this section, the *pater familias.*

The second stage of preparation is more inward-looking and, in consequence, more interesting to literary scholars. It is the spiritual preparation that includes the tripart injunction to die in faith; to die in obedience; to render one's soul into the hands of God (87–97). In this section Perkins lays great store upon the final prayers and the last words of the dying; among them are represented Moses, David, Christ (including his last words to several people and groups), Steven, Polycarp, and Bernard (87–96).

All the biblical types or models emphasize the reliability of the Word, the master text of the Scriptures as the foundation for moral action as well as the revealer of God's historic relationship with his people. Perkins tells an anecdote about Jacobus Latromus of Louvain, who opposed Luther. In the midst of a public lecture he fell into madness, "uttering such wordes of desperation and blasphemous impietie, that other divines . . . were faine to carry him away" (101–2). Perkins insists that the cause of his madness was withstanding, or *standing against,* the manifest truth of God's word.

Perkins finds it necessary to marshal for the comfort of the dying all the most powerful forces of the Word because with his Roman Catholic brethren, he believes that the last combat with the devil can be the most dangerous of all. Characteristically an anecdotal preacher, he illustrates this point in the *Afterward with the death of that saint of Puritanism John Knox.* Except for sobs and groans, Knox on his deathbed was silent for four hours and then spoke to testify to the cruel assault of the satanic lion (1D9–110). Knox's words emphasize two temptations: those to despair and to worldly attachment:

> . . . he set my sinnes before mine eyes, often he vrged me to desperation, often he laboured to intangle me with the delites of the world. (110)

In the mighty battle Knox conquered Satan with the sword of the spirit, "which is the word of God" (110). But Perkins leaves the reader with a final word from Luther, the single most comforting advice before such danger:

> If thy flesh tremble, and feare to enter into an other life, and doubt of salvation; if thou yield to these things, thou hurtest thy selfe: therefore close thine eyes as before, & say with S. Stephen, Lord Iesus into thy hands I commend my spirit, and then certenly Christ will come vnto thee with all his Angels and be the guider of thy way. (111)

When one compares the contents of these books of devotion from the two major traditions, in spite of some differences in emphasis, they still remain remarkably alike. They both share fundamental assumptions about death: its central place in human experience; the necessity to prepare for it; the biblical models and authority for the modes of such a preparation; the spiritual need for the transformation of hearts and minds. Still rooted in the popular imagination of the culture are two important Christian assumptions: that freedom, joy, salvation may be found primarily in fashioning the self after Christ and that what can be gleaned in broad lines from the Gospel is elaborated in other biblical types in the long history of God's relationship to his people.

As for the major difference in their representation of the devotional tradition of the popular Word at the end of the sixteenth century: Verstegan reasserts a more Catholic and traditionally sacramental approach; Perkins in a more Protestant mode stresses the power of the sacred Word to change hearts. However, each sets at the center of Christian experience the *ars moriendi* with its process of final transformation. In both books, as in the devotional tradition as a whole, the deathbed drama is the central representation—a fact that suggests the way in which facing death was a major encounter in the midst of seventeenth-century life—bridging earthly and eternal life. It was for the people of the time the complex nexus of existence, according to custom the time for all friends and relatives to gather, the time for all differences to be reconciled, the time in which the individual would assess all his relationships in the preparation for judgment. The preparation that was hoped for, that was indeed built into the suggested ritual, was one that would reconcile past and present in the light of a glorious future.

Devotional books alone could not have made this instructiton so essential to seventeenth-century preparation for dying if many aspects of the culture had not brought life to the vision. Event, image, and word—the events of dying itself—were not solely the high dramas of execution but deathbed scenes throughout the land, in families of all classes, although the full ritual must have been limited to the prosperous and often the literate. The images of death that even now have survived from that time suggest the pervasiveness of the symbolism in plate, armor, stained glass, woodcuts, paintings, watches.[39] Many of these artifacts bring a kind of shudder to the modern sensibility. Most fully, perhaps, the subject for modern consciousness emerges from many expressions of the Word. Although the art of dying was itself most explicitly treated in the devotional tradition, the concerns expressed recur in every type of literature that survives—from the Bible, epic, liturgy, and sermons to tragedy and elegy. When Shakespeare shows Lear wracked by grief or Donne in a funeral sermon meditates on the powerful hand of the dead James I or years later when Marvell speaks of the leaden slumber of Cromwell, each draws upon attitudes toward time and death that are deep-rooted in English life.

Part 2
The Temptation to Despair and the Art of Dying

4

"A Long Day's Dying": Spenser and Milton on Despair (1590–1667)

As a frame for chapters that explore the responses of Shakespeare's audience to the submerged, displaced commonplaces of the *ars moriendi* in the plays, Spenser and Milton present an interpretation that is inevitably more allegorical, more literary, and more symbolic and theological than that of the commonplace tradition. In order to assess the full relationship between the literature and the rich associations of the seventeenth-century reader and audience, one must be familiar with the popular tradition, verbal and visual, as it survived in artifact, ballad, preaching, and the devotional literature. One must, however, also be conversant with the poetic transformation of commonplace symbolic material into a more formal metaphorical tradition based on Augustine and the Fathers and articulated by such Anglicans as Richard Hooker, William Perkins, John Donne, and Lancelot Andrews.[1] The amalgam of the popular and the ecclesiastical poetic tradition finds fullest literary expression in the English epic: the sixteenth-century style and romantic mode in Spenser's *Faerie Queene,* the seventeenth century in Milton's *Paradise Lost.*[2] The two great epics are expressive of two phases of symbolic expression in the history of English taste and aesthetic and in the English perception of reality itself.

Shakespeare lies between the aristocratic art of the Renaissance epic as practiced by Spenser and Milton and the more popular forms of explicitly religious literature. It is, after all, these two epics of the English Renaissance (one at the height, the other the summation at the end of the period) that most sharply articulate the ideas and beliefs of the Christian humanist tradition. In recent years, under critical reaction to recent theory, historical scholars have come to a reassertion of the full intertextuality of literary study.[3] Just as important as the pervasiveness of popular symbolism and iconography associated with death that Shakespeare's audience would have brought to performances is the sophisticated and paradoxical system of theological relationships between death on the one hand and hope and fear on the other. The two great epics of the period expose most fully the conscious aspects of such a relationship. Shakespeare, who as a dramatist is fully embedded in the culture, interacts with materials from both directions: high art and the popular tradition. We might see the drama on a spectrum between both theology and poetry, giving them a meeting point in ritual act and bodying forth the complexly evocative representation of experience itself.

To examine theological issues in relation to the associations of Shakespeare's audience or as fundamental to art (that is, as allegorical or thematic structure underlying the rich mimetic surface of Shakespeare's plays) is to court the condemnation of many critics—to be accused of reductionism, either of the audience to a single mind or of the plays themselves to naive allegory. It takes even more than the brilliant rhetorical skills of Rosalie Colie or John Steadman to convince many modern minds that it is possible, indeed necessary, to see a rich and fluid hermeneutic relationship between the allegorical and the symbolic structure of one stratum, both as embedded in the plays or equally in the associations of the audience, and the dramatic mimetic orchestration of the fiction itself.[4]

Such a relationship is essential to the Renaissance in England, an age of belief in which empathy for the dramatic situation is always in dialogue with both theological assumptions and the common values of the culture, still, as it was, predominantly Christian. Interpretations must always remain pluralistic, but scholars who cultivate the historic imagination shaped by Shakespeare and Milton as producing the richest image of the work of art must risk abandoning the multifoliate subjectivism of many modern critics. Recognition of the place of belief within the complex and more pragmatic attitudes of history is a necessary risk if only to avoid the countercharge of shallowness. More deeply, it moves us into the central paradoxes of the period that are embedded in the major works of its greatest literary artists. Without recognition of the root Christian values of the period, the scholar is too much in danger of the worst excesses of making Shakespeare "our" contemporary and substituting for his rich affirmation of a complex reality a merely ambiguous and ambivalent exploration of dichotomies.[5] At the same time, of course, the historian must hold in mind all the subversive aspects of experience that qualify the ideals, particularly ways in which patronage and political power created ambivalences.

Because Renaissance persons were close to a worldview largely in conflict with our own, it is difficult for moderns to appreciate the power of the feelings that lie behind many of their assumptions. As Douglas Bush points out in an essay on "English poetry: Time and Man," the difference between Renaissance understandings of time and eternity and our own largely mechanistic view of an almost infinite span of historic time is so great that our feelings have become remarkably different from those of English men and women at the beginning of the seventeenth century. Scholars remind the modern reader that Elizabethans and Jacobeans saw the creation as having taken place around 4000 B.C., and many—even such educated men as Donne and Ralegh—saw the world in its last phase of decline since the Golden Age. For the artists and audiences of the period, time was a somewhat enclosed and a comparatively small unit, a fleeting moment before the vastness of eternity. Within that context, a human life was but the blink of God's eye, and the intense poetic feeling for the transitory nature of the world in both the popular tradition and also in the great poetry of the day becomes understandable. Fed by constant attacks of plague and disease, infant mortality, and early death from general infections, such an idea was in reality part of human experience.

We live in an era when people are troubled by the feeling that although any individual human life occupies a short time, the experience of that time is likely to be repetitive and boring, and we ask ourselves how to restore the sense of meaning to time itself. After all, the infinite (or nearly so far as that) is history itself, a fundamentally Darwinian time scheme stretching back to the origin of things millions of years ago, the age of high technology occupying only a second (technology itself only a moment) within the vast stretch of time that goes forward into an unimaginably long future. Perhaps because there is no perfected end or Second Coming, there is no Augustinian eternal dimension against which historical time is seen and given meaning. Except for those few philosophic supermen who assert the divine power of the autonomous mind against the chaos of reality, modern persons are likely to feel themselves simply swallowed up in it. In the modern view, time seems emptied of divine purpose, one of the corollaries of which is that human will and act are stripped of moral quality.[6] It is this last difference in modern and Renaissance assumptions that makes it difficult for the modern sensibility to grasp fully the importance of death and judgment as a bridge between time and eternity for the persons of the Renaissance. On the one hand, the period in early modern England was one of plagues and political uneasiness, both in the waning years of Elizabeth's reign and the unsettling years under James I. The tides of mortality, both from disease and various forms of conflict, created a nearly constant awareness of the imminence of death. On the other hand, there was also in such a harsh world a spiritual necessity to remind Christians through sermons and devotional literature of the history of God's mercy that would ward off despair.[7]

During most of those bleak years between 1588 and 1600 the promise of the conquest of the Armada was disappointed by continuing agricultural and economic problems for England's people, and Elizabeth's energy for rule began to wane under Time's heavy sickle. In his "Despair Canto" Spenser gave to the last part of the sixteenth century the most vivid instance in high art of the power of despair itself. The great queen's aging was itself a human emblem of the vanity of worldly power after an almost euphoric period when England had emerged as a European nation of stature.[8] Like England in this period, Spenser's knight Redcrosse has been through a period of optimism. It is important to remember that within the immediate context of the poem Redcrosse meets Despayre after he has been imprisoned in the dungeon of Orgoglio, or Pride. Arthur as God's powerful figure of grace has rescued him, but clearly Redcrosse is in a state of unguarded weakness from his sojourn in the dungeon. Arrogance, after all, is the most weakening opposite of humility.

Essential from a spiritual point of view is the knight's full awareness of how far his sin has taken him. Such a confrontation with his own nature makes him especially prey to the temptation to despair. The pseudo-reason with which the hermit speaks is so convincing that while one is involved in the narrative experience of the Spenserian passage it is almost impossible not to be convinced that suicide, not repentance, is the natural order of human response to confrontation with sin; the bony grizzled figure of the hermit within the "darkesome cave" has beside him on the grass a dead man:

> A drearie corse, whose life away did pas,
> All wallow'd in his owne yet luke-warme blood,
> That from his wound yet wellèd fresh alas;
> In which a rustie knife fast fixed stood.

(I.ix.36)

We know almost immediately that this man has somehow followed the advice of the hermit, but the reader anticipates a repetition of the pattern as the hermit begins his rhetoric focused on the knight. He denies responsibility for the death, only insisting that its source was the "guiltie mind deserving death." (I.ix.43) The hermit's explanation of the death of the man on the grass serves, of course, to "hook in" the knight, who becomes increasingly conscious of his sin as the hermit speaks.

The heavy overlay of Stoic commonplace is especially appealing, and we are reminded of the influence of Stoic attitudes exercised by Seneca upon Elizabethan drama as well as the increasing Stoic strain in such devotional writers as Thomas Becon.[9] The hermit's argument for suicide wears the cloak of reason and embodies a powerful human appeal to those weary of the struggle:

> He there does now enjoy eternal rest
> And happy ease, which thou dost want and crave
> And further from it daily wanderest.
> What if some little pain the passage have
> That makes frail flesh to fear the bitter wave?
> Is not short pain well borne, that brings long ease,
> And lays the soul to sleep in quiet grave?
> Sleep after toil, port after stormy seas,
> Ease after war, death after life does greatly please.
>
> (I.ix.40)

Spenser's allegorical answer to the temptation to suicide through despair is not, however, a rational one; the poet knows that rescue from such a trap comes not from personal reason but from outside resources that God has graciously given. Una is the personification of both truth and radical grace (sent by God) when she snatches the knife from Redcrosse's hand. Arthur as well represents grace entering Redcrosse's situation from outside. To meet such temptation to despair on a communal level the instability of the Anglican Church had caused English people to turn to the tradition of private devotion in the sixteenth century, rooted as it was in richness of the fifteenth, yet still marked by the horror of the Black Death in the century before and the recurrences of that devastation.

As we have seen, the publication of the *ars moriendi* books around the mid-fifteenth century seems to have come about as a result of the common awareness that because people often died without the availability of a priest they needed to defend their faith against the last onslaught of the devil. Although despair was only one of the temptations to be expected, that temptation as a challenge to faith was marked by the possibility that the *ars moriendi* arose out of a common feeling that the dance of death was too terrifying as a set of symbols for those who faced death without the comfort of a priest present.

Most important was the assumption that one should make his preparation before the literal time of death. Since death could come at any time there was a necessity (or at least a great desirability) for a daily preparation. Second, one could find solace in being prepared for the particular ways in which the battle would be fought. Legend had it that the devil through demons would make a last mighty assault upon the weakened and vulnerable soul on the deathbed in five ways. Third, the person needed within this instruction to be reassured that the mercy of God was adequate to atone for all the failures of a sinful nature and that God through the mediation of his angels and saints would make his grace available to the *moriens*.[10]

In sketching again the broad symbolic and devotional context we observed in more detail in the last section, students of religious and devotional literature in England no longer have to insist upon the general accessibility of religious symbols and ideas. Within these adjusted attitudes, the fully developed devotional tradition as it applied to death and the other last things (heaven, hell, and the last judgment) is generally accepted as an essential strain in European and English culture.[11] However, the exact relevance of these religious ideas to literature that is not explicitly religious is a complex issue, especially as the religious symbolic tradition is related to Elizabethan and Jacobean drama. Should the emphasis in criticism rest upon the ambiguities and hints of change?[12] Or upon the fundamental, continuing structures? "Both" is the somewhat difficult answer.

First, in order to assess audience response (really multiple audiences) and literary structure, it may be useful to examine the major commonplaces themselves: the components of a good and bad death according to the devotional and literary tradition. On the simplest level, as we have seen, to die well was to live well; thus had repeated every tract on the subject for over a hundred years. But Christian theology and human experience have always furnished little security to the individual in making that judgment; the New Historicists are surely right that the echoing commonplaces do not assure an easy acceptance of death. The struggle continues between the natural fear of death and judgment and the profound efforts of human thought to contain that fear. The conventional pious English Christian of the late sixteenth and early seventeenth centuries had been warned repeatedly of the dangers of pride. Resulting Pauline sins of omission, said the devotional writers, could be far more insidious than the usual vices. In the Middle Ages the seven deadly sins themselves were, as we recall, ranked in a hierarchy of increasing danger so that the sins of the spirit (so difficult to assess) drew one more deeply into hell.

Such a context of values may seem more concrete through the

knowledge that in Spenser's sixteenth-century England, the dance of death, or the "Dance of Machebray," was painted on the cloister walls of the north side of St. Paul's and commonly called the "Dance of Paul's." It was an echo of the original dance painted about St. Innocent's Cloister at Paris. (The meters, or poesy, accompanying the French dance, were translated into English during the reign of Henry VI.) The assumptions such images embody were by the 1590s mostly absorbed into the carefully structured tradition of the *ars moriendi* with its careful balancing and integration of warning, fear, and hope.

Against this set of images and assumptions, and in interaction with it, Spenser's imagination created the hermit Despayre, a character with deep and ghostly influence who causes terror in the reader. Through his emblematic ghostly shadow, he evokes the Renaissance fear of falling into the abyss of despair. When Sir Trevisan gallops across the page with a rope around his neck, the poetry becomes foreboding. When Redcrosse goes to the hut of the hermit, he becomes immediately vulnerable to almost overwhelming temptation. In the scene his defenselessness emerges quickly as the dreamlike imagery evokes an atmosphere of lassitude. Although he argues a fixed term of life, Redcrosse cannot stand up to the powerful ratiocination of the hermit Despayre, who reminds him of his sojourn in the deep dungeon and his earlier betrayal of Una:

> Why then doest thou, o man of sin, desire
> To draw thy dayes forth to their last degree?
>
> (I.ix.46)

> Is it not better to doe willinglie,
> Then linger, till the glasse be all out ronne?
> Death is the end of woes; die soone, O faeries sone.
>
> (I.ix.47)

We are told that Redcrosse is "weake and fraile," (50) that his conscience is attacked by "trembling horror" (I.ix.49), and that "hellish anguish did his soule assaile" (I.ix.49). The hermit, seeing this, offers him the knife of suicide (I.ix.51). And only Una prevails. Helplessness overwhelms before despair; fortunately, the energy and power of the one grace and truth are nearby to break the spell: "She snacht the cursed knife" (I.ix.52).

Spenser's treatment of this theme evokes subterranean fears of human nature and gives important clues to the feelings of Renaissance people. Partially in contrast to *Paradise Lost*, these are not elaborate rational structures developing the allegory toward theology. Here the theology is assumed, but as Kathrine Koller once pointed out, the old temptation to despair is creatively transformed to become a crucial incident in the journey in search of holiness.[13] People in England knew then that touching at least one stage of despair is probably essential to the preparation for holiness, the self-fashioning journey of the Christian for which Adam in *Paradise Lost* nearly a hundred years later marks the beginning:

> O Conscience, into what Abyss of fears
> And horrors has thou driv'n me; out of which
> I find no way, from deep to deeper plung'd!
>
> (X.842–44)

The recognition that one cannot find the way alone is the beginning of salvation. By the time the second great epic appears in English literature the dreamlike atmosphere of an epic played out in a medieval dark forest has disappeared. The theological attitudes toward despair, however, remained much the same, in spite of radical theological and cultural changes. Both Spenser and Milton, two Protestants widely separated in time, seem to come together in trying to combat the enemies of Christian hope with traditional Catholic concepts about death and sin. Perhaps the range of Milton's experience, including the multiple sufferings of political and civil conflict, has brought him to a central and realistic focus upon the power of sin in human history.

By 1667 and the publication of *Paradise Lost,* Milton's exploration of the relationship between hope and despair might be considered on the broadest level to be all of *Paradise Lost.* One might also easily assert Milton's own experience as a literal reconciliation of that paradox.[14] Perhaps even deeper in the theological structure is the way in which the poem is an elaborate encounter between the Trinity of Satan, Sin, and Death and the ultimate triumph over Death. So much has occurred both historically and literarily by that part of the seventeenth century, however, that the mode of representation must differ from that of Spenser. The temptation to despair has been richly played out within the dark trials of the Commonwealth period, and for someone on the earlier winning side, there was, after all, the loss of much in the Restoration. In a profound sense, the "justification of the ways of God to man" is surely the interpretation that in the hands of an inspired poet is designed to bring humankind from despair to hope. The apparent fallen state of existence can only be countered through God's manifestation of the principles of transformation, resurrection, and mercy, in and beyond the incredible suffering and evil of human history. The confrontation with despair on the cosmic level through Satan, Sin, and Death, and the corresponding experience of it on the human level through Adam and Eve are, however, somewhat more manageable windows into Milton's position as it finds expression in Christian humanism. This is not to say, however, that much of Milton does not make a bridge to the new in both poetry and religious thought. It is perhaps not until readers see the horrifying allegory of Sin and Death that they can fully understand the power of evil and the pull into the vortex of despair!

In Book II where we see the setting of hell bodied forth in all its dark and burning horror, Death and Sin are allegorically personified. Ironically the human overlay only serves to make more vivid the lineaments of horror. In her thoughtful essay showing the roots of the allegory of Death in the Psalms, Radzinowicz analyzes the powerful place of Death-in-life in Milton's poem.[15] He is Satan's incestuous child (grandchild) begot by perversion upon his hideous daughter Sin, as we hear when they are described as guardians of Hell-gate. We quickly learn that they will soon inhabit the fallen world with the voracious appetite that would swallow up all the subsequent history of mankind were it not for the merciful intervention of the Son. Hell Mouth yawns for future generations. The reader does not learn more than the allusion to that intervention until Book III.

In Book II both Sin and Death are portrayed (like Error in Spenser) with all their most nightmarish characteristics—she with children painfully hanging on her nether parts; he skeletal, hungry, and horrifying. Critics have often commented upon the embodiment within the character of Satan of "pride, envy, and despair," Milton's "frame" description of Satan's vaunting.[15] For those literary historians who take a non-Romantic attitude toward the fall of Lucifer, the most beautiful of the angels (before his own evil transformed his appearance), the allegorical content of that character necessarily contains the worst spiritual sins among the traditional seven: pride, envy, and wrath. In Book II Satan is characterized as falling into "fear, envy, and despair." Despair, however, is not one of the sins most frequently associated with the pride that dominates the character. "Hopeless" is the original definition given in the OED for *despairing* as it was used in the seventeenth century, and in a strictly literal sense Satan does not seem hopeless at this point in the epic as we see him approach the newly created world. Although by the end of the speech he will be "hopeless" of making peace with the Almighty and therefore hopeless of his own salvation, he struggles with pain and even regret during the length of it. Only near the end of his lengthy tirade (virtually an antimeditation) does he clarify the association between hope and fear.

As we are told by the Argument of Book IV, even when he "at length confirms himself in evil," he still does not seem entirely hopeless. From a modern point of view, there is a measure of hope in his fixation upon the vengeance he will wreak upon God through the persons of Adam and Eve. It is necessary, of course, to remember the roots of the theological tradition and the technical definition of hopelessness as associated with despair in the *ars moriendi* tradition. By this point in the text Satan on the Mount of Niphates may not be literally hopeless, but from the theological point of view (the view essential to English thinking) he is hopeless of reconciliation with God. Another way of putting it is to say that, like Faustus, he has lost faith in the possibility of personal reconciliation with God.

At the same time, however, the speech shows some recognition of the paradox that the temptation to despair from the old *ars moriendi* tradition had a positive side by which one might be moved to contrition over the loss of the original divine stamp, the image of what one had been before the devastation of sin.[16] Satan suffers that "bitter memory." From one point of view, then, as some sixteenth-century theologians had suggested, despair as an initial confrontation with sin could lead to regeneration; but more often, the movement was thought to be a reverse one, leading one deeper into despair, with ultimate loss of all hope and the possible consequences of desperate measures such as suicide. Satan is described in the frame by Milton first in terms that are just short of full desperation:

> horror and doubt distract
> His troubl'd thoughts, and from the bottom stir
> The Hell within him, for within him Hell
> He brings, and round about him, nor from Hell
> One step no more than from himself can fly
> By change of place:
>
> (IV.18–23)

But immediately follows the full experience of desperation:

> Now conscience wakes despair
> That slumber'd, wakes the bitter memory
> Of what he was, what is, and *what must be*
> *worse.* . . .
>
> (IV.23–26; emphasis mine)

Influenced by Calvinism and its popular heirs, Milton has "conscience" trigger memories that body forth despair, perhaps analogous to the "rooted sorrow" we shall note in *Macbeth*. Later, in Adam's despairing speech after the Fall, it is conscience that drives him also into the abyss. Horror and doubt make Satan aware of the hell always within him, but it is ultimately the "bitter memory" that encompasses despair over his whole history—"what he was, what is, and what must be." The past and the future are poisoned by the current desperation; the life is all one and at the same time growing worse: falling deeper into despair.

The reader is reminded of the way in which the story of the passage of a life is built into the old *ars moriendi* tradition. In the temptation to despair, the demons had gathered and concentrated all the sins of the past about the deathbed, and the whole future of the *moriens* hung upon his response. The suggestion of an eternal future hovered about the images of the Communion of Saints in the inspiration against despair. In the fifteenth-century woodcut of the inspiration to hope (against despair) the figures not only of the angel but of the four greatest sinners of the gospel, who were yet redeemed, were explicitly designed to indicate that no sinner, however sunk in evil, should despair.

At the same time that he relies upon the reader's knowledge that Satan represents a special case, Milton plays upon contemporary theological attitudes by building Satan's speech within the structure of meditation, which always allows for transformation. As Martz has reminded us, the meditation embodies a very old psychological pattern by which human time is encompassed, but the mode of meditation popularized by Counter-Reformation technique and aesthetics makes the present moment immediate.[17] The composition of place, the *compositio loci*, awakes the senses and human memory to make vivid the context of the past and bring it live into the present. As Satan tells us, bitter memories are awakened to give him the experience of hell. In this case, it is not (as in the *ars*) his past sins that give him most immediate anguish but the memory of the joys he has given up—the high place among the angels from which he has fallen. Almost as soon as he calls upon the Sun, he distinguishes his voice from that of a friend:

> to thee I call
> But with *no friendly voice,* and add thy name
> O Sun, to tell thee how I hate thy beams

> That bring to my remembrance from what state
> I fell, how glorious once above thy Sphere;
>
> > (IV. 35–39; emphasis mine)

Evil hates the light itself, so closely identified with its creator. As always Milton, however, does not dwell upon the mere sensory description here of Satan's former state. Almost immediately, he moves the appeal to memory into rational analysis. Milton has Satan, though seemingly penitent in lines such as he

> > deserv'd no such return
> From me, whom he created what I was
> In that bright eminence, . . .
>
> > (IV.42–44)

condemn his own ingratitude:

> Forgetful what from him I still receiv'd
> And understood not that a grateful mind
> By owing owes not . . . .
>
> > (IV.54–56)

He rationalizes that his very beauty and high place occasioned his fall, that his hope focused in the wrong direction has brought him to wish himself still higher, even to eschewing gratitude and embracing rebellion. It is important to know that Milton, though a rebel himself in the current English conflict, held Aristotle's view that tyranny consists of being ruled by an inferior. In *The Christian Doctrine* he explains this position. Therefore, from Milton's point of view there was no basis for Satan's rebellion but his own self-generated pride and envy.

Satan's own story parodies the traditional temptation to despair. His rationalization becomes clearly the manipulation of "wrong reason." In it, the speaker twists the stimulants from memory that would ordinarily move one to reconciliation with God into an arrangement for hopelessness. The second section of the speech or meditation is not the normally expected movement of the mind (following the movement of the sense) but the movement into "infinite wrath, and infinite despair," (IV. 74) followed by the famous lines "Which way I fly is Hell," (IV. 75ff). Milton indeed has Satan follow these lines of desperation with the recognition that the only way out is to repent: "O then at last relent" (IV.79). With Donne we should have had at this point a submission to the rod of chastisement and a journey through the straits that are the only ways to God, but

Milton's Satan is under a mythic exigency to present to the reader the warped and lost self of one doomed. Although intellectually he recognizes submission as the only way out of the trap in which he again finds himself, like Marlowe's Faustus, he almost immediately counters the recognition with arguments that will lead him to despair.

Satan tells us that "disdain" and "dread of shame" forbid him to submit. His pride, in short, keeps him from admitting his mistake to his followers, and he consoles himself with seductive false arguments: even if he recanted, immediate ease from pain would bring him to do it again. Trapped in his own anger and hatred, he refuses to believe that reconciliation can occur between two enemies whose hatred goes so deep. Under such circumstances, the fall would be heavier.

Satan moves thus through rationalization to a reversal of the usual movement of the affections by which the meditation integrates sense, intellect, and affection into reconciliation with God. Satan has paradoxically rejected his anguish and fear for a new hopelessness, the full despair that was not visible near the beginning of his address to the Sun:

> So farewell Hope, and with Hope, farewell Fear,
> Farewell Remorse; all Good to me is lost;
> *Evil be thou my Good.* . . .

(IV.108–10)

Here, revealed in their most negative form, the traditional lineaments of despair clothe Satan's speech. Only one of the necessary ingredients from the *ars moriendi* is missing: the final happy ending with its letting go of self-will and the freedom (so essential to Milton's doctrine) of voluntary submission to God's will. The line between fear and remorse is established, from the Renaissance point of view, and it may indicate the "false heroism" of Satan, who throughout the English early modern period was the major type for such a despairing character as Macbeth.

In his falling to the temptation to despair, Milton's Satan is not without literary predecessors. Lucifer was, of course, known throughout theological history as the primary type of one who had fallen unregenerate through sin to despair. Along with Phaeton from the classical tradition and, of course, with Judas, his place in typology was unchallenged. Lucifer frozen in the depths of Dante's *Inferno* is perhaps the most powerful allegorical image of the psychological nature of despair in all of literature.[18]

But just as he was the allegorical figure most steeped in sin and most bound by despair, at the same time Milton's Satan owes something to a view of unregenerate sinners that is particularly English.[19] In a more general sense, elements found in Satan's speech bespeak a common experience with a certain kind of dramatic figure in Elizabethan drama, the most powerful type of which is Faustus. Such characters are largely the embodiments of the fears Renaissance persons associated with the danger of falling to despair. Particularly the ambitious, such as Richard III and Iago, are the types of villains that Milton's Satan echoes in his characterization. Although the *ars moriendi* was originally a tradition of comfort, over the two hundred years of its development it had carried with it the fearsome implications of the other side. If the inspiration of the Good Angel should fail, what then? What if the Good Angel were inexplicably absent? The most common answer in the devotional tradition was the one that Spenser's hermit links to the concept of *suicide*. We shall see more fully how Milton alludes to that tradition in Adam.

Clearly, Satan belongs to another line from those characters who choose suicide. Taking from the great evil heroic figures of Shakespearean drama (and Marlowe as well) the essential characteristics of one who becomes increasingly confirmed in ambitious evil, he constructs rationalizations by which he falls deeper and deeper into an internal experience of hell.[20] Milton recognizes the internalizing of allegorical form through Satan. Does he not move through the three stages of despair? At the same time as he loses both fear and remorse, as Satan himself recognizes, his acts move him outward into greater and greater evil. Both Richard III and Macbeth also follow this pattern until they die in a kind of heroic despair. Satan, of course, not allowed so simple a surcease of misery, must (until the Last Judgment), according to his own lights, continue his vengeance through man upon the Almighty.

It is the speech in Book IV perhaps that is most deeply responsible for the sentimentalizing of Satan: "So farewell hope . . . all Good to me is lost" (108–9). The human empathy it arouses suggests its link with the greatest suffering that sinful human beings have known: the consequences of sin, voluntary and self-willed, that have brought about the loss of a position not truly valued until it was lost. At the same time, Milton was very careful to point out that the end of such anguish was the embrace of evil itself: "Evil be thou my good" (110). Within the large canvas of the cosmic consequences, especially in terms of the suffering caused by Satan in the long history of mankind, the "personal" misery of Satan fades into elaborate literary motivation for his malice toward our first ancestors.

Whatever the residue of empathy, it works within the accumulative reading of the poem most fully as anticipation of the consequences of the Fall for Adam and Eve. When Milton brings the concept down to human scale in Book X, as readers we have been prepared for at least part of the regret that Adam and Eve experience. Built into reader experience is the technique of allegorical contrast that Milton so frequently employs, by which Satan and Adam are shown to respond differently to the temptation to despair that springs from the large remorse *(tristitia)* so inextricable from sin. Adam does not come to this remorse completely through his own imagination of the consequences of sin—such an imagination might have prevented the original fall. But it is after the judgment of the Son and the "alterations in the Heavens and Elements" by the Angels that he speaks. Adam "more and more perceiving his fall'n condition heavily bewails." Just before Adam's soliloquy, Milton says that Adam saw these "growing miseries" in nature:

> Thus began
> Outrage from lifeless things; but Discord first
> Daughter of Sin, among th' irrational,
> Death introduc'd through fierce antipathy:
> Beast now with Beast gan war, and Fowl
>   with Fowl,
> And Fish with Fish; to graze the Herb all,
>   leaving,
> Devour'd each other; nor stood much in awe
> Of Man, but fled him, or with count'nance grim
> Glared on him passing. . . .
>
> (X.707–14)

Like Satan's, Adam's remorse springs in large part from a memory of his better place in an unfallen world. It is characteristic, however, of his more innocent human nature that one of the springs of remorse is his present shame before a God whom once to behold was his greatest happiness. He states explicitly, however, that he could bear such punishment were it not for the sense of future evils, particularly the evil that he as father of the race has brought upon future generations. The first instance of guilt? In more positive terms, guilt is in the seeds of responsibility for the future. As is Satan, he is most grieved by "the sense of endless woes" in such a situation. In his grief over this multiplication of curses on his head, he accuses the terms as too hard, the terms by which he was to hold "The Good I sought not" (X. 752). He did, after all, not ask to be born. Adam shows, as he has earlier in his new sinfulness, a tendency toward buck-passing, but he comes to recognize that both justice and grace have been granted to him:

> Be it so, for I submit, his doom is fair
> That dust I am, and shall to dust return.
>
> (X.769–70)

In accepting, however, God's judgment of death upon him, he in turn opens himself to despair, masking itself, as in Spenser, with the all-too-human weariness of life that seems to come when life itself demands absolute submission to iron necessity.

> O welcome hour whenever! why delays
> His hand to execute what his Decree
> Fix'd on this day? Why do I overlive?
> Why am I mockt with death, and length'n'd
> To deathless pain? How gladly would I meet out
> Mortality my sentence, and be Earth
> Insensible, how glad would lay me down
> As in my Mother's lap!
>
> (X.771–78)

And yet within a few lines Adam answers his own question: perhaps his "pure breath of Life, the Spirit of Man" (X.784) cannot die, and perhaps he may be doomed to endless misery. Conscience has indeed through fears and horrors plunged him deeper and deeper into what resembles despair. It is within the context of this nightmare without boundaries that Death becomes the supreme punishment for the Fall. Adam and Eve know nothing until afterward of its character except the abstract promise of it as punishment. The great bridge that humanity will tread on its weary way to hell until the "Greater Man" redeems the path is an emblem of how powerful Death is without Christ's sacrifice.

As Milton moves away in Books XI and XII from the ancient poetic structuring of the epic into the human tragedy and then into theology and history, Satan, Sin, and Death gradually lose something of their fearful power. Radzinowicz talks about the change from poetry into rationalizing, theologizing, and historicizing. Actually Milton draws back the curtain for Adam through the prophecy of Michael. The abstraction of the punishment becomes horrifying in its own ordinary and fallen way as Adam is shown the murder of Abel by Cain, both his progeny, and the larger vision of conflict and death that permeates the history of the Hebrews until Noah is the only righteous man left to field a new beginning. Nevertheless, the many faces of death are in some sense history, especially as the promises of rescue emerge typologically in Noah and Moses.

But it is only in connection with the fulfillment of the Son's voluntary sacrifice that Death is transformed into the "wafting" of the soul into heaven. And that comes later. Though Milton describes Eve (in Book X) as *desolate,* when she hears Adam lamenting to himself she approaches him with soft words. Adam, however, falls into a tirade of blame, accusing her of "pride and wand'ring vanity" (X.874) and asking God why he admitted to creation the feminine principle. Eve, constantly weeping, replies that she will beseech God to place the whole blame on her alone for the sake of peace between them. Her humble submission moves Adam to relent toward her, says Milton, and to counsel her that they accept the inexorable and strive

> In offices of Love, how we may light'n
> Each other's burden in our share of woe;
> Since this day's Death denounc't, if aught
>   I see,
> Will prove no sudden, but a slow-pac't evil,
> A long day's dying to augment our pain,
> And to our Seed (O hapless Seed!) deriv'd.
>
> (X.960–65)

In this speech Adam moves upward from despair to a measure of acceptance of Death—to more than acceptance, to the fortitude that is for the seventeenth century a combination of patience and hope. For Adam and Eve represent the only immediate aid for each other; Milton must have had in mind the modest promise that Ecclesiastes offers: that two are better than one. In a harsh world if one stumbles, the other can keep him from falling. "Again, if two lie together, then they have heat; but how can one be warm alone?" The promise of "sharing woe" is hardly a glittering one for lovers about to face a world that tends toward Death, the "slowpac't evil." The "long day's dying to augment our pain" will most require the elaborate tradition by which an art of dying develops.

Milton's perspective is profoundly traditional in this point: only the redemptive act of Christ can transform the plight of Adam and Eve from despair to hope. In Books XI and XII Michael reveals the promise more fully. The imperfect human love they share is only a dim foreshadowing of that love to come. Like the human beings who follow them throughout history, however, such a mature love in response to the redemptive act can only be glimpsed through a glass darkly. Indeed, it is that truth that makes the efforts of the *ars* meaningful. It is only on the deathbed, reasoned seventeenth-century Christians, that the epic perspective can triumph—after they have been at a long day's dying through a lifetime. Only after that span will they let the old selves die and will the new be released into the arms of eternal love.

5

"Despair and Die": The Ultimate Temptation of Richard III

Richard III (1592) is a convenient play with which to begin a more text-based study of Shakespeare's evocation of attitudes embodied in the commonplaces from the *ars moriendi* and inherited by the late Elizabethan and early Jacobean periods. This one and the next few essays will focus on scenes from several of Shakespeare's plays that provide windows into the tradition of death and dying in the period. Although formally *Richard III* lies between the genres of history and tragedy, it is an early Shakespearean tragedy concerned fundamentally with the encounters between life and death, good and evil, that the tragic form requires. It is from just such a drama of evil that Milton generates his own dramatically conceived epic. The importance to Shakespeare of the theme of death with its cosmic reverberations emerges in the original title of the play in the First Quarto, *The Tragedy of the Life and Death of Richard III*. The allegorical thrust of the play, with its dominant evil character, provides the modern reader with a mirror of symbolic values. For the study of the relationship between evil and despair, particularly instructive are two stunningly theatrical scenes: one the courtship scene between Richard and Anne; the other Richard's "deathbed" scene before the Battle of Bosworth Field, when he undergoes the temptation to despair.[1]

During most of the play, Shakespeare's Richard III undergoes little temptation in the usual dramatic sense; in the manner of the conventional dramatic Machiavel, he announces his evil course to the audience and systematically and bloodily carries it out. No audience of any time could doubt the wickedness of Shakespeare's character. Even the twentieth century with its sympathy for those physically deformed instantly recognizes Richard's evil.

Given the lack of internal conflict in the character, the audience of any time, but especially Elizabethan audiences with their sense of life as a Pauline battle, would focus dramatic interest in the external conflict between Virtue and Vice that runs throughout the play and reveals the downfall of Vice as embodied in an evil king. Familiar to critics and scholars are the bloody Senecan conventions of ghosts, dreams, murders, and vengeance. Thus far neglected, however, has been Shakespeare's use of the popular symbolic tradition of the *ars moriendi* to dramatize the example of a wicked king who has lived badly and who must be shown to die badly. The conventions of the *ars moriendi* tradition are most clearly illustrated in the famous third scene of Act V, where Richard is visited by a succession of ghosts. For a Renaissance audience most striking are the psychological and dramatic implications of this scene. These implications emerged not simply from the obvious references to murder, death, and the supernatural but also from the iconic structure given the scene by its relation to the temptation to despair, part of the last battle of Satan for the soul.

Shakespeare, as usual, however, gives the convention new vitality by integrating it into the dramatic context so that it enlarges both the vision of history and that of personal experience. Not only does he place it at the climax of the action, thus drawing upon the natural high feeling to which the audience has been brought, but he builds into the staging the familiar iconography of the deathbed scene, which supports emotionally the metaphorical language from the *ars moriendi*. A modern audience, however, misses a good deal of the power of the scene (and thus the play) because it is insensitive to the fusion of the iconographical implications of both staging and language.

Though Shakespeare also makes brilliant and original use of the popular *ars moriendi* tradition in both *Othello* and *Lear*, his most traditional and explicit re-creation of its conventions occurs in the history plays.[2] Dignified by their relation to the history of England, these plays appropriately contain formal conventions that embody many of the questions and answers in the allegory of salvation and the ongoing struggle between good and evil that shaped Elizabethan attitudes toward history.[3] To the early modern mind, even the popular mind, history was always related in good Augustinian fashion to a typological understanding of biblical truth and was therefore close to the great questions of the salvation of the soul.[4] For a person in early modern England, the four last things were essential concerns. One should not be surprised, therefore, that elaborate constructions built upon the theme of death would appear in *Henry V* and, in parodic form, in the end of Falstaff in *The Merry Wives of Windsor*.[5] But the most illuminating use of the art of dying well appears in the scene the night before Richard's death—and the earlier wooing scene that prepares for it—in *Richard the Third,* often entitled *The Life and Death of Richard the Third,* a title that suggests the powerful Renaissance belief in the centrality of the moment of death to a man's life and character.[6]

In the second scene of *Richard III* a demonic hunchback brings a grief-stricken woman full circle from hatred and anger to acceptance of his marriage proposal. The scene is augmented by the presence of a corpse, interrupted in the ceremony of its own funeral. The scene is still one of the most bizarre in Shakespeare, but for Elizabethans the allusion to the iconography of death would have heightened even further the dramatic intensity. The visual suggestions alone with Richard and Anne in opposition on stage and the corpse of Henry between them would have underlined on a mimetic level the irony of the swift courtship and its macabre interplay with Elizabethan *memento moris.* The symbolic language of heaven and hell that emerges from the dialogue would also have enriched the visual paradox of eroticism and death, calling forth reverberations of the dramatic struggle between Virtue and Vice that lies at the heart of Renaissance attitudes toward death and the salvation of the soul.

At the beginning of the scene, when Richard stops the funeral procession, Anne turns to the bearers of the corpse:

Anne: What do you tremble? are you all afraid?
Alas, I blame you not, for you are mortal,
And mortal eyes cannot endure the devil.

(I.ii.43–45)

In her next speech, Anne addresses him as "Foul devil" and tells him to go away "for God's sake," for he "has made the happy earth thy hell" (I.ii.50–51). A few lines later she climaxes her attack upon him and his fiendish murders by saying,

Anne: Villain, thou know'st nor law of God nor Man,
No beast so fierce but knows some touch of pity.

(I.ii.70–76)

When he wittily answers that because he knows none, he is not a Beast, she replies:

Anne: O wonderful, when devils tell the [troth]!

(I.ii.73)

In this stychomythia, Richard caps the opposition of the two figures with his answer:

Richard: More wonderful, when angels are so angry.

(I.ii.74)

Though readers in general have seen this language as the commonplace language of anger (and of calculated palliation on Richard's part), Shakespeare's audience, I believe, would have responded to it as metaphorical in a much more lively sense. Eyes that had looked at so many representations of the battle between the good and bad angels for the soul of the dying would have not failed to register the root metaphors of the *ars moriendi* tradition that underlies the scene. Anne herself reminds the audience of the traditional form of the battle:

Anne: Avaunt, thou dreadful minister of hell!
Thou hadst but power over his mortal body,
His soul thou canst not have. Therefore be gone.

(I.ii.46–48)

Anne's words denying the possibility of Richard's gaining the soul of the corpse would suggest for the Elizabethan the image of that mighty conflict which must have been part of the visual effect of the scene.

Like ours, Shakespeare's audience, however, would have been quick to see that in this scene Richard as the devil was intent on gaining the body and soul of one living, Anne herself, and the corpse on stage would serve primarily as a visual reminder of the old tradition. Here, as often, Shakespeare employs old conventions, but he employs them freshly to enrich the particular erotic drama of the encounter. Even in a play that lies as close to the medieval stylized allegory as this one, he displaces the conventions to heighten dramatic and plot values. The fusion of the death imagery with courtship and sexual implication intensifies the immediacy of the mimetic surface and heightens the audience's empathy with the drama.

Though theology is always subordinate to drama for Shakespeare, in this scene the theological structures just beneath the surface underline the major conflict between Anne and Richard as incarnations of the principles of good and evil. On a historical level, as well, the conflict between the two hints at the opposition of good and evil at moments in the historic flux, and in this particular scene the sometimes irresistible power of evil. Shakespeare's scene 2 makes this apparent point dramatic for the audience only to foreshadow its reversal in the ultimate fall of Richard the Vice to his true historic opponent and Virtue, Richmond, a fall that does not occur until the end of the play.

By suggesting the richness of iconographical associations and a bone structure of allegorical opposition between virtue and vice in the play, I do not mean to be reductive. On the contrary, Shakespeare's thematic reverberations have been too often silenced by critics in a one-dimensional mimetic image, and I do not wish to correct that oversimplification by moving toward the opposite extreme. *Richard III* is neither a full, nor naive, allegory; nor is it a simple morality play.[7] If anything, the sophisticated comedy in the treatment of evil is not so much explained by reference to the medieval notion of *evil as comic* as it is by analogue to modern black comedy. Such a comparison is reinforced by the dominance of the mimetic image, the richly incarnate surface of the play. But Shakespeare's genius was multidimensional, as was the perspective of the Renaissance in general, if we are to give credence to the scholarship of the past forty years such as that of Panofsky, Wind, and Gombrich that reveals the submerged value structure in the plastic arts during the period. Artists of the period moved easily between a surface texture of particularized image and universal values just beneath that surface.[8]

Certainly Shakespeare's creation of the drama was no less accessible to such a fluidity among dimensions. *Richard III* as a linguistic and dramatic structure is particularly suggestive of the balance between particular and universal, momentary and eternal, such as one sees in the Flemish tradition of art. "The Marriage of Arnolfini," by Jan Van Eyck, just for a single instance, is a parallel Northern example of the harmony of a detailed mimetic image and the structure of hidden symbolism, as Panofsky argued convincingly in his exposure of disguised symbolism. Religious attitudes toward the sacramental nature of marriage that find expression in ordinary objects in the painting parallel the themes of salvation which are bodied forth in the events of a particular life in Shakespeare's history, events played out on the battleground of power politics and kingship. It is this interweaving of the dimensions of particularity and universality that contributes to the ironic concentration of the play. That a character can both be himself and a demonic representation at one and the same dramatic moment imbues the drama with power of two kinds: that of the specific, individual human image and that of the force of evil in the universe.

However much Shakespeare's audience responded to the dramatic structure of Richard's particular rise to power and the seeds of destruction sown in that rise, it must also have felt in differing degrees the Pauline interpretation of life it brought to such a theme. It was not necessary for such an audience to be learned (though we are told that many were); it was enough to have been literate enough to read the Bible, much less Augustine and his heirs in the history of theology. For those who *could* read, such major commonplace themes as life as a battleground and place of testing for the soul; the opposition of virtue and vice in such a context; the fallen nature of the world that often makes the virtuous appear vicious and the vicious appear virtuous; the salvation of the soul as the end of life—all these appeared in various manifestations in current devotional literature. And for those who could not read at all, whose intellectual or social power did not allow them access to popular devotional literature, the sermons that they were required to hear weekly embodied these ideas. Examples of popular iconography that appeared in stained glass, armor, embroidery, plate, and stone all kept alive the religious sensibility that was not to disappear from England until at least the end of the seventeenth century, probably as late as the mid-eighteenth. This is not to say that everyone in the audience would have felt the same about these themes. The notion of a single interpretive community does not hold up in a fully developed class system. The nineties were a time of various interpretations, and Shakespeare's audience was a varied group. But no one could fail to be aware of the pervasive iconography of death, and, more, the awareness provided emotional depths.

To return to the dramatic scene that veritably sparkles with implication, Anne's husband Edward had been slain some three months before by Richard, and now her father-in-law lies dead in an open coffin, also by the hand of Richard; she is the chief mourner for the corpse. At the beginning of the scene (I.11.14–28) she utters a long and bitter curse on Henry's murderer, whom she knows to be Richard. Critics have always wondered, however, at the daring of Shakespeare, who has Richard win her love, or at least her acquiescence, by the end of the dramatic encounter. This startling change of heart may, of course, be understood in contemporary psychological terms: the strong passions of vanity and love drive out the passions of hatred and loyalty. Adding dramatic tension to Renaissance psychology, however, is something older, an opposition essential to allegory. In this scene, Richard and Anne, in addition to their bold and interesting particularized characterizations, would have been seen by a contemporary audience to suggest the virtues and vices eternally in conflict on the Pauline battleground of life. The crooked Richard, emblem of wickedness, facing the beautiful young woman, suggests the allegory of good and evil in opposition on stage with the coffin between them; as suggested above, such an opposition would probably have reminded the audience of popular representations wherein virtue and vice are bodied forth in the frequent image of a divided path as moral choice (usually the choice of Hercules), with one direction a road to virtue, the other, to destruction.

As numerous literary historians have pointed out, Elizabethans were familiar with various representations of the psychomachia. Perhaps the most popular image of the high point of battle between virtue and vice—and the necessity of the battle to the death— was that of St. George and the Dragon.[9] As England's patron saint George was portrayed everywhere in English painting, but major Italian painters had found the subject an interesting one as well. Both Raphael and Carpaccio come to mind, the latter's painting especially as an iconographical parallel to Spenser's use of the theme in Book I of *The Faerie Queene*. Graphics based upon paintings such as theirs were a major instrument for the dissemination of iconography throughout Western Europe. As one finds in the photograph collection at the Warburg Library, many graphic representations brought major artists into England.

But the Renaissance ideal of the Christian knight and the Christian prince was celebrated in both image and word. Erasmus had written about both; earlier he had used the essentially Pauline image for an influential book, *Enchiridion Militis Christiani, or The Manual of the Christian Knight,* introduced by the "Printer to the Reader" with a bad poem that contains the commonplace imagery of the tradition. Richard is in some measure the antitype of such an ideal. Shakespeare makes broad use of the tradition, this time reversed, to gain power from a familiar image. In Tudor history and in Shakespeare's play Richard is the very antithesis of the Christian knight. As one may see, he is close to being the knight's antagonist, the devil mentioned by the "Printer to the Faithful Reader":

> The mortal world a field is of battle
> Which is the cause that strife doeth never fail
> Against man, by warring of the flesh
> With the devil, that always fighteth fresh
> The spirit to oppress by false envy,
> The which conflict is continually
> During his life and like to lose the field.
> But he be armed with weapon and shield
> Such as behoveth to a Christian knight,

> Where God each one, by his Christ chosseth right
> Sole capatin, and his standard to bear.
> Who knoweth it not, then this will teach him here. . . .[10]

Certainly in this scene with Anne, Richard plays not the knight's part but that of a demonic opponent as he undermines her virtue. And throughout the play, his actions are the very opposite of the ideal posited by Erasmus as that of the true prince in *Praise of Folly*:

> Whoever did but truly weight with himself how
> great a burden lies upon his shoulders that
> would truly discharge the duty of a prince . . .
> would consider that he that takes a Scepter
> in his hand should manage the Public, not his
> Private Interest;

In presenting the image of Richard, Shakespeare is indeed playing upon the reversal of moral expectations. He relies on the fundamental cultural assumption that the values of the good are always in combat with vice. Erasmus lists the commonplaces associated with the virtuous prince:

> study nothing but the common good; and not in the least go contrary to those Laws whereof himself is both the Author and Exactor: that he is both the account of the good or evil administration of all his magistrates and subordinate Officers; that, though he is but one, all men's Eyes are upon him, and in his power it is, either like a good planet to give life and safety to mankind by his harmless influence, or like a fatal Comet to send mischief and destruction: that the vices of other men are not alike felt, nor so generally communicated; and that a Prince stands in that place that his least deviation from the Rule of Honesty and Honor reaches farther than himself, and opens a gap to many men's ruine. (138–39)

At the center of the old *ars moriendi* tradition, both in the fifteenth-century woodcut series and in the individual examples, as we have frequently seen in the sixteenth century, lay the great image of the deathbed scene, events within which appeared in visual as well as verbal popular texts. Here the popular theme of the struggle between virtue and vice emerged in the combat of demons and the guardian angel for the soul of the dying. Behind that image was the Pauline concept that life is a perennial trial; the individual soul must put on the whole armor of God and do constant battle, always aware that he must enlist the virtues that together will overcome the vices.[11]

Within the iconography of death, specifically, the manifestation of the warfare between virtue and vice appears at its most dramatic in this crucial deathbed scene, in which demon and Guardian Angel battle for the soul of the dying one. As we have seen, death was, after all, for the medieval Christian, a great moment of life—perhaps for the Renaissance man even more essential now that the doctrine of immortality had been declared in the Council of Trent. An eternity hung upon the penitence of the last moment, and folklore had it that the devil marshaled his forces for attack at this moment of greatest human weakness.

Although the original artist of the block-book eschewed images of worms, hellfire, and damnation, the intensity of the conflict between demons and the Good Angel was maintained by the symmetry of what is essentially tragicomedy. In the eleven woodcuts five temptations by the devil alternate with five inspirations by the good angel. The soul must face and overcome (with help, of course) temptations to loss of faith, to despair, impatience, vainglory, and avarice, before, in the last woodcut, it is received out of the mouth of the dying into the hands of an angel.[12] It is, of course, a displacement of the simple battle between virtue and vice that is fundamental to the Pauline experience of the warfare in this life.

But the conflict does not always end there. In a manuscript illumination from *The Book of Hours* of Catherine of Clèves, the demon and the angel hover over the corpse, immediately battling over a large book, but apparently still in conflict over the soul of the dying.[13] However defective the theology involved, the continuation of the battle after death becomes one of the more macabre variations. The most beautiful illuminated painting of this dynamic process is that in the Rohan Book of Hours, which shows a large image of God the Father, apparently observing the attempt of a devil to seize the soul of a corpse. In line, however, with the more comforting use of the *ars moriendi* tradition, the archangel Michael is on his way to rescue—perhaps sent by God himself.[14] Salvation is apparently assured and so, then, is a happy ending.

Shakespeare's image, however, as we might expect in the more particularized stylistic surface of Elizabethan drama, is obviously more earthbound, though surely as intense. Like Shakespeare's "two loves of comfort and despair" in Sonnet 144, Richard and Anne are in deadly combat with each other, and in both sonnet and play the possibility exists from the beginning that vice will overcome virtue, at least temporarily. The death imagery within the language of the scene, made more pointed for the audience by the visual image of the two confronting each other over the coffin, must have suggested further to an Elizabethan audience the above-described conflict of virtue and vice manifested in the battle of the good and bad angels over the soul of the dying.

As critics have long recognized in this scene, Shakespeare's rhetoric persuades the audience that Richard is a devil, or in this instance, *the* devil, and that Anne, who begins the scene as an angel, becomes eventually, in the context of Elizabethan attitudes, the daughter of Eve as she succumbs to the human temptation of power and romantic love. In short, the scene begins as a fairly equal battle between virtue and vice, but as it proceeds, Richard becomes more skillfully demonic, and Anne loses her angelic cast to feminine vanity and fleshly temptation rather than remaining the true warrior or good angel. On one level, the very power of evil seems to triumph. It is an interesting displacement here, however, that neither character is yet on his deathbed, and Henry is past his. Death lies in the future for both; the scene comes to be more strongly associated with the Dance of Death than with the *ars moriendi*.

In addition to the theological, a specifically erotic form of the tradition must have added associations for some in Shakespeare's audience. One of the most startling themes in sixteenth-century graphics is an extension of the *memento moris* into erotic variation. Holbein's Dance of Death, structured upon the Chain of Being and underlining the theme of death as leveler, is in the visual tradition elaborated in a subcategory that plays with associations between love and death. One important example in the period is Dürer's heraldic version of "Love and Death," 1503, with woman, satyr, and skull. Another, more comic, treatment is that of the well-known student of Dürer, Hans Sebald Beham, whose woman herself walks with a skeletal death (1541). The engraving has the motto: "*Omnem in Homine Venustatem Mors Abolet.*" But some woodcuts by the same engraver take the theme to a more erotic focus upon the flesh in contrast to the skeleton. Bartsch annotates a woodcut by Beham of three voluptuous nude graces and the figure of death who holds one of them by the hair, a study in contrast that jars the viewer into awareness of corruption in the very midst of life. In one sense, the erotic becomes most vivid in the face of death. Perhaps the most shocking image of all is that rendered in a graphic by Beham (IsB), 1548, of death coming for the soul of a fleshy nude asleep in a wanton posture that obviously exposes the pudendum. Perhaps the suggestion there is the old idea that through Eve lies the means of passing on original sin and its consequent mortality.[15]

"Omnem in Homine Venustatem Mors Abolet." **Woodcut by Hans Sebald Beham, 1542. Permission to reprint is from the Board of the Warburg Institute, The University of London.**

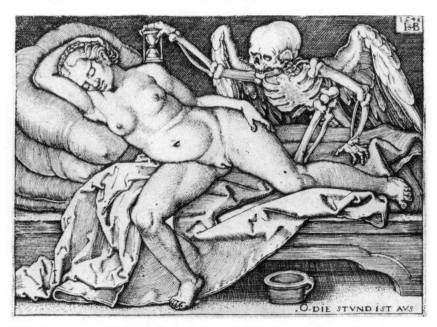

"O Die Stundist Aus." Woodcut by B. Beham, 1542, in Bartsch. Permission to reprint is from the Board of the Warburg Institute, The University of London.

Such juxtaposition of flesh and corruption laid the foundation for an interpretation of the connection between the macabre and the erotic that eventually blossomed into some of the more decadent imagery of death and sensuality in Jacobean drama, but which remains in Shakespeare's *Richard III* restrained and subordinated to the political thrust of the play. In this scene, when Anne shifts her original, angelic posture to the more earthly stance of the woman Eve in her acceptance of Richard's proposal, the eroticism in this shift is scarcely submerged. In line with Renaissance devotional attitudes toward lust, Anne seems drawn into eroticism through Richard's demonic power. Shakespeare's audience would have been sensitive to such associations in a way somewhat different from our own. Graphics were the most frequent means by which European art was disseminated in England. Although the specific graphics I have mentioned may not have been widely available in England, the mingling of love and death was so frequent a theme in the popular graphic tradition that English audiences by the end of the sixteenth century could hardly have avoided the association.

Shakespeare's Richard wooing Anne over a corpse must surely have borrowed even by 1592 associations from a tradition already so elaborated in the graphic arts. On the one hand, the impropriety of the courtship with the corpse between them must in itself have stirred Shakespeare's audience to surprise. On the other hand, erotic excitement was already a common association with love and death. At the same time the most profound irony in the shift is that though Richard may seem to offer life he remains throughout, like the devil he plays, the emissary of death itself.

In addition to the visual image on stage that intensifies irony by bringing into contrast the theological implications of salvation with the seduction of Anne by Richard, the scene would have been understood by many in Shakespeare's audience to foreshadow some of the major themes and events of the rest of the play. The most comprehensive foreshadowing is, of course, that of the death of Richard himself, which, in terms of Renaissance attitudes toward salvation, is a bad death at which the devil will be victor. When Anne speaks near the beginning of this encounter,

Anne: Fouler than heart can think thee, thou canst make
No excuse currant, but to hang thyself.

(I.ii.83–84)

and Richard answers

Richard: By such despair, I should accuse myself.

(I.ii.85)

he is not literally foreshadowing his own suicide but rather the state of despair to which he will be brought on the night before his death. Although the exigencies of history demand a battle scene, the religious tradition would show that the nature of his evil life brings him in that night to the mood of self-destruction, a mood that foreshadows the destruction of the soul that the audience would see as the subsequent damnation of his evil life. In this regard, the Elizabethan would remember the constant mention by popular sermons and current devotional literature of two kinds of death, that of the body and that of the soul, the latter far more to be feared than the former.[16]

Any Elizabethan would also have recognized the language of suicide, which was a much graver threat to salvation than any modern can realize. If the frequency of discussion in devotional treatises means anything, the temptation to suicide was most feared by Renaissance playgoers. Despair was widely known as a sin against the Holy Ghost leading to suicide, and it became for some in the Renaissance the ultimate sin of cutting oneself off from the mercy of God.

Particularly, the allusion to hanging oneself as an act of despair by which one would accuse himself was a richly commonplace association for Shakespeare's audience, both educated and uneducated alike. Judas, for example, was the familiar type of despair, who had gone forth to hang himself after betraying Christ. In the emblem tradition, as well, the association between despair and hanging was common, and Whitney shows a female figure of despair with a rope around her neck. In the *ars* series it is suggested in the Temptation against Faith and by this period in the knife of the Temptation to Despair, actually presented with the sin of murder.

The second, and most interesting, foreshadowing in the scene between Richard and Anne is that of scene 3 in act 5, where Richard and Richmond form an iconographical opposition on stage in stunning displacement of the *ars* woodblock illustrations. In some ways, the latter scene reverses the present order of things as they exist in act 1, scene 2. Just before the major battle of the play at Bosworth Field, Richard lies on stage in the position of the *moriens* of the woodcuts, himself being tempted by the Devil to despair by the parade of his past sins, while Richmond represents the Future-Good-King, beloved of angels. In the later scene, of course, he is not only tempted to despair; he *falls* to it and to the devil.

In act 1, however, Richard takes the role of the devil, or more literally, thinks of himself as having the devil on his side. He gloats over his conquest in amazement:

> *Richard*: And I no friends to back my suite [at all]
> But the plaine devil, and dissembling looks?
> And yet to win her! All the world to nothing!
>
> (I.ii.235–37)

Though Anne has tempted him to an act of despair, ultimately she has yielded to his erotic rhetoric. As Good Angel, she has rescued him from despair, but Shakespeare suggests the profound ironies of the "seeming" victory. Richard, however, is the aggressor and the victor in the scene in act 1, his pride whetting our moral appetite for his eventual downfall at the hands of Richmond. There is a tragic structural balance between the first scene of Richard's triumph and the scene the evening before the battle in which his confrontation with conscience brings him to genuine despair.

In act 5, scene 3, which balances and opposes the earlier scene, Richard is no longer the demonic aggressor or the conqueror. Although he has accomplished all his ends, mainly through the vices traditionally most closely associated with evil, deceit, and murder, his past sins, namely the murders he has committed, rise up to accuse him and to bring him to despair. Ironically, his victories have brought him to defeat. Partly because this is a dream scene, Richard is passive. His passivity, however, becomes part of the great theatrical image of the familiar deathbed scene that would have struck the chords of memory in an Elizabethan audience. The night before his actual death, he lies in the posture of the *moriens* in the woodcuts and dreams that he is visited by all those that he has murdered, including Henry VI, who in the early scene lay as a corpse between him and Lady Anne.

Tom Driver has interpreted this scene in terms of the forces of history coming together in judgment upon Richard and England. There is no question that the historical and cosmic cohere, especially as the scene is built upon a broad contrast in which both Richard and Richmond are seen in bed on the stage, and the ghosts treat them again so as to suggest the old opposition between virtue and vice. For this audience, of course, the scene plays up the contrast between the bad king and the future good king, a favorite opposition in the Renaissance and built firmly upon the literature that deals with the education of the prince. To an audience whose literate members were familiar with Elyot's *Book of the Governor* and Castiglione's *Courtier* (to name only the most influential examples), the divine working through history must be seen to pass its inexorable judgment upon such a king as Richard, who broke many of the laws of political philosophy as well as the laws of nature.

Shakespeare's interest in the morality of kingship is in evidence in all the history plays and continues into the tragedies, where his most mature and complex treatment of the theme occurs in *Antony and Cleopatra* in the brilliant comparison of Antony and Octavius. Because both these characters appear in his sources, Shakespeare is not free of Plutarch any more than he is free of Tudor history when he portrays Richard, but his originality in developing the theme is obvious. Only in the tragedies does Shakespeare follow the history of kingship to its logical tragic conclusion—that often the fully sympathetic human being must fail as a great leader, lacking sufficient control over his passions, sometimes lacking even sufficient judgment in his own character, in order to recognize deceit or evil.

In *Richard III*, however, the opposition remains simple. The wicked king has built his kingdom upon sinfulness and the cosmos will not tolerate him. Ultimately the goodness of Richmond must triumph and restore the normal order to the state. Throughout the drama the contrast between the two men is played upon. Insofar as Richard as king signifies sinful England, a potentially virtuous England as summed up in Richmond must triumph in order for Renaissance theological and political expectations to be fulfilled. But more than the judgment of God in history in this scene, Richard comes to an internal judgment upon himself, or at least his mind forces him finally to a judgment, which must of necessity include his past. In his waking speech, Richard labels this judgment *conscience.*

Leading up to the internal judgment, however, is the crucial dream that culminates in Richard's meeting with conscience. Shakespeare, although always concerned with the outward struggle between virtue and vice, always returns to Tuve's more personal allegory of salvation. It would be foolish in the instance of a history play to argue the superiority of the spiritual allegory that this scene plumbs. Clearly, the moral allegory is most often dominant in the plays that interpret the facts of history. But it is Shakespeare's dramatic genius to go also beyond the historical into the depths of a personal conflict that produces the spiritual sources of the tragic.

In this scene, the strength of Richard's personal sense of damnation is imparted to the audience through the rich adaptation of several aspects of the *ars moriendi* tradition. As indicated above, the visual images of Richard and Richmond in bed on the stage and the procession of the Ghosts of those murdered by Richard would in themselves have brought for his audience immediate associations with the temptation to despair, as we have seen, the most powerful scene in the *ars moriendi* series of temptations and alternating inspirations.

Although this traditional image is obviously in the background of the stage image and would undoubtedly have been seen as such by an Elizabethan audience, here, as usual, Shakespeare selects and adapts his material creatively to enrich the particular. The inspirations of the Good Angel in the woodcuts are absent as far as Richard is concerned. No figures of forgiven saints appear to soften the parade of those he has murdered. Shakespeare seems to say that Richard has already gone so far toward damnation that he cannot see or hear his own Good Angel. The inspirations of the Good Angel, however, are drawn upon fully in Shakespeare's scene as a whole; they are part of the woodcut series that is placed to comfort and encourage Richmond. This is obvious, I think, in the visual and rhetorical structure of the scene, but if anyone should miss it, Shakespeare has the Ghost of Clarence associate with angels the "wronged heirs of York" by his "Good angels guard thy battle! Live and flourish!" (V.ii.138) and, later, Buckingham with his "God and good angels fight on Richmond's side" (V.iii.175). Shakespeare with this adaptation maintains the visual balance of temptations and inspirations that is part of the *ars* tradition. The *ars,* after all, was historically a tradition of comfort, in which the Good Angel through inspirations wins the soul of the *moriens*, though in *Richard III* Shakespeare, never content with the commonplace alone, reverses the outcome, or uses the reversal to underline the contrast between Richard and Richmond.

In addition to the striking visual use of the *ars moriendi* through the image of Richard abed on stage, Shakespeare has structured his scene rhetorically to invoke the powerful emotions associated with the theme of damnation in the Elizabethan mind. The most obvious reference to the temptation to despair is the repetition of the refrain "Despair and die" (V.iii) by all those Richard has murdered: the Ghosts of Prince Edward, son of Henry VI; King Henry VI; Clarence; Rivers; Grey; and Vaughan in a group; Hastings; two young Princes; Anne; and Buckingham. The repetition of this refrain, with such minor variations as Edward's "Despair therefore and die" (V.iii.120) or Grey's "let thy soul despair (V.iii.141)," sounds a somber bell of judgment throughout the scene, especially as it contrasts with the alternative words of comfort and life addressed to Richmond. The scene is played liturgically, the repetition creating a ritual of enforced remembering by which Richard's hard heart is moved to encounter conscience.

It was also commonplace to show the contrast between the death of the virtuous man and that of the wicked man. Here Richmond is not literally upon his deathbed as Richard is close to being, but the opposition of virtue and vice balances that in the earlier scene between Anne and Richard and suggests the kind of contrast often shown in death scenes. One of the earliest, and most clearly allegorical, instances appears in the beautiful early fourteenth-century De Lisle Psalter, now in the British Museum, which was acquired by Lord William Howard, of Naworth, Cumberland, in the late sixteenth century. An illumination of the twelve articles of faith shows the soul of Lazarus being received by good angels and that of Dives by bad angels.

Shakespeare's refrain suggests the relentlessness with which Richard's past sins accuse his conscience and ultimately overwhelm him with despair; it also suggests the commonplace revelation of past sins being paraded before the sinner on his deathbed in the temptation to despair. As Shakespeare handles it, however, it has the narrative formality of ritual procession or masque rather than the visually simultaneous presentation of the sins as shown in the woodcut. The liturgical repetition builds gradually to the appearance of the last ghost murdered, who is Buckingham:

> *Ghost to Richard*: The first was I that help'd thee to the crown;
> The last was I that felt thy tyranny.
> O, in the Battle think on Buckingham,
> And die in terror of thy guiltiness!
> Dream on, dream on, of bloody deeds
>   and death,
> Fainting despair; despairing, yield
>   thy breath.

(V.iii.167–172)

His curse implies that dying in despair would result in damnation.

From the numerous allusions to the *ars* tradition, one might speculate that Shakespeare did not consider this a unique or unusual dream but an instance of the preparation for death that every man must be concerned with. Though the earliest form of the *ars* might suggest that it be relevant primarily to those dying in bed at home safely and calmly, the tradition had been adapted in the hands of preachers and devotional writers to people who lived less safe or stable lives, as in Perkins's "Salve for a Sicke Man," and . . . "Souldiers when they goe to battell."[17] Shakespeare himself in *Henry V* (IV.i.78–85) gives Henry lines on the equal necessity for preparation for death by the soldier and the man who will die at home in bed.

In fact, Shakespeare's dream scene in *Richard III* picks up from the devotional tracts the familiar idea that a man's whole life must be a preparation for his death (live well and die well), though the *ars* also insists that there is always time for repentance on his deathbed. Ironically, Richard's preparation has been a series of heartless murders that might under ideal circumstances lead him to radical conversion but which in this instance leads only to the despair of the Ghosts' counsel. Though the *ars* has throughout most of its manifestations insisted that the grace symbolized by the Good Angel is always available to the sinner, Shakespeare's scene, like the end of *Dr. Faustus*, makes the dramatic point that Richard's preparation for death through murder has cut him off from the mercy of God. Major sins have led him to such depths of despair that he cannot throw himself upon the mercy of Christ, having rejected it throughout his life. He simply cannot believe that so great a sinner can be forgiven—such is the hopelessness of despair. In short, it is his own state of mind and soul that causes the Good Angel to be absent from his consciousness, for the dream is an image of the state of Richard's soul.

This internal dimension, which is more characteristic of the allegory in dream poetry than drama, is underlined by Richard's waking speech in which he reveals to his audience the judgment of his conscience:

> *Richard*: Give me another horse! Bind up my wounds!
> Have mercy Jesu! Soft, I did but dream.
> O coward conscience, how dost thou afflict me?
> The lights burn blue. It is now dead midnight.
> Cold fearful drops stand on my trembling flesh.
> What do I fear? Myself? There's none else by.
> Richard loves Richard, that is, I [am] I.
> Is there a murtherer here? No. Yes, I am.
> Then fly. What, from my self? Great reason why—
> Lest I revenge. What, myself upon myself?
> Alack, I love myself. Wherefore? For any good
> That I myself have done unto myself?
> O no! Alas, I rather hate myself
> For hateful deeds committed by myself.
> I am a villain; yet I lie, I am not.
> Fool, of thy self speak well; fool, do not flatter.
>
> (V.iii.177–192)

As it is, Richard's self is divided—close to taking vengeance upon itself.

> My conscience hath a thousand several tongues,
> And every tongue brings in a several tale,
> And every tale condemns me for a villain;
> Perjury, perjury, in the highest degree,
> Murther, stern murther, in the direst degree;
> All several sins, all us'd in each degree,
> Throng to the Bar, crying all, "Guilty! guilty!"
> I shall despair; there is no creature loves me,
>
> (V.iii.193–200)

I have quoted this speech at such length because as Richard's answer to his dream, it sums up many elements of the tradition. A few lines on, at the actual end of the speech, he resolves to battle to the death with Richmond, and that final section of the speech moves us forward into the battle itself. But it is this earlier major section that is of the most importance. We notice, to begin with, that it seems a rather long, set speech, following the formal, near allegorical, structure of the dream itself. Examined internally, however, the speech is a microcosm of Richard's confrontation with his past sins and the only scene through which he may be demonstrated to have a conscience. The very use of the phrase "O coward conscience" reveals Shakespeare's sophisticated use of the "Temptation to Despair," whereby the ancient allegory of the devil struggling for the soul of the sinner against his Good Angel becomes the more internalized struggle within the individual soul.

Expressive of this struggle are lines that suggest technical or formal elements within the *ars* and that together form a rhetoric through which the speech moves. Line one, of course, suggests that upon waking, Richard conflates the reality of his dream with the reality of the moment and even that of the future. He thinks that he is in the battle scene the next day, that he is wounded and in need of a horse, just before his actual, as opposed to psychological, deathbed scene. The immediacy of death gives point to his calling upon the mercy of Jesus. From a modern point of view, this appeal to Christ may seem odd in a character who, throughout the play, has been allied obviously with the devil; but here again, Shakespeare's audience would have found commonplace the *ars* convention that recognized the name of Jesus as the most powerful and present help against despair. In the woodcuts and in most of the visual representations, a crucifix hangs before the eyes of the sinner to remind him that the mercy of Christ is available to the sinner until the moment of his death, specifically the moment at which his soul goes forth out of his mouth.

Richard, however, like Faustus, hears no answer from his Saviour but turns inward to find only himself present. Shakespeare makes the experience dramatically powerful by portraying Richard's profound sense of aloneness. Unlike the figure in the woodcuts, who is surrounded by companions supernatural and human, Richard wakes to find himself alone. The loss of all companionship is perhaps the strongest foreshadowing of hell as well as the hallmark of tragic isolation. The ghosts have come and gone—the demons have disappeared—and Richard is left with himself: "Is there a murtherer here?" (V.ii.184).

Throughout the rest of the speech he vacillates between despair and the last shred of self-esteem that keeps him from literal suicide. *Despair* here at the end of the speech is used in the technical theological sense familiar to Elizabethans. It was not considered simply a state of very deep distress but the loss of faith in the mercy of God toward oneself that ultimately leads to suicide. Throughout the speech, Richard has battled with himself lest he revenge himself upon himself. To the Elizabethan, this meant a struggle against the impulse to suicide, usually considered the worst of sins because it did not allow of time for repentance before death. The allegorical elaboration of this struggle may be seen at its most frightening in the "Despair Canto" of the *Faerie Queene*" and at the end of *Dr. Faustus,* but one would not have had to turn to poetry or drama to be aware of the theological and human implications of despair. Devotional literature had sounded its dangers. So strong, apparently, was the fear of being overcome by sin at the last illness that some devotional manuals for the sick, such as the one attributed to Luther, had become a compendium of comforting biblical passages that emphasized the unquenchable mercy of God. In the oldest conventions of the *ars* in the blockbooks, the Inspiration against Despair shows the Angel pointing to Paul and Peter as the archetypes of great sinners who have found mercy.

Although Richard retains enough of conventional piety to call upon the mercy of Jesus in the second line of his speech, he persuades himself by the end that the accusation of all his sins that "Throng to the Bar, crying all, 'Guilty! Guilty!'" results in despair. Most damaging of all is his realization that he can find in himself no pity for himself:

> And if I die no soule will pity me.
> And wherefore should they, since that I myself
> Find in myself no pity to myself?
>
> (V.iii.201–3)

The entrance of Ratcliff cuts short Richard's speculations, and the plotted necessities for battle preparation leave little time for introspection. The next time Richard speaks of conscience he is seeking to encourage his forces before the battle. However, his desperation remains clear as he defies the very things that are moving his thoughts.

Although to a modern audience he may seem heroic during the battle, his loss of heaven and the acceptance of damnation expressed in his speech to Norfolk would mark him as despairing and demonic to an Elizabethan audience:

> Our strong armes be our conscience, swords our law.
> March on, join bravely, let us to it pell-mell,
> If not to heaven, then hand in hand to hell.
>
> (V.iii.311–13)

For it is at this point that Richard is shown by Shakespeare to have turned his back utterly upon his conscience. From a modern point of view we are tempted to see this behavior as a kind of brave whistling in the face of insurmountable obstacles, and certainly I can think of no instance where Shakespeare is totally devoid of sympathy. But the overwhelming force of Richard's speech as prepared for by the temptation to despair and its judgment of conscience is to show the desperation in Richard's soul—a desperation that shows him to be utterly lost. The ghosts have urged him to carry in his mind the despair that they have counseled; it is within this context that the battle takes place next day.

It may seem curious that in this very formal Ghost scene with its terse speeches and many repetitions, the major one the refrain "Despair and die," the play rises to its emotional climax, culminating in Richard's great soliloquy. It is, indeed, one of the best instances of the way in which nearly liturgical formality seems necessary to contain the most passionate emotions. Vice is finally overcome; the devil as always is seen to be his own worst enemy; historical providence overcomes. Richard dies later, literally by the hand of Richmond, but the dream scene has bodied forth the death of his soul. His death, in the spiritual sense, has been brought about by the wickedness of his own past. Always within the *ars moriendi* tradition the *moriens* is counseled to remember that the death of the soul is far more serious than the death of the body. And just as a good death is dependent on a good life, the life of the soul depends on dying a good death. Horror at the death of the soul is one of the emotions that would be aroused in an Elizabethan audience sensitive to this tradition.

At the same time, the vast majority of the Shakespearean audience would respond to a justice in the conventional use of the temptation to despair, which shows the past sins finally being visited upon their executor. After the capitulation to despair, it would have been no surprise for Elizabethans that Richard no longer is in control. Even the despairing final burst of courage is only to be taken for that. More importantly, virtue and Richmond are personally and historically in the ascendancy. The ethical present dominates the dramatic text. Richard is slain on Bosworth Field without being given a final speech. If during the final reconciliation of the play, the audience thinks at all of him, it is only to visualize hell-mouth gaping for the hell-hound. But that is not in the play.

6

Othello's Angels

A Prayer to be sayd at our going into bed.

When the day is ended, we geue ourselves to rest in the night so when this life is ended, we rest in deth. Nothing resembleth our life more then the day, nor death more then sleepe, nor that graue, more than the bed. Vouchsafe therefore, O Lord our gouernour, and defender, both to shield us now lying unable to help ourselves from the craftines and assaults of our cruell enemy: and also to call us then unto thee, when we shalbe yet more unable at the finishing of the race of this life, not for our own deserts, but for thy own mercy sake: that we may liue and walk with thee for ever.
—Richard Day, *A Booke of Christian Praiers*

The second scene of the last act of *Othello* (1604) invokes another allusion to the *ars moriendi*, the comfort for the dying which, as we have seen, stands in ironic contrast to Othello's own violent and possibly despairing death. The most familiar prop in the iconography of Renaissance death is the bed, and in this scene the bed is the dominant presentational image, a bed that should probably be both well downstage and as massive as possible while still capable of being rolled forward. In many of the woodcuts that accompany the *ars moriendi* tracts and in the sixteenth-century paintings of deathbed scenes, the bed is inclined to be massive and rectilinear, in contrast to the curvilinear voluptuous couch hung with tent-like draperies that appears in representations of amorous scenes.[1]

Supporting this dominant icon of the deathbed is a network of verbal images, especially those associated with angels and devils, the contestants for a dying man's soul.[2] There is no great elaboration; the details are commonplace; but by 1604, the projected date of the play's first performance, such a long and popular Christian tradition as the *ars moriendi* needed only to be hinted at, as we have seen.[3] The Judeo-Christian view of life as a trial or a series of temptations is familiar to medieval and Renaissance scholars. The patterns of temptation and fall, or temptation and victory, appear throughout the history of literature. The great archetypes are, of course, biblical; the pattern for tragedy to the Renaissance mind was the narrative of Adam and Eve falling to the devil in the Garden; the tragicomic pattern, however, was exemplified by Job and Christ, both of whom came to ultimate victory over the world, the flesh, and the devil.

Some scholars have seen Othello as a type of Adam in his fall through uxoriousness to the temptations of Iago in the main body of the play, but no one has seen act 5, scene 2 as a parallel temptation and fall underlined by the allusions to the *ars moriendi* tradition. This chapter argues that Shakespeare, by the use of this tradition, intensifies the tragic fall of Othello. As he has lived and fallen earlier to temptation, embodied in Iago, so he dies, confronted by his own sins as they seem to be embodied in Iago, from the traditional point of view falling into the sin of despair and taking his own life. I shall argue later that the overlay of stoicism combined with tragic heroism onstage qualifies and perhaps transforms the effect of this, but it necessarily must play against the tradition. The most explicit allusion to the tradition, made by Gratiano, reminds the audience of the deathbed struggle between good and evil in which the stakes are very high:

> Did he [Brabantio] live now,
> This sight would make him do a desperate turn:
> Yea, curse his better angel from his side,
> And fall to reprobance.

(V.ii.206–09)

By the time Gratiano speaks these lines, Othello is facing his own struggle with the temptation to despair, suicide, and probable damnation. Critics have found it impossible to believe that Othello is both damned and heroic. On the one hand, those who see his damnation seem to lose sight of the heroic proportion of his struggle and the very human glory of his ending. On the other hand, those who respond to Shakespeare's dramatic portrayal of the struggle try to minimize the theological implications of Othello's suicide. Somewhere in between are the scholars who discuss the play as something of an allegory of fortunate fall; they see many theological allusions to damnation in the language of the play, but at the same time they find in the final scene a structure of redemption, often built upon Desdemona as a Christ figure and upon Othello's sincere repentance of her murder.[4]

All three positions seem to me to ignore at some point the text of the play as it would be apprehended by a Shakespearean audience. In his professional knowledge of the theater and of the need to communicate immediately to an audience, Shakespeare often speaks explicitly. When he is using allusions to suggest a dimension other than that of the particular, he frequently gives his summary clue. In *Othello*, perhaps his most carefully wrought play, Gratiano, horrified at the murder of Desdemona, brings explicitly into the context the long *ars moriendi* tradition as a comment on what would have been Brabantio's response to the scene.

The explicit reference to the *ars* tradition operates dramatically in two ways. It throws into relief the contrast between the tragic suffering of Othello in Act V and the ordinary suffering of one who dies well.[5] By juxtaposing the ideal of dying with something very near its opposite, Shakespeare suggests the possibility of Othello's damnation. At the same time, however, by showing the heroic intensity of the struggle and the suffering that results from the recognition of his guilt against the conventional background of the *ars*, Shakespeare evokes dramatic sympathy for the human Othello. Perhaps paradoxically, Othello's damnation is supported by the references to the *ars* tradition at the same time that he becomes more dramatically sympathetic in the quality of his suffering—so much so that one feels that Shakespeare has used the conventional theology to overturn it.

At the heart of the *ars*, as we have seen earlier, is the actual deathbed scene, viewed as a climactic struggle between the forces of evil and the forces of good for the possession of the dying one's soul. In the oldest, simplest, and most iconographic terms, as it is seen in the woodcuts, or in early medieval drama such as *The Castle of Perseverance,* this struggle takes place between one's Good Angel and demons sent by one's Bad Angel (or the devil). The struggle between the two angels in five temptations and five inspirations, as we have seen, and the accompanying instruction attempt to aid the dying one to overcome the devil and to die peacefully, so that his soul may be received out of his mouth and into heaven by the Good Angel. Sections other than the temptations were usually included, of course, and sometimes in the seventeenth century the central struggle disappeared so that the instruction consisted of comforts alone.[6] Many popular devotional writers of the late sixteenth century, however, such as Cardinal Bellarmine and the Protestant preacher Christopher Sutton wrote *ars* books that expand the original treatment to contain the instruction against temptation.[7] Often, the first section of an *ars* book was an extensive treatise on accepting death as the gateway to life and preparing for it; instructions were elaborated for those attending the sick: questions to be asked, prayers to be said.

In spite of the dramatic sympathy that arises from the recognition by the audience that Othello has not fallen through malice but rather, like Adam in the Garden, through uxoriousness, the audience could hardly fail to see the manner of his dying against the long and popular tradition of the *ars moriendi*. The counsel of the *ars* against impatience in the face of suffering or against despair that might lead to suicide could hardly have failed to present a contrast to Othello both earlier in the play and also in his last moments. According to conventional Renaissance theology, Othello dies badly; like Faustus, he does not follow the accumulated wisdom of Christian theology; and as Roland Frye has said in his *Shakespeare and Christian Doctrine*, there was nearly universal agreement in the sixteenth century that damnation resulted from suicide committed willfully, consciously, and successfully.[8] Shakespeare reminds his audience of this contrast between the ideal death and that of Othello by commonplaces. By this time, Shakespeare had only to refer to traditional images and theological themes to bring before the mind's eye of the audience the ordered and optimistic ideal for the art of dying. But Shakespeare always complicates the commonplaces.

By far the greater number of religious devotional books in the *ars* tradition began with a section on the necessity for accepting death joyfully and preparing oneself for it. As part of this preparation, many writers gave copious advice on how to die. Christopher Sutton's *Disce Mori: Learne to Dye* (1600) reminded early moderns that an essential part of the preparation is self-knowledge:

> Well, the perfection of our knowledge is to know God and ourselves: ourselves we best know when we acknowledge our mortal being . . . by our dying to the world, Christ is said to come and live in us, and by our dying in the world, we are said to go to live with Christ.[9]

Devotional writers warned against just such sudden death as Shakespeare's audience finds in *Othello*. This warning arose out of the recognition that human beings desire a leisurely death in order to prepare their souls; even so sophisticated a preacher as Richard Hooker said that the virtuous must desire the leisurely death in old age, both for their own joy and for the example that they can give to the many who surrounded them on their deathbed:

. . . because the nearer we draw unto God, the more we are oftentimes enlightened with the shining beams of his glorious presence as being then almost in sight, a leisurable departure may in that case bring forth for the good of such as are present that which shall cause them [joy] for ever after . . . and let our last end be like theirs.[10]

Probably the suddenness and violence of the deaths in the last act of *Othello* were in themselves enough to arouse horror in an audience warned against being caught unprepared. At the same time, however, that devotional writers warned men to guard against sudden death and indeed to aim for a leisurely dying, they also warned them not to judge the future of the dying one, presumably because one could not know whether the *moriens* might have time for repentance between apparent dying and the actual going out of the soul. With characteristic pithiness, Erasmus says,"For it may be, that he, which for treason, is hanged, drawn, and quartered, passeth into the company of aungelles, where as another, the whiche dyeng in a gray friers cote, and relygiously buried, departeth downe into hell."[11]

Although even the sophisticated desired a leisurely death, the tradition allowed for a "good" sudden death under one essential condition: that of a good life. Clearly, this is the traditional justification for Desdemona's good death and, in less ideal terms, for Emilia's as well. Neither has time for the traditional preparation, yet the audience would have seen Desdemona's death in perfect charity as ideal and Emilia's in heroic truth-telling as nearly so.

Clearly, the instructions for deathbed behavior were aimed more surely at those who had doubts about having lived well and who envisioned a last epic struggle with the devil. The tradition was designed to comfort especially those who needed the assurance of ritual. In fact, as we have seen, the great set of eleven illustrations that accompany the *ars* block-books narrates what I have already called a "tragicomedy," in whose final scene is illustrated the happy dying of the sick man.

The effect of the series is not, however, to frighten the reader with the mightiness of the struggle but rather to reassure him that with the aid of his Good Angel he will be able to overcome the devil. The Good Angel suggests aids against the devil in some of the inspirations, in which one sees the vestige of a smile on the face of the *moriens*; particularly essential is the patterning of one's death on the Passion of Christ and the remembering of his mercy. The literal expression of this counsel is to fix one's eyes on the figure of Christ on the cross. In the Inspiration against Avarice and in the final scene of the dying well, the figure of Christ on the cross is prominent.[12] In "The Craft to know Well to Die: the following advice is given:

> [Item] there ought to be presented to the sick person the image of the crucifix, which always should be among the sick people, and also the image of our Blessed Virgin and of other saints which the sick man hath most loved and honored in his life.[13]

Certainly, compared to the *danse macabre* and even the *memento mori*, which stemmed from that, the *ars* tradition had a particularly kind and encouraging tone. For the most part, the writers of the *artes moriendi* shunned images of damnation and hellfire and sought to encourage the dying one lest his bodily weakness cause him to fall prey to the devil's temptations, especially the sin against faith and the sin of despair, both of which might lead to suicide.[14] Almost all the authors of these numerous books on the art of dying attempted to give very practical instructions. In vivid contrast to their optimistic tone, the end of *Othello* is filled with passion, murder, recrimination, and a barrage of temptations for Othello. Anyone familiar with the medieval *exempla* of good Christians facing their death would recognize in Othello's ending a near antithesis of the ideal. Certainly the ironic contrast is the point. Shakespeare is using the order and tradition to underline the tragedy.

The popularity of the theme of preparation for death had led, of course, to several levels of writing on the subject: the old *ars* tradition focused on the struggle, symbolic and visual; the intellectualized books of meditation; and pious treatises that tended to focus more on practical instructions for setting one's property in order than upon the great spiritual crisis. As we have seen, Shakespeare chose the older tradition to which the deathbed struggle was central, a tradition that was still very much alive in the popular folklore of the day. No doubt his reasons for choosing this older tradition had to do with the visual or iconic qualities that make it especially appealing for the stage.

This visual quality in the *ars* suggests Shakespeare's presentational use of the tradition. Inevitably, one recalls the woodcuts mentioned above, which had appeared first with the block-books but had been reproduced and imitated elsewhere throughout the sixteenth century. The excellence of the representations suggests that they would have imprinted themselves on the imagination of all who saw them, and the quantity of their reproduction supports that suggestion. There is evidence that originally many considered the graphic representations central to the *ars* and the text of explanation and instruction a mere accompaniment. At least we know from the closing lines of the introduction of one of the early block-books that the author intended the words and pictures *to work together* in the emblematic tradition to teach a man how to die.[15] Since these books were not designed for the clergy but rather for the uneducated layman, one may deduce the primary importance of the illustrations.

For these reasons, one may speculate that the visual dominance of the bed in act 5 was to Shakespeare's audience pervasively suggestive of the deathbed scene in the *ars*. At the same time, it was obviously a marriage bed. Also in visual terms, the traditional gathering of the central characters about the bed as the scene progresses, first with the entrance of Emilia, after Desdemona's almost-death, then with the entrance of Montano, Gratiano, and Iago after l.207, culminates with the final entrance of Lodovico and Cassio. The scene's associations with the *ars* are displaced for the particular drama, but the audience would have had suggestions of the *moriens* surrounded by friends and foes of a supernatural or symbolic nature as well as by members of his earthly community.

The art of dying also informs the structure of the scene. Act 5, scene 2 is divided into two major parallel sections. The first presents the murder and "good" death of Desdemona and the second the discovery by Othello of his monstrous mistake and his consequent suicide, or what critics have seen as a "bad" death. In the first section, the contemporary audience agreed that Desdemona's death was extremely affecting.[16] This is true, not only because of her innocence and loveliness but because in exemplifying the ideal of Christian forgiveness, she brings into the context of the play a great body of emotional associations with a good death intensified by an unjust murder. During the first part of the scene, before he is overcome by jealousy and rage, Othello behaves as just avenger. Still softened by his first sight of Desdemona asleep and the kiss with which he has wakened her, he himself remembers the advice of the *ars* tradition that the soul should not depart out of the world unprepared; he admonishes her to think on any crime that she has not as yet confessed because he would not kill her "unprepared spirit," her soul (V.ii.30–31). A few lines later he utters the conventional phrase, "Think on thy sins" (V.ii.39).

However, when Desdemona does not confess, he advises her not to commit the sin of perjury, since she is on her deathbed. This last remark is, of course, a further suggestion of the visual icon of the bed in the scene. The seeming peace of the scene, with its echoes of traditional phrases and kindly advice, is merely a thin ironic overlay for the increasing tension as Othello grows more and more angry at what he believes to be Desdemona's dishonesty. As the scene builds, Othello shifts his role from that of fatherly adviser or confessor to that of the accusing Bad Angel of the *ars* series. At the end, he is too overcome by his own passion to allow her even one prayer. He does, however, retain some measure of sympathy from the audience by his attempt to keep Desdemona from suffering when she seems slow to die.

The first section of the scene, Desdemona's good death, is linked with the second, Emilia's entrance, by her poignant and momentary waking, which critics have long seen as an emblem of perfect Christian forgiveness and a final attempt at reconciliation with Othello. Asked by Emilia who has committed the murder, she replies: "Nobody; I my self. Farewell! / Commend me to my kind lord. O, farewell!" [*Dies*] (V.ii.124–25). Ironically Othello remarks: "She's like a liar gone to burning hell" (V.ii.128). He sees her as having damned herself by telling a lie on her deathbed. Only as the scene progresses would the audience, recognizing the dramatic necessity of Othello's death, begin to see Othello take the place of Desdemona as the *moriens*. In some measure, Desdemona remains the central figure evoking the *ars* simply because she remains in the posture of the *moriens* (and finally the *dead*) on the deathbed. During the earlier part of the scene, one remains still conscious of Othello as demonic in his murder of Desdemona; this is underlined in one sense by Emilia's line: "O, the more angel she, / And you the blacker devil" (V.ii.130–31). The veriest commonplace of commonplaces, the opposition may imply further that Desdemona as Good Angel has sought to save Othello by one inspiration and that in killing her, he has played the role of Bad Angel against himself.[17] His shift to *moriens* becomes more obvious in the scene's ironic structure when Gratiano makes the *ars moriendi* tradition explicit a hundred lines later in his reference to Brabantio, already cited:

> Did he live now,
> This sight would make him do a desperate turne:
> Yea, curse his better angel from his side,
> And fall to reprobance.
>
> (V.ii.206–8)

Gratiano is glad that Brabantio is dead because the sight of Desdemona murdered would have brought him to despair; in this state, he might curse his Good Angel from his side and fall into reprobance, or reprobation, defined by the OED as "a state of rejection by God," and so be condemned to eternal misery.[18] Here the text makes explicit for the audience one of the strongest warnings of the *ars* tradition, the avoidance of despair and suicide.

Gratiano's speech is extremely important in several ways. First, it makes clear that Shakespeare is thinking of the *ars* tradition, not referring loosely or metaphorically to angels and devils. Second, the implied analogy turns the focus of the audience to Brabantio as the dying one—and perhaps thereby to Othello, even though he has not yet begun to die physically. Third, the speech sums up symbolically what Othello has done and foreshadows the tragedy of what he will do: he has by killing her actually cursed Desdemona, his Good Angel, from his side, and the full revelation of his sin in doing so will lead him to the despair that ends in the suicide usually seen by Renaissance theology as resulting in damnation.[19] Suicide itself is, of course, not mentioned explicitly in Gratiano's speech. As earlier sections have shown, the connection between despair and suicide was very close in the associations of Shakespeare's audience. For this reason, the *ars* tradition placed almost inordinate emphasis on this temptation and the means of overcoming it. In some measure, too, this explains the increasing emphasis in devotional literature on the comforts for the dying. In the little manual attributed to Luther, for example, the whole notion of the great struggle has disappeared, and the book is wholly comprised of comforting bible verses, meditations, and prayers.[20]

That Iago parallels the Devil of the *ars* is suggested in a number of places, both before and during act 5. The association is most obviously prepared for by Iago's lines early in the play:

> Divinity of hell!
> When devels will the blackest sinnes put on,
> They do suggest a first with heavenly showes,
> As I do now.
>
> (II.ii.350–53)

Critics have long recognized the quality of Iago's character as diabolic in its love of evil and deception. Othello's own superstitious response to the depth of deception that Iago has practiced upon him is an explicit suggestion in act 5 itself: "I look down towards his feet; but that's a fable / If that thou be'st a Devil, I cannot kill thee" (V.ii.286–87). One should not press it too far, but one can hardly help remembering that Othello finally only wounds Iago. The association between Iago and the devil is reinforced a few lines after the reference to his cloven hoof when Othello calls him demi-devil and asks him why he has ensnared his soul and body (v.ii.368–69). In terms of the deathbed scene of the *ars* Iago becomes for Othello the cause and embodiment of the sins of faithlessness and jealousy that have led him to murder and despair.[21] The discovery of Iago's perfidy is the means by which Othello confronts his own sins. One remembers the temptation to despair in the woodcuts that shows the *moriens* surrounded by six demons pointing to the sins of his past; one of the six carries a scroll that bears the inscription: "*Ecce peccata tua,*" or "Behold thy sins." The others point to various representations of those against whom the *moriens* has sinned through fornication, avarice, and murder.

Because the tragic force of the revelation of his own sins finds Othello without any of the supports recommended by the *ars* tradition, the leisurely deathbed with its time for meditation and repentance is impossible. Desdemona, after one attempt at inspiration, is dead. There are no friends about Othello to encourage him in the conventional ways by mentioning the thief on the cross or other examples of sinful men who died saved. Indeed, before her death, Emilia lashes out with fury to judge his guilt. Even as the truth is revealed and Iago shown to be the villain, there is among those present pity for Othello's rashness but no real comfort for his grief and no mention of Christ's mercy. Because the devilish Iago remains largely inarticulate through the scene, one feels that Othello's despair stems primarily from his own confrontation of his sins.

In these circumstances, Othello's despair seems inevitable. After he wounds Iago but does not kill him, Othello remarks, "I am not sorry neither, I'ld have thee live: / for in my sense, 'tis happiness to die" (V.ii.289–90). These lines are ironic in terms of the *ars* tradition in which one well prepared should be happy to die. The irony is given its despairing cast, however, by Othello's previous speech:

> Here is my journey's end, here is my butt
> And very sea-mark of my utmost sail.
> Do you go back dismay'd? 'Tis a lost fear;
> Man but a rush against Othello's breast,
> And he retires. Where should Othello go?
> Now—how does thou look now? Oh ill-starr'd wench,
> Pale as thy smock! when we shall meet at compt,
> This look of thine will hurl my soul from heaven,
> And fiends will snatch at it. Cold, cold, my girl?
> Even like thy chastity. O cursed, cursed slave!
> Whip me, ye devils,
> From the possession of this heavenly sight:
> Blow me about in winds! roast me in sulphur!
> Wash me in steep-down gulfs of liquid fire!

Oh Desdemon! dead, Desdemon: dead.
O, o!

(V.ii.267–82)

Not only does Othello see himself cast out from heaven, as his earlier lines foreshadowed: "O, I were damn'd beneath all depth in hell: / But that I did proceed upon just grounds / To this extremity" (V.ii.137–39), but he also desires to be cast away from the vision of Desdemona's innocence. At the "compt," the Last Judgment, the sight of Desdemona will hurl him to hell. The presumably purgatorial imagery of winds and fiery gulfs notwithstanding, the strongest suggestion is that of hell.[22]

It is only a short step from the surmise that Othello's sin is unforgivable to suicide. We need to remember, however, that the surmise is Othello's at the worst point in his encounter with himself. One is reminded of the figure of the demon in the woodcut temptation against faith; the right hand of the demon rests upon the shoulder of the *moriens*, and his scroll reads "*Interfecias te ipsum*" or "Kill thyself." But before he kills himself, Othello makes his dying speech, his final justification and one that dramatically redeems him. One must say with Siegel that all the imagery of the play, and certainly that of the final scene, suggests Othello's damnation. This is not to say, however, that he cannot remain humanly sympathetic, or more accurately, tragically heroic.[23] The dignity of his final speech surely projects the classical image of a man and a general who was once a hero. That the suicide is conventionally unacceptable is suggested by the comments of Lodovico and Gratiano:

Lod. Oh bloody period!
Grat. All that is spoke is marr'd.

(V.i.356–57)

That the dramatic dimension, the human dimension, takes emotional precedence in the play, however, is shown in Cassio's comment, which comes in the last and most emphatic position: "This did I fear, but thought he had no weapon: / For he was great of heart" (V.ii.360–61). One's tragic sympathy remains with Othello and the strong indication that he is damned in conventional terms only intensifies the tragic loss of potentiality. Shakespeare's genius, however, is that he intensifies dramatic irony by opening for Othello in the minds of many more sophisticated members of the audience a larger vision than he has for himself. By recovering his former self in his final speech—the dignity he regains in encountering the madness of the jealousy manipulated by Iago and his own betrayal in his murder of Desdemona—he actually becomes himself. In short, the justice by which he judges himself would probably bring most of the audience to the same mercy that Desdemona herself has shown. The dominating theological implication, of course, is that God (more merciful than any audience) would accept Othello's judgment upon himself and grant him mercy. But that is outside the play—a speculation on the richness of dramatic irony. In the actual scene Othello is judge and executioner of himself.

Pointing out these theological commonplaces of Renaissance thought should not imply that Shakespeare's audience would be preoccupied with eschatological considerations while it viewed the last act of Othello. The play is not an allegory, and one must agree with Roland Frye that Shakespeare is primarily concerned with the now, the ethical present.[24] Drama is closer to religion in its ritual form than in its theology. No doubt Shakespeare's audience was immediately involved in the murder of Desdemona, the discovery by Othello of Iago's diabolical scheme, and the recognition by Othello of his personal guilt that leads him swiftly to suicide by self-execution. At the same time, however, remembering what scholars have learned from art historians Gombrich, Panofsky, and Wind about the Renaissance ability to move back and forth readily between the particular and the universal, one can hardly doubt that the audience was from the beginning aware of universal implications. The great bell of the *contemptus mundi* tradition had already rung so insistently across the ages that men knew the scallop shell of the pilgrim as the emblem of life. Erasmus had sounded the subordination of this life to the next in the most conventional phrasing:

> We be wayfarynge men in this world, not inhabytants,
> we be as straungers in Innes (or to speke it better) in bouthes or
> tentes, we lyve not in our countrey. This holle lyfe is nothing
> but a rennynge to deathe, and that very shorte, but death is the
> gate of ever lstynge lyfe.[25]

It is difficult to define precisely the effect of the allusions to the *ars moriendi* in the final completely articulated scene of *Othello*. Clearly, the scene is not a simple allegory of dying badly. The suggestions are neither frequent nor elaborate. It is consistent with Shakespeare's artistry, however, that he deepen the emotional response of his audience to a particular image of life by suggesting analogues from experience and history. In this case, the introduction of the ideal for dying quickens the emotional response of the audience to the "tragic loading of the bed." What creates the dynamic power is the play of that loss against so much life. "In me thou see'st the glowing of such fire," says Shakespeare in Sonnet 73, "that on the ashes of its youth doth lie / Consum'd with that which it was nourish'd by."

The paradoxical key to much interest in the final powerful scene of a tragedy, as in this tragedy, is parallel to the interest felt by much of the culture in the deathbed. For a brief time the curtains of the massive bed are drawn back and the secrets of a lifetime are revealed. The passions central to that life glow most brightly in the examination at the end of it. Here the curious contradictions that turn a life to tragedy draw Othello into the ritual of self-examination. The event of the murder, the heartbreaking innocence of Desdemona, the shocking discovery of how deceit and treachery have brought him to such love, loss, and self-blame—all together, the components of his life—show forth most vividly in Othello's recognition of who Desdemona is.

He was blinded, and now he sees. It is this tragic recognition of the innocent and forgiving—but wronged, killed, murdered by himself—woman that inevitably calls forth in Othello the dignified general. The experience of a lifetime as a leader calls out for justice. In his last speech, the deathbed examination of self becomes not so much an assessment as a recovery of the created self written upon the human heart. That, after all, in the last scenes of the *ars*—surely for a great general—is the aim of religious transformation. For the man of action, such a transformation and healing is more than intellectual; the word and image of the devotional tradition is wedded to the eloquent *act* of drama. Is it desperate suicide or just execution? Those present in the scene leave the question open. As audience, we are stirred by ambivalences but ultimately moved to cathartic reconciliation.

7

Lear, Gloucester, and Dread Despair

In act 1, scene 1, when Lear opens the play (1605) with the announcement that he is giving up his kingly responsibilities and dividing the kingdom in order to "Unburthen'd crawl toward death," Shakespeare calls forth a rich set of associations with the familiar *ars moriendi* tradition.[1] His audience, at all levels, even if at varying degrees of sophistication, would have been aware (and many would have anticipated) that Lear in the complex process of facing his own death must ultimately confront several temptations, among them the temptation to despair. That Gloucester is the character who comes closest in the play to representing the dread image of despair brings the audience to see by contrast how narrowly Lear avoids falling to that temptation. Since the Gloucester subplot has no historical relevance to the Lear story, it seems obvious that Shakespeare is using it consciously for dramatic and thematic purposes.

As Gloucester smells his way to Dover a broken and blinded man, the larger dramatic structure visibly broods over the shadow line between pessimism and hope and on the mystery of human relationships in their potentiality for love. Father and daughters, father and sons, sister and sister, brother and brother, husband and wife, servant and master—the drama exposes the deepest loyalty or the blackest betrayal of these fundamental human relationships. In this instance, the despair of Gloucester, brought on largely by the perfidy of Edmund, is held in balance with the pure selflessness of Edgar's love for his father. In the heart of the play pulses the fundamental tragic question: Is the suffering demanded by the knowledge of good and evil worth the cost? Or put in terms of the devotional tradition widely known by Shakespeare's audience, can such knowledge be bought even after a lifetime's experience without the soul's falling prey to the temptation to despair? The play—perhaps of all those in western civilization—exposes the worst consequences of mistaken love while ultimately affirming its opposite.

It is no wonder that this play above all of Shakespeare's tragedies has a history of criticism that swings in a weighty pendulum between pessimism and hope. Probably few historians would express surprise that pessimism seems to dominate twentieth-century interpretations of *King Lear*, the major exceptions being those of Harbage and Kermode.[2] At its most optimistic, relativistic philosophy breeds an acceptance of ambiguity such as that presented persuasively in Rabkin's critical approach.[3] In our current critical context Renaissance paradoxes easily become discrete pairs of contradictory elements, and the whole play becomes deconstructed. It is difficult for many scholars to accept Andre Chastel's intuition that such disparate elements as nature and art, soul and body, faith and reason, hope and despair, were brought into reconciliation largely by illusion—even so powerful an illusion as the belief that Englishmen could rediscover Paradise by recreating the Golden Age.[4] After subtle qualifications many scholars would come down on the side of pessimism and cosmic chaos.[5] It is only when one assumes that Shakespeare's audience was sophisticated enough theologically to apprehend the profound paradoxes of religious skepticism that *King Lear* as a dramatic affirmation becomes credible.[6] Strip away the authorities of the world to expose faith alone as safety.

With minor qualifications, we know that the English remained Christian at least well into the Enlightenment. In spite of scattered records of a few university wits who toyed with agnosticism, most critics are aware that in defiance of the deep insecurity caused by the disintegration of the great Roman monolith and attendant shifts in Tudor religious loyalties, both the courtier and the man on the street spent an inordinate amount of time listening to sermons and arguing theology. As we have seen, worldly men like Essex and Ralegh died in the Christian tradition of making a good death, even at their executions, and the most naive middle-class-citizens bought countless religious tracts. The subtler religious underpinning in such tangible activity is more difficult to prove. Many critics still feel that religious attitudes were merely conventions supported by powerful authorities while the opposite camp argues the roots of these conventions in a profoundly sophisticated experience of Christian paradox.

Such paradoxical associations on the part of Shakespeare's audience were rooted in a more fundamental experience of the sacred in the created world than moderns are accustomed to associate with the religious perspective. It is just such a sense of paradox and the fundamental ambivalence of human experience that imbued Elizabethan and Jacobean tragedy with its dramatic power. That these feelings went hand in hand with a religious skepticism profoundly distrustful of reason is another instance of the paradoxical nature of the period. To the religious skeptic, such as Montaigne, faith in God emerged fully only after all worldly and rational supports were stripped away. Such a bold vision of the sufferings of this life can easily be confused with modern ideas of a capricious and cruel god. For Montaigne and others, however,the full confrontation with mortality sometimes allowed the mysterious discovery of the relationships between faith and love.[7] This is not to say, of course, that Renaissance Christians lived ideal lives. We know enough of their problems with ambition, greed, and violence to know the similarity of Renaissance Christians to modern, secular persons. But beneath the ordinary struggles of everyday lay a complex religious worldview that had at its center an ultimate trust in redemptive reality.

Particularly relevant to the tragic experience of Shakespeare's audience, however diverse, was the old tradition of the *ars moriendi*, and within that large tradition the temptation to despair. Behind this set of assumptions with its focus upon the moment of death as a kind of humanized last judgment lay centuries of theology, devotional practice, and symbolism related to the last things, many of the conventions of which survived in the early seventeenth century and were inevitably part of the response of Shakespeare's audience. *Hamlet*'s questionings move more toward large allegories of good and evil in the tragic form of *King Lear*. Whatever its makeup (and controversial scholarship such as Ann Cook's *The Privileged Playgoer of Shakespeare's London* suggests that it was more educated than scholars originally thought), fundamental attitudes of the commonplace tradition of death and its symbolic expression were widely available to the English culture. As we have seen, English culture, in fact, was saturated with various reminders of mortality, both visual and verbal, in the first quarter of the seventeenth century. But mortality was itself deeply embedded in a Christianized world view that included immortality, the way into which was structured through an elaborate process of judgment, justice, and mercy.

Donne's ringing call to the last judgment in Holy Sonnet 4 (At the round earth's imagin'd corners . . .) is a composition of place still much alive in the seventeenth-century meditative tradition, as Martz and others have reminded us.[8] The importance of meditation on death and judgment has also been duly pointed out within that tradition, and there are few Renaissance scholars today who are unaware that English poets and dramatists of the early seventeenth century were urged to die daily through meditation; Shakespeare's plays are filled with allusions to such a tradition. Once that pervasive exhortation has been recognized, however, scholars and critics have been slow to assess the effect of this tradition upon the central literary and emotional reality, especially as reflected in reader and audience experiences of Jacobean drama and poetry. Most critics seem unaware, for example, that the *ars moriendi* was a tradition of comfort, an art of dying *well* to be set against the more macabre (but continuing) heritage of the Dance of Death. Little criticism has appeared that probes the relation in the literature of the period between the potentiality for despair and the existential necessity for trust in the mercy of God.

A few scholars, however, have noticed that the sophisticated Anglican demand for contrition preached in the reign of James I by preachers like Donne and Andrewes and that included the full play of fear, love, and sorrow reflected literary structures so as to bring these discordant opposites in concord. It has been argued, for example, that Donne's Holy Sonnets represent a working through of the meditative process, a strategy by which fear, contrition, and death are integrated; and one could argue for *King Lear* (and dramatic form) as a more indirect but more fully developed and incarnate experience.[9] Within the contemporary Renaissance understanding of the "last things," the final context to which all these issues having to do with death and dying were referred was that of the last judgment. One's life and the moment of death were preparations for the final assessment of the quality of one's soul. Psychologically, the importance of the moment of death for Renaissance Englishmen could not be minimized, as we see in many instances—perhaps the most dramatically in the political executions of Essex and Ralegh during the first fifteen years of the period. An English audience would have been quick to see the importance of such an assessment for both Lear and Gloucester in their old age.

On the one hand was the necessity to arrive at detachment from material power and possessions; on the other hand lay the danger that the inevitable pain of the "stripping" process might lead to a premature and unwarranted hopelessness. The self-discovering itself was known to be radical. Death was the last chance to experience and express the appropriate humility, and, with the help of the Guardian Angel, friends, family, and even the Communion of Saints, to chart one's course between the Scylla of Pride and Vainglory and the Charybdis of Despair. The shock of the encounter with death was known to transform perspectives. Well into the seventeenth century the art of dying well survived as a sailor's map for such a journey.[10]

It is no surprise then that scenes of Elizabethan and Jacobean tragedy have rich associations with the old *ars moriendi* tradition. The ancient folklore surrounding the tradition had it, as we have seen, that the devil was making a last mighty attempt to capture the soul on its deathbed, at the moment when it was weakest. But the tradition also dramatized one's guardian angel as an opposition to demons—God's mercy against diabolical forces of temptation and therefore an ultimately positive reconciliation of the negative and positive feelings surrounding death. In the tradition, especially in the latter half of the sixteenth century, friends of the dying were urged to function in the manner of the guardian angel, as Thomas Becon counsels. The heroism of virtue was softened by the suggestion of a shared dependence upon a communion of love. Shakespeare plays a number of variations upon such a tradition.

It seems clear that the temptation against faith gradually became conflated with the temptation to despair and that impatience and avarice were often seen as temptations that must be dealt with well before the last heroic necessity for struggle. Perhaps, after all, it is part of the same pattern by which Renaissance literature was continuing to some degree, but always simplifying, the elaborate medieval symbolism of Christianity. For example, the temptation to suicide with a dagger that is part of the temptation to loss of faith in the original *ars* series had become closely associated with the temptation to despair, as in the frequent emblematic figure of despair with a halter around his neck. Dramatists especially appear to have known instinctively that the essential conflict in the final moment lay between the temptation to despair and the inspiration to faith in the mercy of God.[11] Despair, as Aquinas had pointed out, was not simply a loss of hope but one of six sins against the Holy Ghost by which one lost faith in the mercy of God.[12] At the same time, it was very close to that abyss into which Augustine saw the soul descend before the experience of rescue by radical grace. The full encounter with one's own dying or even the battering experience of mourning brought one close to the poles of feeling.

In the original woodcut from the *ars* series the demons tempt the dying to despair by bringing before his eyes all his past sins. Especially by the late sixteenth century suicide came to be the feared response to such a state of mind. "Kill yourself" is the imperative counsel of the demon who offers the *moriens* a knife as the dying one views his sinful past; such a one is not worthy of the mercy of God. The inspiration of the angel then suggests the double remedy against such destructive remorse. Both the visual and the textual advice of the inspiration woodcut might have been translated into this: "You who think yourself a sinner unworthy of the mercy of God can look for comfort to St. Peter, who denied the Lord three times; to St. Paul, who had to be struck down blind on the road to Damascus for persecuting the Lord's people; to St. Mary Magdalene, called from a life of sinful lust to devotion." In sum, if all these were worthy, *why not you*? Second, the figure of the thief on the cross is also prominent in the woodcut, with the manna of grace raining from heaven as an instance of last-minute forgiveness. In many devotional works the *moriens* is also instructed to keep the image of Christ on the cross ever before his eyes. In fact, the crucifix placed over the eyes was early considered an efficacious protection against demonic images.[13] But many of these images were blunted by use by 1605.

In the hands of such a major artist as Shakespeare, the elements of the tradition do not often appear in their most conventional and popular forms; as we have seen, *Richard III* was most explicit. But more often his genius effects changes by which commonplaces are integrated (and deepened) into a particular dramatic structure. At the same time, however, Shakespeare's use of the symbolic material even in displaced form in *Richard III, Hamlet, Othello,* and others of his plays shows a deep familiarity with both assumptions and symbolic elements from the iconography of death. The frequency of allusion to the tradition may well suggest a less than conscious acceptance of some of the fundamental values embedded in it, especially the way in which death brings about the evaluation of a life. It is easiest perhaps to assess Shakespeare's treatment of a bad death, as in the "conscience" scene in *Richard III* or, less close to *ars* conventions, with the figure of Macbeth.

It seems clear that Macbeth died in heroic despair. The image of his life throughout the play is bodied forth as a life of tragic mistakes and agonizing punishment. The imagery is apocalyptic in its suggestion of an inner experience of hell as the consequence of evil choice. Lady Macbeth is the even more typical figure of despair in the play as we shall see. The audience knows that she may have died by her own hand, the suicidal epitome of the sin. It is also clear from his response to her death that Macbeth has lost his sense of connection with God's mercy; indeed, throughout the play he serves increasingly and descendingly the gods of his own ambition and necessity. The justly famous soliloquy by which he uses his wife's death to comment upon reality and life as "walking shadow," the frail light that shows us the path to "dusty death," is magnificent poetry and the essence of bad philosophy, from a contemporary perspective. From the point of view of the *ars moriendi* tradition such attitudes speak lack of response to the created world and therefore a dangerous state of mind in its response to its creator. The overlay of heroic convention at the end does little to transform Macbeth's despair, though superficially he dies bravely.

Lear's death, however, is more subtly presented than that of Macbeth and more interesting to explore. The play's greatness lies partially in Lear's portrayal as a king who learned to be wise through tragic error, suffering, and madness. He is not portrayed as a grand, but somewhat stereotyped, ambitious Renaissance figure such as Macbeth. The simple conventions of the *ars* are not obviously present in *King Lear*; there is no scene like the ritualized displacement of the medieval temptation to despair with which Richard III is beset the night before the battle of Bosworth Field, when the ghosts of all those he has murdered visit him like a liturgy of past sins. But Lear's death is so close to despair that we need to reassess it in relation to some of the assumptions of the *ars* tradition.

Like all of Shakespeare's great tragedies, *King Lear* has no conventional deathbed scene. It is, in fact, part of the tragic irony that this old king dies out of bed—without his family gathered in kindly comfort to take him through a ritual of assurance. Shakespeare's bleak improvisation of this scene throws into relief the tradition of a happy death. Only the small remnant of friends is left. I suspect that a Renaissance audience would have been struck by the death of Cordelia and the absence of a context of comfort. Many critics have equated the absence of all ritual comforts with a despairing view of the whole nature of reality. Certainly the Peter Brooke production of the play in 1962 in London stressed the absurd contemporaneity of the play, presenting it as if Lear had never come out of the storm on the heath; similarly the BBC video production in 1977; perhaps not so clearly the Olivier version.

On one level, the complex blending of hope and despair makes the argument for ambiguity unanswerable. Literature almost never allows for final or absolute answers; dramatic form is always to some extent ambiguous as well as ambivalent in its treatment of reality. Drama lies too close to the ritual modes by which we seek to heal the deep ambivalence of human experience for it to find a simple solution. At the same time, however, dramatic structure as well as poetic language itself is historical, and it is a modern fallacy to assume that Shakespeare created his plays outside a frame of moral judgment. The power and pervasiveness of the contemporary religious perspective were still far too deeply ingrained in early seventeenth-century poetic structure to allow for such a possibility. The still vital image of the last judgment that we see strong in the imagination of a poet so worldly as Ralegh, among others, argues the corresponding place of moral judgment in this life. There is, of course, no such moralistic didacticism in Shakespeare as one is offended by in *The Mirror for Magistrates,* but as Tuve long ago argued in *Elizabethan and Metaphysical Imagery,* the commitment to a larger (less explicit) neoplatonism that saw in art the enlargement of knowledge and moral truth in the universe is part of the Renaissance aesthetic.[14] Doran, more relevantly and specifically, argues in her essay "Command, Question, and Assertion in *King Lear*" that Lear's own style of language moves away from simplistic command through agonizing question to greater conditional complexity and finally to some simple, profound assertions—all on the basis of what he learns from experience and Cordelia about the nature of true love and false reason.[15]

As Doran says, "Lear is discovering who he is."[16] Such a discovery is impossible, believed Jacobeans, without an understanding of good that implies an objective context, a structure of morality that emerges from the play—however sophisticated that structure may be. As Doran points out, the devastating vision of a corrupt world is shown ultimately and mercifully to house those large images of love and reverence: the outcast Edgar, who saves his father from despair, and Cordelia herself, whose tender and courteous questions contrast with Lear's incredulous questions at the behavior of Goneril:

> Does any here know me? This is not Lear.
> Does Lear walk thus? speak thus? Where are his eyes?
> (I.iv.226–27)

Images of love such as those of Edgar and Cordelia tilt the balance toward hope in spite of the agonizing losses of worldly comforts and even in spite of the disturbing question at the end of the play.

In characterization, plot, and imagery, the play balances the old assumptions of the *ars moriendi*: sin and forgiveness, suffering and release, damnation and redemption. The very depth of despair an audience must feel when confronted with what the false children Edmund, Goneril, and Regan can be, stripped of loyalty and true reason, undeserving of mercy, is designed to offer the opposing necessary glimpse of the manna of grace. The false children are on one level displacements of demons tempting to despair, while the true children are displacements of the guardian angels. The moral and allegorical interpretation is also supported by Renaissance sociological and historical attitudes toward the family. Regan, Goneril, and Edmund are exaggerated examples of what children should never do or be. Holding the structure in balance, both Edgar and Cordelia shine forth in goodness as extraordinary as the evil of Edmund and the pelican daughters.

Several explicit details support the redemptive interpretation of reality in the action of the play. After the heath we see Lear wondrously restored to Cordelia's loving kindness. The "no cause, no cause" response to his plea for forgiveness is, as Harbage points out in the preface to the Pelican edition, the supreme example of what love at its best is capable of. This play explores the relationship between despair and redemption, even if the final affirmation is far more qualified then it appears in the wonderful example of Cordelia's love.

Although the pre-Christian setting of *King Lear* prohibits the full development of *ars* imagery, the same themes underlie the structure—the necessity to know oneself more than "slenderly," to face all human potentiality for evil uncushioned by rank or title, to recognize the embodiment of the opposition between Good and Evil, and to throw oneself with all one's imperfections on the mercy of a mysterious and loving god. But the last is at the end of an agonizing process. Renaissance thinking of the period assumed that typological images of the primitive or pre-Christian times clearly prefigure fundamental truths of the universe.

More specifically, the paradox of despair and hope is built into the very structure of the action. The profound probing of nature—especially human nature in relation to the nature of the cosmos—is central to the imagery of the storm scene and would have been recognized by the more theologically sensitive in the audience as embodying a frequent theme of temptation from the devotional tradition. Facing fully the limits of human nature is likely to lead to despair. Devotional writers following St. Paul had long emphasized that facing one's frailty in living according to the law also required knowing the gospel of redemption. That writers frequently expressed this abstraction by pointing to its incarnate forms in such sinner-saints as Peter and Mary Magdalene makes more understandable Shakespeare's giving his audience Cordelia as an opposite to Regan and Goneril and Edgar as an opposite to Edmund.

In the pre-Christian setting of the play, the absence of Christ makes little difference to the fullness of the overall theme. Lear himself perhaps comes closest to the explicit Christ figure when Edgar comments upon him as a "side-piercing sight." Lear learns most about transcendent values from Cordelia, however, in that scene in which he wakes thinking he is in heaven (IV.vii). Here the imagery has always been recognized as explicit in presenting the Christian theme of redemption. This is Lear's moment of learning the nature of the real love that he so mistook in act 1, scene 1, in his ritual demands for flattery. This scene with Cordelia foreshadows his literal death scene and draws both into what a Renaissance audience would probably have thought of as the communion of saints. Lear has learned to despise the false world of appearance and is ready for death, as suggested by his belief that he is awakening from death to life eternal.

Near the beginning of the play his rough notion that he was ready to crawl toward death has had to undergo a seachange. With the *contemptus mundi* theme sounding in their ears Jacobeans would certainly have recognized his spiritual immaturity in Scene 1. The early scene contrasts strongly with the newborn Lear who wakes from his madness into the loving presence of his true daughter and thinks that he is in heaven and she an angel. Suddenly remembering the cruelty of Goneril and Regan, Lear can hardly believe that Cordelia, who has some cause for anger, will not turn on him in hatred. Instead, she acts with the fullest generosity possible. Instead of grinding in his past injustices; instead, even, of granting the forgiveness that inevitably implies moral superiority, she pretends that she has never been wronged. She simply blots out the past with her magnificent "No cause, no cause." The doctor then points out that the "great rage" is "kill'd in him," and Lear, a man broken in genuine penitence, says,

> You must bear with me.
> Pray you now forget, and forgive; I am old and foolish.
> (IV.vii.82–83)

The rash and absolutist authoritarian father becomes as a child to the daughter, adoring her newly apprehended brilliant truth and love.

One senses that two things have saved Lear from despair: the madness that kept him from facing fully the lack of mercy in the world of Regan, Goneril, and Edmund and, from a positive perspective, the loving redemptive acceptance of Cordelia. Gloucester confirms in act 4, scene 6 the possibility that madness operates as this sort of cushion:

> The King is mad. How stiff is my vild sense,
> That I stand up, and have ingenious feeling
> Of my *huge sorrows! Better I were distract;*
> *So should my thoughts be sever'd from my griefs,*

And woes by wrong imaginations lose
The knowledge of themselves.

(IV.vi.279–84; emphasis mine)

The theologically sophisticated members of Shakespeare's audience were aware of the danger of "huge sorrows," the *tristitia* that
could lead to despair and the misuse of reason (or "thoughts") that
is so persuasive in the powerful poetry of Spenser's false hermit,
Despayre. At this moment, Gloucester moves toward despair for a
second time in the sorrow with which he confronts Lear.

Gloucester's parallel character institutes major means by which
Shakespeare's audience would have seen Lear as avoiding despair,
even if partially through madness. While Lear in his anguish and
rage has come to grips with the cruelty of his daughters and with
nature in the storm scene, Gloucester has faced the harrowing experience of rejection by his son Edmund. He discovers his own de-
lusion in having believed through appearance and manipulation that
nature's child was more loving and true than his legitimate son "Got
'tween the lawful sheets." In the most painful scene in Shakespeare,
his defense of Lear and his particular discovery lose him his eyes,
and the audience of any age is hardly surprised to find him wending
his way toward Dover in despair. Critics have often remarked upon
the superstition that might well make him the victim of fated doom.
His helplessness fully ritualized in the plight to which his defense
of Lear and his resulting blindness have brought him, Gloucester is,
as every audience recognizes, stripped of all hope, all faith in the
mercy of the gods, when he says,

As flies to wanton boys are we to th' gods,
They kill us for their sport.

(IV.i.36–37)

In act 4, scene 1, where Gloucester enters led by an Old Man,
Edgar disguised as Mad Tom speaks with choric wisdom upon
Gloucester's excessive sorrow. His own compassion is reflected in
his initial aside:

O gods! Who is't can say, "I am at the worst"?
I am worse than e'er I was.

(IV.i.25–26)

Gloucester links him quickly with the beggar in the storm scene:

> I' th' last night's storm I such a fellow saw,
> Which made me think a man a worm.
>
> (IV.i.32–33)

This bleak reflection is followed directly by his famous statement of despair directed toward the cosmic relationship between the human and the divine. Edgar expresses his own desire not to exacerbate such a loss of faith in the redemptive aspects of reality:

> How should this be?
> Bad is the trade that must play fool to sorrow,
> Ang'ring itself and others.
>
> (IV.i.37–39)

Like most Renaissance people, the virtuous Edgar was conscious of the dangers of his father's *tristitia*. Unlike Lear, who balances a proper respect for the stars with a measure of responsibility for his actions, Gloucester feels himself totally victimized. He has called upon the gods, and they have not answered. Gloucester's inability to act out of hope in relation to the gods would have seemed the true measure of the despairing state to a Renaissance audience.

His resolution to suicide emerges as Gloucester arranges for Poor Tom (Edgar in disguise, of course) to lead him to Dover:

> There is a Cliff, whose high and bending head
> Looks fearfully in the confined deep.
> Bring me but to the very brim of it,
> And I'll repair the misery thou dost bear
> With something rich about me. From that place
> I shall no leading need.
>
> (IV.i.73–78)

Later in act 4, scene 6, the mysterious allegorical episode by which Edgar has him act out his suicidal desire ends happily; both Edgar (and surely the audience) recognize and defeat the suicidal impulse. Edgar says (aside) when he is pretending to lead his father to the very height of the cliff:

> Why I do trifle thus with his despair
> Is done to cure it.
>
> (IV.vi.33–34)

How this action performs a cure remains partly a mystery, but surely it indicates the way in which Renaissance persons believed profoundly that suffering must be encountered fully in order to come out the other side. It is not, as some have said, a fake miracle that makes it come out right for Gloucester, but rather an existential experience of lament and healing. Equally important is the presence and guidance of loving persons. Even after the pretended fall, Gloucester holds to his despairing desire for death, asking if the final misery were not deprivation of the possibility of ending life by death. Edgar attempts to convince him that the beggar was the devil and that the gods have mercifully preserved him. "Thy life's a miracle," he says in line 55, speaking the reassurance that one needs to avoid despair. But the love of the son is the greater miracle. He succeeds in bringing Gloucester around to an appreciation of Christian stoic endurance:

> I do remember now. Henceforth I'll bear
> Affliction till it do cry out itself
> "Enough, enough," and die. That thing you speak of,
> I took it for a man; often 'twould say
> "The fiend, the fiend!"—he led me to that place.
>
> (IV.vi.75–79)

In this mock suicide, especially, Shakespeare draws upon the commonplace folk associations of his audience. The reference to the fiend with a thousand noses and "whelked horns" suggests the displacement of the old *ars* image in which the beggar is a disguised demon and Edgar functions as the angel of inspiration. After the suicide attempt, he points out the divine mercy for Gloucester's benefit:

> Think that the clearest gods, who make them honors
> Of men's impossibilities, have preserved thee.
>
> (IV.vi.73–74)

The miracle wrought by Edgar is an existential experience of the availability of mercy that brings Gloucester to acceptance; although later he indicates some backsliding, he returns to a more positive acceptance. The constant and unfolding love of his true son is the incarnate mercy here, such as we see paralleled by Cordelia in the forgiveness scene with Lear. But Gloucester has provided the image of despair that Lear in his madness only inclines to.

The dangerous intractability of Gloucester's earlier state of mind emerges both later in act 4, scene 6, and also in his last appearance with Edgar in act 5, scene 2, when he comments bleakly on the political situation. After the heartbreaking encounter between the

two old men, Gloucester reminds the audience of his predilection
for suicide:

> You ever-gentle gods, take my breath from me,
> Let not my worser spirit tempt me again
> To die before you please!
>
> (IV.vi.217–19)

At the same time, however, his prayer confirms his radical change
of heart toward the gods and his new willingness to accept their
benevolence. Later, however, when Edgar tells him that the battle
is lost by the king's forces, Gloucester again shows his tempera-
mental lack of hope: "No further, sir; a man may rot even here"
(V.ii.8). It is only when Edgar has "nursed" his father's despair again
with his famous speech about men enduring their going hence as
their coming hither—"Ripeness is all" (V.ii.11)—that Gloucester
answers somewhat ambiguously, "And that's true too" (V.ii.11).

Pulled down by new suffering, Gloucester seems so battered by
sorrow and his trust so frail that only Edgar can keep him from
despair. Like our own, Shakespeare's audience must have breathed
a small sigh of relief when Edgar reported Gloucester's death off-
stage as one that rejoiced in learning the loving "pilgrimage" of his
son with him (V.iii.189–200). His heart, we are told, "Burst smil-
ingly" (V.iii.200), and the account perhaps moves even Edmund to
good. Love triumphs on the spiritual plane.

As Edgar wins the tournament and speaks his own loving history
as the good angel of his father, both the order of the kingdom and
that of the drama seem to move out of the bleakness that courts
despair into hope. If Gloucester can be finally rescued by kind gods,
Shakespeare's audience may well have hoped, perhaps Lear, too,
can find a happy death.

The rapid action of the ending, with recognition that Goneril and
Regan are *desperate*, also supports the opposition between good
and evil and suggests the triumph of good. Gloucester has died
happy; those who have fed on power, hatred, and deceit die in despair. Says Kent,

> Your eldest daughters have fordone themselves
> And desperately are dead.
>
> (V.iii.292–93)

The audience has been shown several hints of the curious indirect
way in which hope is given to the good.

And yet the failure of Edmund's good deed remains a question both for scholars and audience. When Lear brings in Cordelia dead, any audience must feel that *too late* the change of heart comes. When we turn to Lear himself, the death of Cordelia seems still to be a major stumbling block to the more affirmative interpretation of Lear as having escaped despair. Why could they not go away to prison together? Perhaps because, in a sense, as Harbage tells us, the two become part of the ancient sacrifice of tragedy that goes even beyond the popular religious order of the *ars moriendi* tradition. Stoicism and skepticism fuse with Christianity and bring a darker, more ancient, vision of the world. Tragic heroes must suffer more than they deserve for order to be restored. The clothing of this world must be stripped away garment by garment: all the human comforts of civilization and power must go before human beings can "see better." Even according to the old *ars* tradition, one must face death finally as separation even from family. Otherwise Shakespeare's audience (and we ourselves) would never see. Only in the naked Bedlam beggar does the audience begin to join Lear in compassion for the poor forked naked human, and perhaps only when Lear is denied his last comfort in this world, Cordelia alive, could even the faithful see the full metaphysical dimension of the play.

Death for Shakespeare's audience, however ethical and fundamental the emphasis on dramatic action, implied not merely the loss of human survival on this plane but the translation of the soul into a transcendent world. The love that emerges between Lear and Cordelia belongs to a plane other than that of the earth, and it seems proper for her to die, too, in order for them to sustain the pattern of such a relationship. The preparation for death is embodied ultimately in Lear's turning away, but only through suffering, from the false, self-willing images of love, and the gradual emerging of the "love that moves the sun and other stars." Such was still the deepest vision of the time.

The end of the play, however heartbreaking, would have illuminated for Shakespeare's audience the life that transcends the material. Lear does not, as we might expect, fall into the kind of madness he has shown earlier. Grief and anguish, his near agony, the anger inherent in grief that the meanest animal has life while Cordelia has "no breath at all" (V.iii.308)—all these emotions play within his realization of her death. The saddest line in all of Shakespeare is that which includes the five *nevers* and underlines the human loss. But the second part of his speech is the crux. The button business and the attendant hope of life from a worldly point of view feed illusion; Cordelia is indeed physically dead. The Shakespearean audience was aware of all the warnings about spiritual death and had experienced the full triumph of redemptive love between father and daughter in the reconciliation scene: there could be no death of the soul. For audiences who had seen numerous last scenes of *ars* series in which the soul is received into the Communion of Saints as a small child from the lips of the dying one, Lear's last lines surely had special meaning:

> Look on her! Look her lips,
> Look there, look there!
>
> (V.iii.311–12)

As Bradley and many later critics have thought, Lear died in joyous affirmation of Cordelia's life. Unlike Gloucester, he knew his good angel as his child before he was too bruised. From the beginning Lear trusted more in the stars than most of the characters had done. He ultimately refused to despair. He counseled Gloucester to patience—the old medieval patience before the sorrows of an imperfect existence—and he clung to hope with the expectation of the life it brings. The *ars moriendi* tradition would have made such assumptions understandable to his audience. Although I should not like to see it pushed too far, I can imagine the scene played as if Lear sees that newborn soul of the woodcuts coming out of Cordelia's lips. I could almost imagine it when Olivier gave his performance for the BBC.

In summary, then, despising the world, living a good life, meditating on death as a way of self-knowledge, coming to an existential experience of the necessity for mercy through facing one's sin, and finally overcoming despair by throwing oneself on grace, mercy, and love—all these devotional assumptions are part of the structure of understanding Shakespeare's audiences must have brought to *King Lear*. The despair scene with Gloucester and Edgar points up and deepens the links between the *ars* tradition and the more complexly displaced *Lear* plot. Whatever the horror, the pitiful suffering, the agonizing blow that comes with Cordelia's death, Shakespeare's audience must have found hope with Lear in the promise of new life in that liminal dimension he inhabits on stage.

8

"Rooted Sorrow": The Metaphor

Cure [her] of that!
Canst thou not minister to a mind diseas'd,
Pluck from the memory a rooted sorrow,
Raze out the written troubles of the brain,
And with some sweet oblivious antidote
Cleanse the stuff 'd bosom of that perilous stuff
Which weighs upon the heart? (V.iii.39–45)

In Shakespeare's *Macbeth* (1606) when Macbeth so orders the physician to cure his wife of a diseased mind that springs from a sorrow rooted in the memory, he is asking, according to early seventeenth-century religious and medical thought, that the physician cure a disease of the soul, a pathological imbalance of the emotions that is finally the result of impenitence.[1] The physician recognizes the complexity of the demand and his own lack of qualification for the task when he answers, "Therein the patient must minister to himself." (V.iii.45–46).[2] The audience would have been aware, however, that such a self-ministry must relate the person to the long tradition of spiritual healing both within the church and within private devotional literature. As we have already seen, this highly elaborated tradition had found expression in literature intended for both clergy and laymen.[3] A goodly number of the audience would also have sensed that the bitter sorrow of Lady Macbeth's mind was close to that of the sin of despair, which was thought in late-medieval and Renaissance popular theology to lead to the more final one of suicide.[4] Excessive sorrow for past misdeeds was thought to be so rooted and intense a consciousness of sin that it might bring about a virtual disease of hopelessness and loss of faith in the efficacy of mercy instead of moving the individual to contrition, penance, and reconciliation with God. Such a quagmire of loss of faith became for the age of Shakespeare the crux of the human spiritual journey. An assessment of the quality of a life and a proper preparation for death involved necessarily, as perhaps it has for other generations as well, a confrontation with human imperfection. A good death must show the *moriens* overcoming the tendency to allow that sick imperfection, or sinfulness, to overwhelm one's faith.

The aim of this chapter is not, however, primarily the analysis of Lady Macbeth's particular spiritual problem. Although the immediate dramatic portrayal is altogether gripping, this study will emphasize the contemporary intellectual background in order to illuminate her state of mind and to suggest the response of her audience(s). Most pertinent are commonplace associations with the old temptation to despair, a survival from the *ars moriendi* tradition. Chew points out, for example, numerous instances in fifteenth- and sixteenth-century drama in which the hero is sorely tempted to despair. Toward the end of the sixteenth century it becomes apparent that the temptation to despair dominates the other temptations in the series as the major obstacle to salvation, and contemporaries began to wonder whether the delicate balance between fear and hope that was so essential to the *ars* tradition were not in jeopardy. By the early seventeenth century such a tilting toward despair might even be seen as necessary background to the agonizing consequences of evil in *Macbeth*. Despair is only one aspect of the preparation for a good death, but in many ways it becomes a focal point in the development of the *ars*. The unholy trinity of death, sin, and despair is at the heart of the forces of evil that must be overcome in a fallen world within the devotional tradition we have surveyed.

In spite of the frequent assertion in word and symbol of the principle of redemption, a major theological assumption of the period from 1590 to 1630 was the recognition by the Christian of the necessity to balance a healthy fear of judgment with the appropriate degree of faith in mercy. Such an emphasis was related to the increase of secular power and the accompanying conservatism—perhaps even conservation of authority through a process of containment. Essential to the experience of this elaborate reconciliation on a theological level was the knowledge that despair of salvation was a dangerous possibility for a person who faced his own sinful nature in its full manifestation and in relation to God's laws. As Thomas and others had warned, and as we saw in the dramatic instance of Richard III, a person was in danger of despair when he saw the impossibility of salvation by merit through having fulfilled the law.[5] Othello was a more complex case than that of Richard. At the same time, everyone recognized the need for constant awareness of the fallen nature of the human context—a need that justified a solemn bell of warning throughout the devotional tradition. That the bell sounded more solemnly about the turn of the century suggests some disturbance of the theological equilibrium after the religious turbulence of the 1500s. After the pendulum swings of the English Reformation in the 1600s a clearly authoritative center of faith was unlikely.

Perhaps even more important in what some critics have seen as the increasing melancholy of the seventeenth century (within literature an increasing emphasis on decay of the world) was the growing sense of corruption in high places, as Goldberg and Orgel have exposed. Well into the seventeenth century, John Donne elaborates in his second penitential sermon on Psalm 38.3 the importance of scriptural memory as the means to balance the human sense of sin and failure.[6] Many popular devotional works echo the themes of sin and failure. Donne himself must have been well aware of the depth of the cultural need for faith by the twenties, when most of his sermons were written. In his position as Dean of Paul's and with his associations with the gentry and aristocracy, Donne was surely in touch with some of the immediate decline of values among members of the Court. What this impression or atmosphere meant in concrete terms has been documented by recent scholars and will be explored more fully in the final section of this book. Even Donne's own attempt to gain the patronage of a man like Somerset casts a shadow on the system. On a broader level, perhaps, the court of James I has been shown in its practices to be more drunken and more sexually corrupt than that of Elizabeth, reflecting in an overall way the loss of aristocratic self-confidence.

Donne's own personal history, however, drew him more deeply into an affirmation of Christian idealism, as we shall see developed more fully later in this text. Scripture was to Donne the storehouse of Christian memory, beginning with the mythic event of Exodus by which Yahweh had created for his people a pattern of deliverance. Donne points out that just as memory is the source of knowledge for the Platonist, it is the source of religion for the Christian. The Bible is a record by which all God's mercies in the history of his chosen people become public memory for the Christians. For Donne and other explicitly religious writers of the seventeenth century the correspondence of this document of love, the Bible, and the individual remembrance of God's mercies in a lifetime was an ever-present source of comfort by which one might avoid despair, even in the dark moments when memory of one's sinful nature might seem to overwhelm. The need, however, to assert comfort so strongly and so frequently suggests that in early modern England people were deeply aware of the danger of despair not just personally but as part of a national mood. The *ars moriendi* tradition in its fifteenth-century inception had presented vividly the psychomachiac opposition between the devil's use of memory for the dying one as temptation to despair and the Good Angel's reminders that draw upon the recorded memory of God's grace and mercy to mankind.

Throughout the sixteenth century, numerous writers had developed themes that drew together the despair and hope of the *ars moriendi* tradition. But as we saw in an earlier section, Spenser in his "Despayre Canto" had given the preceding century the most vivid instance in high art of the power of despair itself. It is important to remember that Redcrosse meets the Hermit Despayre after he has been imprisoned in the dungeon of Orgoglio, or Pride. God's powerful figure of grace, Arthur, has rescued him, but clearly Redcrosse is in a state of unguarded weakness from his sojourn in the dungeon. Essential from a spiritual point of view is his full awareness of how far his sin has taken him. Such a confrontation with his own nature makes him especially prey to the temptation to despair. As we saw, Spenser's allegorical answer to the temptation to suicide through despair is not, however, a rational one: rescue comes first through Una when she snatches the knife from Redcrosse's hand.[7]

Lady Macbeth's story lacks, of course, such a rescue. Tragedy always underlines the powerful inevitability of consequences. In *Macbeth* the consequences of wrong action become dramatically painful in the inner world of both of the two main characters. For one, the inner world of Lady Macbeth that culminates in this scene is revealed earlier. Everyone who has ever seen or read the play remembers the chilling and exotic lines: "Here's the smell of blood still. All the perfumes of Arabia will not sweeten this little hand." (V.ii.50–51). The allusion to the indelible blood of Duncan in act 5, scene 1 is in ironic contrast to the early scene just after Macbeth has murdered Duncan and the scornful Lady Macbeth urges him to return to the scene of the murder to smear "The sleepy grooms with blood" (II.ii.1.47). She goes herself to "gild" their faces when he refuses to go back. In the earlier scene she scoffs at Macbeth's near-hysterical comment on bloody hands:

> Will all great Neptune's ocean wash this blood
> Clean from my hand? No; this my hand will rather
> The multitudinous seas incarnadine.
>
> (II.ii.57–59)

By act 5 she is in the agonizing grip of guilt, whereas Macbeth himself has become hardened to the deepest sin.

Most people would agree that the inner consequences of sin in *Macbeth* are the worst manifestation of evil. Macbeth's earlier fear of blood on his hands must take second place to his terror over the Ghost of Banquo, his murdered friend, and all the fear of community that murder unleashes. The murders of Duncan's wife and sons that follow are, of course, themselves a consequence of the earlier sin and take him deeper.

Alciati, among several images, shows in an emblem Despair with a rope around his neck and thereby emphasizes the association of the state of mind with suicide.[8] It is not surprising that sixteenth-century representations of Despair have looked more and more like the figure of death as the century progresses. At the end of act 5, scene 3, Macbeth says despairingly, "I have lived long enough: my way of life / Is fall'n into the sear, the yellow leaf (22–23)." Perhaps the fear of spiritual death became more intense in the latter sixteenth century as the general atmosphere of optimism waned. At the same time the increasing influence of Reformation forces in the English church brought about a shift from the apocalyptic images of hell and hell-mouth of the late Middle Ages to the more psychological images of deprivation that one finds in the earlier seventeenth century, for example, in Donne's sermon that defines hell as the absence of God.

For Shakespeare, also, who contemplates the absence of God in hell in the imagery of *Macbeth,* the bleakness of despair was on a profound level an experience of awful and hellish absence. Shakespeare articulates the full embodiment of the experience in Lady Macbeth's history: If hell is ultimate separation from God, despair is the closest we come in this life to such radical emptiness. It is the dangerous type of hell that Satan leads the dying to experience, in order that he may trap *them* into the permanent state of separation from God.

One hundred years earlier, in a 1519 sermon "Preparing to Die," Luther had indicated the importance of the visual as part of the psychological preparation for a good death. In his own strong verbal imagery pertaining to diabolical possession, he suggests the need to avoid the powerful negative influence of such images of despair as those mentioned above. He underlines the source of despair in Lucifer, the epitome of hopelessness, and warns against Lucifer's technique of pictorial seduction. His advice expressed one of the major fears in the symbolic tradition of the next two centuries:

> . . . in this affair we must exercise all diligence not to open our homes to any of these images and not to paint the devil over the door. These

foes will of themselves boldly rush in and seek to occupy the heart completely with their image, their arguments, and their signs. And when that happens man is doomed and God is entirely forgotten. The only thing to do with these pictures at that time is to combat and expel them. Indeed, where they are found alone and not in conjunction with other pictures, they belong nowhere else than in hell among the devil's.[9]

Luther goes on to say, however, that the fight against such demonic forces must take place in a curiously indirect way if they are not to prove too strong. He advises his congregation to "look at death while you are alive and see sin in the light of grace and hell in the light of heaven." The paradox, however, is that one must look at death with its potential for destruction only as Christ and the saints triumph over it. The popular notion of looking at a crucifix and placing it over the eyes functions as more than an amulet against evil. As Bosch suggests in his painting *The Death of the Miser,* it is a way of meditation, especially favored later by counter-reformation technique but represented as well in reformed churches.[10] It is a way of focusing all the senses upon the picture and person of Christ, who is all-life, according to Luther. If one's eyes and heart are filled with life, then there is no room for the devil and his deathly images. In Shakespeare's darkest plays we see a reversal of this idea; through the displaced representation of evil, the audience could see what the consequences of filling one's mind with death might be.

Such a way of meditation is, of course, the opposite to Macbeth's (and Lady Macbeth's) concentration on evil. The witches and their embodiment of his ambitions in their prophecies become an early focus for his imagination. And once he has shared that demonic hope with Lady Macbeth she becomes the goad to ambition and murder that he needs to allow the forces of evil to overcome him. Increasingly the minds of both are filled with death, not life, and it is no wonder that the death of the soul triumphs in the end. As Macbeth says in the last act:

> I have supp'd full with horrors;
> Direness, familiar to my slaughterous thought,
> Cannot once start me.
>
> (V.v.13–15)

By the end of the sixteenth century, it seems likely that an English poet had only to allude to common symbols from the tradition for the audience to respond out of a rich context of devotional attitudes by which they had developed their faith against the spectre of death, so frighteningly present in a world of plague, infection, and political

instability. However great a "Prince" Elizabeth had proved herself
her entire reign had been under various threats of dissolution, but
especially from her excommunication by the Pope in 1570 to the
Essex Rebellion in 1601. One might remember, also, that the coronation of James I was postponed because of the severe plague in
London in 1603 and that the reign of James himself was increasingly
disappointing. Obviously, different social levels of Shakespeare's
audience would have responded in varying degrees to the temptation to despair.[11] The more subtle theological issues would have
eluded some of the less educated; nevertheless, the commonplace
tradition of the *ars moriendi* in its darker assumptions was understood by a great range of Englishmen within such a period.

The darkness of the dangers of evil associated with death and
dying in the first decade of the seventeenth century is particularly
reflected in Shakespeare's major tragedies. If *Richard III* is a bit
early, the writing of the major tragedies (*Hamlet* around 1600 with
Macbeth rounding out the period in 1606) embodies the profound
probing of that darkness. The explorations of the heroic villain
(Richard), the pure villains (Edmund and Iago), and finally the vil-
lainous hero (Macbeth) all contribute to the examination. Overlap-
ping those years and extending into the second half of the decade
are also the "problem" comedies that record especially the social
presence of evil that Shakespeare seems able to transcend only
within the redemptive magical powers of romance. In the great
tragedies themselves there is ample recognition that the art of dying
is not simply a tradition of comfort, but one in the later sixteenth
and early seventeenth centuries that contains the terrifying working
of the dance of death. But the unfolding is gradual. Hamlet's Ghost
and Hamlet's own soliloquies that embody the fullest expression
of the fears and anger of the grieving contain only glimpses of the
mysterious agonies of the afterlife. Ophelia's and Othello's suicides
both are romantically transformed: hers by lyricism, flowers, nature; his by his own heroic repentance and self-execution. In *Macbeth,* however, the absence of good during his reign in the kingdom
(Malcolm and Donalbain must flee) provides an image of the consequences of evil power that evoke the hell and damnation that must
be avoided by the full practice of the art of dying.

Within this long *ars moriendi* tradition that found expression in
so many sources of cultural symbolism, by the late sixteenth and
early seventeenth centuries the deathbed had become the greatest
moment for testing complex issues surrounding salvation—partly
because it came at the end of a lifetime of living well or not, partly
because it represented that last opportunity for tuning the soul. Ac-

cording to the old folklore surrounding the fifteenth-century version of the tradition, the devil made a last mighty attempt to capture the soul at the deathbed moment when the human being was weakest, especially through the confrontation with all his remembered sins. It is the powerful presence of sin as deep spiritual illness that dominates *Macbeth,* of course, though the deathbed is absent. But the tradition also dramatized the presence of one's guardian angel in opposition to demons—God's mercy against the diabolical forces of temptation. During the latter half of the sixteenth century and continuing late into the seventeenth, friends of the dying were urged to function in the manner of the guardian angel.[12] But the Doctor in *Macbeth* nevertheless rightly underlines the individual responsibility of Lady Macbeth.

The theology at the heart of the deathbed ritual, developed by symbolism in all major churches, usually balanced fear and promise. In the background was the old opposition between virtue and vice, or the structure of the psychomachia. On the one hand, the warning to prepare for the demonic onslaught was constant; on the other, the promise of mercy had always been essential to the symbolism. Even though the visual and verbal iconography did not always show both sides of the equation—fear and comfort, hell and heaven, justice and mercy—the reconciliation of those opposites had been built into nearly two hundred years of visual and verbal expressions. Nevertheless, it is not unprecedented that the evil forces in *Macbeth* have such weight; it is important to notice that the woodcuts of the temptations were more frequently reprinted than those of the inspirations. In *Macbeth* there is little of the good; Malcolm and Donalbain are clearly subordinated to the vision of evil. Although Chew's *The Virtues Reconciled* makes the point that the concept of justice was always balanced by mercy, increasingly voices of melancholy disturbed such a happy symmetry.[13] English attitudes between the Elizabethan and Jacobean periods supports such a change in atmosphere. The change could (and did) result in the probing of a fully evil world, such as that in *Macbeth,* and a kind of embodiment of the last judgment and its condemnation.

Parallel to the general changes in religious cultural attitudes, tragedy as a form tended to underline the darker side of the equation. *Macbeth* as a tragedy of evil, like *Richard III,* exposes the lineaments of despair with the loss of hope for mercy which seems the dark consequence of the fall of the hero who was once like us but who is now fully evil. Not surprisingly, the inspiration of the Good Angel, even in some sort of mimetic displacement, is absent from the personal experience of Lady Macbeth and Macbeth himself.

The answer of Macbeth to the announcement of Lady Macbeth's death—possibly by suicide—is the most despairing comment on human life in the annals of great poetry:

> It is a tale
> Told by an idiot, full of sound and fury
> Signifying nothing.
>
> (V.v.26–28)

Both of them have defied the limits of nature. Both have devoted themselves so fully to evil—especially to its contemplation—that despair and death are the only possible consequences, determined by their choices from the beginning, as the witches foreknew.

The redemptive principle in a communal sense must transfer to the renewal of the proper order of the state or, in more human terms, must find expression in the character of the good and future king, Malcolm. Even so, Malcolm has a less vivid role than that of Richmond lying onstage beside Richard, visited by guardian angels in the great dream where Richard encounters only despair.

In the old series the Good Angel points to four great sinners of the New Testament: Peter, Magdalene, Paul, and the forgiven thief. The implications are clear, as we have seen. Peter is shown with the cock, and the dying one is thereby reminded of his three-time denial of Christ. The sins of the flesh forgiven in God's mercy are subsumed in the figure of Mary Magdalene. A persecutor of Christians and "chief of sinners," as he calls himself, Saul (later Paul) is shown falling from his horse as he is struck down on the road to Damascus. The obvious message is the good news that no sinner is too deep in sin to receive the gift of mercy.[14] It there is any doubt even of last-minute forgiveness, the dying one should fix his eyes upon the forgiven thief upon the cross, shown with manna raining from heaven upon him. But here in *Macbeth,* all such grace is absent.

All the *ars* books make the point, explicitly or implicitly, that the loving nature of God must be known in order for the sinner to face his own fallen human nature, and the old woodcut structure makes the point of saving grace numerous times. In many ways, the popular tradition of the *ars* foreshadows the Reformation emphasis upon faith and grace over works. The ministering messenger, the Guardian Angel, shows the dying one that the nature of God is one of loving mercy and forgiveness. Within the tradition, the person is not only informed theologically of the nature of God, but the angelic image of the woodcut series (not to mention the presence of the saints) illustrates the way in which God's grace reaches out to rescue the sinner from despair.

With the more mimetic representation the Doctor in *Macbeth* explicitly rejects such an angelic function of the *ars moriendi* for himself: the patient must in such a situation cure himself. The lack of such comfort exposes a world absent of comfort; these are the bleak tragic consequences of evil in *Macbeth*. Both Macbeth himself and Lady Macbeth, like Marlowe's Faustus, have moved beyond the reach of grace into the large sorrow *(tristitia)* that leaves no room for repentance.[15]

By the time we see this encounter between the Doctor and Macbeth in act 5 the morally reprehensible choices of the pair, arranged in a descending vortex of evil, have all occurred, from the death of Duncan to that of Lady MacDuff and—worst of all—her children. In some sense Shakespeare in the progress of evil echoes his treatment of Richard III's increasingly evil acts. But in that play Richard's inner sense of evil remains almost totally absent until the dream and conscience scene, whereas Macbeth is tormented in the early part of the play and Lady Macbeth, as the action progresses, becomes increasingly an icon of the agonizing consequences of deepening sin. The sleepwalking scene has just occurred, and the Doctor is aware of the "despairing" disease that wracks her.

Devotional writers did not allow for the possibility of God's denial of mercy to the wicked. Rather, they recognized that the individual failed to reconcile himself to God when he found that he was personally unworthy of mercy. The insistence with which the tracts proclaimed radical and ever-present grace even to deathbed converts reflects the uneasy sense of many Christians of the day that the circumstances of life might bring them to despair at the critical moment of death. Given the pervasive quality of such assumptions, Shakespeare's audiences would have brought many of the complex visual and verbal associations with the temptation to despair to their experience of *Macbeth* and to other Jacobean tragedies. Such named and unnamed fears of despair would have deepened their experience of themes of judgment at the same time they intensified the weight of tragic warning against unscrupulous ambition. The audience could hardly have failed to be moved to pity and fear by the despairing queen who substituted for the gentle hospitality of her sex and social place the bloody violence of regicide.

It is the undermining of the themes of hope and redemption that would make increasingly evident then and in the decades to come the need for a poetics of comfort—more fully articulated expressive forms by which evil and death might be overcome in the individual psychology. Certainly redemption exists politically, socially, and cosmically in *Macbeth* in the overturning of the reign of wickedness but not here for the individual. The powerful rush into ambition and murder by a couple all too human and the inevitability of the inner consequences surely moved Shakespeare's audiences to fear and the need to search out some "sweet oblivious antidote."

Part 3
Poetics of Comfort

9

A Case Study in Dying: Donne's Poetics of Preparation and Comfort

No one can write a book on the art of dying in the English Renaissance without encountering concerns of seventeenth-century culture for the comforting of the survivor. The earlier essays on Shakespeare and his tragic vision come together in their focus on preparation for death. Scenes all circle about the shape of a composed life: the nature of a peculiarly Renaissance pilgrimage of selfhood that culminated in the profound rite of passage of the deathbed. That was the moment at which all earthly power and possessions met the great spiritual powers that had been in interaction with them over a lifetime—Satan and God in a last combat for the soul, as Zachary Boyd, adapting St. Paul in the title of his devotional work, *The Last Battell of the Soule in Death,* dramatizes the encounter.[1]

In the plays we have examined, Shakespeare's characters all experience this moment of summing up, of searching out the true self, the crucial personal summation, in various degrees of displacement. The characters see themselves in preparation for the great judgment, at least by implication, that theologians had projected for centuries, those trumpets at the "round earth's imagin'd corners" that Donne in his Holy Sonnet very humanly wanted to postpone: "Let me mourne here a space."[2] In the plays, however, there is a secular shaping of the encounter in the sense that drama creates an eternal *now* in the focus upon its own incarnate representation of life in the midst of earthly power: politics and society.

How these essentially personal and theological attitudes turned back on the particularities of life and society remains something of a puzzle. Scholars in this age must still worry the paradox that the contemplation of death puts life back into an always-dying life. Most scholars believe these days, insofar as anyone can speak for general assumptions of a pluralistic field, that cultural context was far more important in shaping literary reality than scholars believed in the past. Whether full ideological cultural materialists like Dollimore at one end or those more simply impressed with the implied interactions of power and patronage with literature, like Goldberg, most literary scholars today do not treat the literary document as a world apart.[3] In *The House of Death: Messages from the Renaissance,* Arnold Stein probably comes closest to privileging particular literary passages as textual center in his book, although he, too, in most ways a traditional humanist critic, bows to cultural contexts with a section of intellectual history titled "What Renaissance Poets Would Have Known."[4] Many modern scholars, however, do not privilege their literary document among cultural texts but view all kinds of texts as equally dynamic in cultural interaction.

No longer is it possible to maintain the position of either of the main camps of literary studies dominant twenty-five or thirty years ago. On the one hand, the historical scholars like Tillyard were busy with historical scholarship as "background" for literature. The effect of that careful delineation of convention, according to one modern scholar, was to make literature seem embedded in a "morass of Elizabethan commonplaces." One might say the same (however unfairly) of the greatest woman scholar of the fifties, Rosemund Tuve, as, indeed, the supporters of Empson came near to saying of her reading of Herbert's "Sacrifice."[5] On the other hand, the neo-Coleridgean critics, the imagery people like L. C. Knight and those who sought to make of poetry in general and Shakespeare in particular a great treasure trove of subtle ambiguities and paradoxes set within a kingdom of poetic language, stimulate another cry: "aesthetic, sterile, privileged elitism." For those who attack new criticism most frontally, literature becomes lifeless if seen as too remote from history and ordinary humans. The aesthetic bone structure seems meaningless outside the flesh of culture.

Noting the general need felt by many scholars to make literature present in society and society present in literature, Stephen Greenblatt puts it this way: we need to reveal "the social presence of the world in the literary text."[6] Like traditional critics, Greenblatt often continues to keep the literary texts central, but he assumes that the text has its own full life only when it is understood within the full dynamic of the time, and, perhaps most characteristically, moves outward from text to explore culture. It is not enough to explicate ideas of intellectual or literary history as a single aspect of background or context; current methodology must create the illusion of a literary text interacting dynamically with an image of history. Time is established as many in the Renaissance believed, that is, as the "revealer of truth" or (in more modern terms) as all we know of it. Perhaps this explains also the aptness of the metaphorical interchange between theater and world that was central to baroque sensibility: the emergent sense of *improvisation* (Greenblatt's term) in life that brought to many among the audience the illusion of stage experience in their lives and concomitantly the experience of plays themselves as shimmeringly real.

That sense of seventeenth-century ideas being acted out in various art forms (even large arts of living and dying) echoed still within a world of corresponding experience, microcosmic and macrocosmic models, and established the multiple relationships that scholars and critics still struggle to define. Attitudes toward authority have eluded definition as critics seek to measure subversion and containment in literary forms.

What impels the change in England within religious attitudes that explodes into civil war in the 1640s has still not fully been explored by scholars. The seventeenth-century English sense of self is surely primarily still a social and a religious self. Montaigne and Descartes and the influence of the French notwithstanding, the self was determined in large part by a closed image of reality in which one must find a place or function, however great the stresses of new science and exploration that threatened explosion.[7] Crucial to what continued to be a hierarchal society structured along strong class lines was a sense of authority stemming from a single source in monarchy. The God-and-church focus of that authority had eroded to a great degree with Reformation splintering—certainly, however, more gradually for the English. They after all, having come to rest in king and state, saw king as the head of church but in some measure above it. Perhaps also by the first decades of the seventeenth century, ordinary people identified the king more fully with the divine as agent of Providence. Roy Strong, Stephen Orgel and others have chronicled the subtle and not-so-subtle movements of propaganda that issued throughout the Tudor dynasty in a symbolism of power.[8] By James's reign the idealism shifted from church to crown, so as to give him a "divine right" he might have really had in the popular mind if he had not insisted so irritatingly upon it. Englishmen were never as influenced by such theory or such absolutism as the French, and English literature built within its forms various modes of representation, as Goldberg phrases it, that allow for varying degrees of subversion and reflexivity.[9] And most importantly, side by side with such representation, or underlying it, was a gradual questioning of hierarchal structures that still retained power.

More than lip service was given by all, however, including literary artists under James I, to the continuity of several ideas: (1) that God ruled his created world through a worthy and anointed agent, James I; (2) that the king ruled by law, which was itself divinely ordained; (3) that whatever vicissitudes one found in this life, their presence was designed to test and develop the soul to prepare it for its eternal life in God. All of these ideas or assumptions were theological commonplaces still alive in the devotional tradition, however threatened by immediate events and evidences of James's imperfections. Such assumptions were intended to create a sense of order and comfort within a world fraught with far different realities: political conflict, economic hardship, a church already exploded and fragmented by conflicts between worldly and spiritual powers, a king who seemed distant from his people and wrongheaded in his values.

In short, what seemed to be optimistic moral clichés were the most frequent ideas mentioned in a particular time and place where despair cast its shadow everywhere, where violent political, religious, and economic changes seemed just outside the door or around the turn of the narrow London streets. That sermons and devotional books from 1603 to 1630 seemed to echo again and again the old answers indicated not that those answers were fully integrated or fully accepted into the consciousness of the English people, but rather that they needed to be stated again and again in a world where they were not apparent. They were given a particular poignancy in the midst of a life where death came in many guises to threaten the order of every day.

Death had always been the ultimate threat to human order and stability, and the English in the early seventeenth century recognized its inescapable presence. Literature itself, like religion, always seeks to transform mortality, to shore up human loss. The rituals of confrontation with death and the redemption from it came into the English Renaissance in many guises, but they were certainly reflected in tragedy, and less directly, in comedy and romance. In poetry the elegy and the pastoral tried on their powers to comfort; Shakespeare's sonnets had made a variety of efforts to place the potentialities for the death of love in a context of immortality. The more explicit forms of popular literature, the devotion or the sermon, followed some of the same patterns: the recognition of mortality and the probing of metaphors that moved it into hopes of immortality. Obviously, life itself, like literature, contains forms by which transformation can be supported by rituals of preparation for dying, the art of dying itself, patterns of dying at executions, and so on. During the first thirty years of the seventeenth century all these cultural events shape and are shaped by literature as well.

This penultimate section examines several examples of Donne's last writing: devotions, sermons, and a few poems, instances of literature that was most explicitly focused on comfort. The sermon especially represents the authority of God's voice as mediated through the preacher: the most fully accepted representation of preparation and personal comfort for the human condition within the seventeenth-century culture. On the personal level, perhaps, *The Devotions upon Emergent Occasions* had the most to say about the comfort of Christian community.[10] In the concluding chapter, I will examine lamentation as the paradoxical way to such comfort.

Several questions surround the fact of death as interpreted within the framework of the seventeenth century. How did people view its relationship to the ideas surrounding death in the past? What happened to the conception of death when the comforting rituals of the Roman Church were under attack or vanquished? Perhaps the most radical question is that of how death can be transformed from the great destructive ax of life itself into a rite of passage, a bridge to greater life, Milton's "gentle wafting to immortal Life" (*PL* xii.435). How can such a view be brought into line with the old metaphor of pilgrimage of the self? In what ways can history, the communities of the self, and the individual self come together into an integrated harmony? Moderns have somehow ceased to have such a harmonious vision, clinging often to the last shred of meaning in the precious unique Romantic self, but there are still indications of the hard-won answer in seventeenth-century literature.

Donne is perhaps the most representative of such an answer. In the last six or seven years of his life, Donne took important structures from the continuity of inherited theology and practice and, using them, built a literary place of comfort in his writing of religious culture. It is this place he celebrates when he finally came to tune his soul before the journey his faith projected into harmony.

Since modern critics have come to question the conversion psychology of Isaak Walton, they have suggested various explanations of the radical tensions between individualism and community (and between orginality and tradition) in the work of John Donne that finally came to resolution in the last years of his life. Particularly controversial has been the distance between his arrogant, witty, and, at times, heretical voice and that of the devoutly humble Christian "involved in Mankinde." The modern reader, however, may come to an easier understanding of the relationship between such voices by listening to them within patterns of change as defined by a modern anthropologist, Victor Turner. Although Turner's theory focuses upon culture as dominant over the individual, his cultural analysis of change actually projects a parallel pattern for both society and the individual. From a more anthropological perspective than that of Donne or other poets of the English Renaissance, Turner nevertheless assumes virtually the old macrocosm-microcosm relationship between society and the individual. At the same time he accounts for the ongoing thrust of change by means of what moderns might call a "culturally based modification of the Hegelian dialectic." Renaissance persons and scholars would tend to see the process as a paradoxical providential movement in history, the sides of the paradox resulting ultimately in *discors concordia.* Nevertheless, Turner's explanation provides a fresh perspective, one that critics might move through analogically to a more fully historical understanding of Donne's context and personal growth. At the same time there is the theme of life as a "long-day's dying" that paradoxically tracks self-discovery within the process of the individual's journey.

The thesis stage of the process Turner calls *structure,* or culture with all its inherited forms and institutions that are representative of the continuity and stability of human effort. On an individual basis, that most relevant to a consideration of Donne, the person beginning to mature initially accepts an inherited structure made up of elements such as these. Inevitably, however, structure in society tends toward rigidity and decay at the same time that new possibilities emerge, or, in the instance of the individual, the maturing adult begins to experience both himself and society in this way. Structure must, therefore, always be moving into something of an antithesis to itself—virtually yearning toward a meeting with what Turner calls *communitas,* a yeasty state of communal relationship that is spontaneous and regenerative, without fixed structure, tending usually toward the antitraditional. The final reconciliation of the opposing stages is the resulting *societas,* the healthy and harmless society that is a product of the dialectic between *structure* and *communitas.* On a personal level, the anthropologist speculates that maturation of the individual occurs in a pattern parallel to his culture, away from convention or inherited structures into a freer state of individualism and communal relationships and finally into a mature reconciliation of the two. It is interesting to consider in relation to Donne particularly the theory that creative individuals who might be seen as "threshold people" by Turner produce their most interesting ideas in the liminal or transitional period between these phases.[11]

Such a process provides, then, not only a linear model of changes but also patterns of simultaneous tension between opposites. Obvi-

ously, any period in history itself can be seen from both these perspectives. For example, the early seventeenth century in the
broadest terms is both a transition between the structure of the tradition it inherits (in this instance, the high Renaissance of the sixteenth century) and the emerging society of the next phase (English
rationalism and enlightenment as it begins to grow out of the first
half of the seventeenth century) and at the same time a live orga-
nism that at any moment includes interaction between the structure
of the former and the hints of the future that flow from *communitas*.
In some sense, the tremendous energy of the period can be assigned
to such paradoxical interaction.

Donne's personal development or maturation covers a shorter,
less dramatic transition. It spans the last twenty years of the sixteenth century and the first thirty years of the seventeenth, a period
that includes on a parallel sociopolitical level the transition between
the last waning of the greatness of Elizabeth and the uneasy, partially doomed grafting of the Stuart monarchy onto the elaborate
English civic conventions of the Tudors. From this perspective, history may be seen as moving from a comparatively fixed set of structures at the end of the Tudor dynasty into a more experimental,
yeasty community that circled around James's court. As the Jacobean drama reveals on many levels, it is a period of questioning or
even search for new values. At the same time, however, one can
see it as fundamentally a clinging to the old underlying religious
structure, as for example, a continuation that is one strand of the
communitas phase on a political level.[12] It is not until the Civil War,
or perhaps the decade leading up to it, that the Tudor reconciliations
come entirely undone.

The late poems, the devotions, and the last sermons of Donne
reflect both the end of the breaking away from the structure of his
early beliefs and the gradual moving through a more vital relation
to a *communitas,* a process and a state that in turn eventually moves
him into the larger society that reconciles structure as a principle of
order and convention and the warmly spontaneous and ambiguous
phase of community. The specifically Anglican and spiritual nature
of Donne's corresponding personal change—a change reflected in
his work—shows several modifications in Turner's patterns.

One important adaptation is that the resulting society, the ideal
reconciliation of the principles of inherited order and regeneration,
seldom exists for Donne in his personal vision of the world. He was
always a "liminal' or "threshold" person, to use Turner's termi-
nology. The dialectics of social experience with its paradoxical
movements between high and low, *communitas* and structure, ho-

mogeneity and differentiation, equality and inequality, appear, one might argue, in most of Donne's great poetry and in varying degrees in all his work. Critics have long recognized that there is more of this sense of paradox, tension, moving *between* poles, however, in the poems that we believe were written before he took orders. One is tempted to see in the period after his marriage the need to give up the vocational expectations he had for himself in relation to his culture. We see both from his letters and his poems that he is forced to live without clear structures as he grapples with a changing personal religion and a growing family. Donne himself, not surprisingly, sees his own struggle within a Christian context of struggle with sin.

In the bustle of everyday the images of reconciliation come occasionally through glimpses of the ideal in the presently incarnate world, but they come most fully in the paradoxically momentary vision of the New Jerusalem, which he gives to his readers in his sermons and divine poems. The most crucial metaphor in these texts seems to me to be the "communion of saints." For Donne, of course, the communion of saints is much more than metaphor or synecdoche for heaven: it is a natural and theological symbol of the continuity among souls who have lived, as Augustine put it, in terms of the spirit, not the flesh, some of whom live now in this world, some in the next. This is the true Church Triumphant. For Donne there is also virtually continuous tension between the sometimes libertine, even heretical, stance with which he views the "structures" of society in this life—the London life of his world—and the "pure submission" with which he struggles to approach the Anglican ideal of Christian society.

For seventeenth-century Augustinians, the City of God existed both in a kind of veiled dimension within time, as perceived in divinely inspired or sacramental moments, and also as it was more fully revealed to the saved when they took their assured places in the New Jerusalem at the end of time. That they had a present place in the Communion of Saints is of course true, also, as they partook of the mystical body in the eucharistic celebration. In the popular Vives edition of Augustine's *City of God* translated by J. Healey, the presence of such a reality is emphasized in the variety of symbolic forms it may take in history:

> This Mistery of Eternall life, even from the first original of mankinde, was first by the angells declared unto such as God voutchsafed, by diuers signes and maisticall shadowes congruent to the times wherin they were shewed.[13]

Devotional books and elegies of the seventeenth century such as, for example, *Great Brittans Mourning Garment,* which was created for the funeral of Prince Henry, often use lyrical traditional descriptions of the heavenly life as major sources of comfort to the grieving.[14] *Societas,* the third stage in the process of change, is accessible for both Donne and other Augustinians of his period mainly through similar moments of spiritual vision, not as an actual phase in the process of societal change as, later, Marxists would view it. The New Jerusalem exists fully for Donne and other Christians only at the end of time or in a purely spiritual or eternal dimension, but the Communion of Saints experienced in the sacrament of the eucharist in the English Book of Common Prayer exists throughout and beyond time as well as in the individual consciousness.

Like Augustine, Donne sees all of history moving toward the culminating point when God's will for mankind will be fully revealed in the City of God, but he finds much of daily existence an imperfect tension between the rigidity of structure and the chaotic spontaneity of *communitas.* Nevertheless, the sensitive modern reader may see in Donne's work a gradual growth (even if somewhat erratically expressed) into *societas* with an ever-stronger sense of human concern as Christian *caritas.* Even in Donne's secular poetry, the beginning of such a spiritual growth finds expression in the cultural encoding of his idealized love poems such as "The Canonization," which ends by affirming the saints of love described by the speaker-lover as models for a community of lovers.

I have selected for the section dealing with the early Donne perspective two poems that speak with those voices by which Donne moves through the yeasty liminality of *communitas* toward *societas:* "The Exstasie" and "The Canonization." In each, the paradoxical images of individualism and communion are strong. Although "The Exstasie" and "The Canonization" are usually classified with the secular poems, they also represent serious encounters with spiritual values. They reflect, respectively, cultural and communal codes that prepare the reader for Donne's fullest image of belonging, the one that moves him most deeply into the resolution of *societas,* the Communion of Saints. In both poems, several distinctive metaphors of union are strong, and in both, the transcendent experience of communion is central. It is not, however, until the actually explicit "divine" poems that Donne speaks of a new world and a new society.

"The Exstasie" is Donne's most Neoplatonic vision of body and soul. It was deeply influenced, as Donne's editor Dame Helen Gardner suggests, by the Neoplatonist Leone Ebreo, whose views of the relationship between body and soul embraced a characteristic Hebraic vision of human integration and incarnation. Such a modified

Neoplatonism was the appropriate background for a poem whose wit moves it between the erotic images of seduction and the profound theological examination of the connections between body and soul. At the same time, the images affirm the link between transcendence and the immanence that was so important to Donne. In the opening metaphor of the joined lover's souls, that of a mystical *ecstasie,* the reader is shown that experience of communion by which time and physical separation are transcended. The lovers are (at least momentarily) content to lie there merely holding hands while union takes place in a nonphysical dimension; ultimately their united soul parts to return to their respective bodies, "Else a great Prince in prison lies."

Behind such an assertion of relation and connection is always paradox—Donne's original experience of the gap between body and soul and the joy in the discovery of paradoxical connection through deconstruction. The joy of connection rests in large part upon the anguish of felt separation. Of all the idealized poems, "The Exstasie" reminds us most strongly of the two sides of Donne's experience: one sensual, demanding; the other spiritual, agonizingly conscious of the separation between body and soul, lover and beloved, but both, through love expressed in this poem in a unique "voice" of vision, dynamically united in this poem. In contrast, the libertine poems such as "Song," "The Flea," and even so Petrarchan a poem as "Twicknam garden" show the bitterness of the failure of love. In that last poem, the end of love is not union or communion but the bitter anguish of separation. The anguish is underlined most deeply by the metaphor of religous transformation moving in a direction opposite its usual one:

> But O, selfe traytor, I do bring
> The spider love, which transubstantiates all,
> And can convert Manna to gall,
> And that this place may thoroughly be thought
> True Paradise, I have the serpent brought.

(11.5–9)

Again, Donne plays with paradoxical inversion. Such inversion comes out of a fundamentally paradoxical sense of reality, for Donne a mode of perception of the way things are and a mode always close to the liminal or "threshold" personality. As Colie has commented in another context:

All things are intimations both of mortality and immortality, everything and nothing are sufficient for salvation: as Folly says, "what outwardly seemed death, yet lokying within we should fynde it lyfe: and on the other side what seemed life, to be death. . . ."

In "Twicknam garden," the anguish of love's failure—separation and isolation—is communicated through images that normally suggest union or communion: transubstantiation and the eucharist, the image of Paradise before the human separation, through sin, from God. The violation that language does to reality by underlining separation and differentiation is partially healed through paradoxes that make connections. It is this failure endemic to life under time that makes *societas* possible for Donne only in brief moments until his soul resides in the Heavenly City. And yet the full experience of isolation can be known by a personality such as Donne's only against a background of the most profound appreciation of communion, just as conversely in the idealized poems one almost never loses sight of Donne's anguished awareness of the obstacles to community.

In such a poem as "The Exstasie," the diverse modes in which the body may function, as both sensuality and as the vessel for spirituality, interact with each other to enrich and concentrate meaning. It would, however, be a mistake to read the *double entendre* as entirely ambiguous. While playing the whole range of suggestion, by the end of the poem Donne comes to serious meditation upon body and soul within a theological framework in which soul remains the essential master, the privileged link with the divine reality, but fully experienced only through body:

> To' our bodies turne wee then, that so
> Weake men on love reveal'd may looke'
> Loves mysteries in soules doe grow,
> But yet the body in his booke

(11.69–72)

The modulation of the poem to Donne's spare and serious voice from the more playful and extended erotic sense imagery of its beginning ("Pregnant upon a bank") is a subtle movement, musical in the flow of its articulation. The delicate ringing of the changes may be one of the reasons for widely diverse interpretation among critics. There is a clear disparity between the images of sense and vegetation in the beginning and the images of "book" and "revelation" in the last third of the poem. Such a contrast parallels the contrast in voice and focus. Nature is ultimately metamorphosed into revelation through the moving structure of Donne's rhetoric. The book of the body of the creature—nature and, in more general religious terms, the Book of the Creatures—is transformed within the unfolding structure of the poem to become the Book of Revelation for saving knowledge.

When one turns to "The Canonization," the radical movement within the poetic structure from the worldly to the celestial, from the particular to the universal, from separation to union, is so much more boldly and strongly articulated than in "The Exstasie" that there are few disagreements over what Fish has called the "dialectic" of Donne's poem. A movement out of conflict between world and lovers into a reconciliation that provides a temporary window into the eternal truth is necessarily ineffable and tentative. When Donne's poet-speaker strikes the explosive "For Godsake hold your tongue and let me love," the irascible, mutable world of "forward springs and plaguey bills" merges in opposition to the true lovers. Community is broken by the conflict between the values of loving and the mercantile, litigious values of the world. Unfortunately, as the "I" of the poem recognizes, the lovers do not live in Paradise but in the social context of the seventeenth century, a world constantly in conflict with itself and dominated by commerce and litigation.

But, nevertheless, the power of the quality of their love to transcend such a context builds firmly toward consummation in the last half of the poem from

> Call us what you will, wee are made such by love;
> Call her one, mee another flye,
> We' are Tapers too, and at our owne cost die
>
> (11.19–21)

to the glorious baroque trumpet of the last lines:

> Countries, Townes, Courts: Beg from above
> a patterne of your love!
>
> (11.44–45)

The movement from the isolation of the lovers against the world to an affirmation of their union as a model for the world is ultimately mysterious. It probably grows out of the power of the lover-speaker to use language in such a way that his consciousness is strengthened and empowered by his own definition of the quality of the love shared. It finds expression in the phoenix in which "neutrall thing both sexes fit," an image that sounds boldly and joyfully through the last three stanzas. And the phoenix is the dominant image of integration and transformation. Significantly Donne loses angry self in the physical and spiritual union of the lovers. He has lost himself to find it, a necessity in human love as well as the Christian love of God.[15]

In Turner's terms, he has moved through an attack upon the structure of the world and an assertion of love to a full experience of *communitas* in the language. There is in that communal celebration little preservation of the individual except in the symbolic delineation of distinctions between the Eagle and the Dove. The reconciliation of strength and concupiscence, Donne's own marriage of Mars and Venus, is subordinated not only to the phoenix riddle but to the "wee" and "us" that is the point of view of the last two stanzas. Human love at its best expressed through the idealized celestial Venus of Neoplatonic mythology is raised to transcendent heights in the union of lovers. Pride and isolation are healed by a theology of voluntary human love. The breaking of *structure* in the conflict implied in the beginning of the poem moves into full *communitas* by the end. The opposing world at the beginning has become a world of lovers looking to the saints of love for pattern.

In his later work, poetry and prose, Donne's sense of *communitas* is seldom represented by Neoplatonic or Petrarchan images. It is metamorphosed into more explicitly religious metaphors of integration, such as that of the Communion of Saints, that both participate in and look forward to a *societas* only possible in preparation for and after death. Ultimately, Donne's fullest sense of community seems to be experienced in a metaphysical context that allows him, both through his theology and his increasing understanding of the relationship between experience and biblical types, imaginative experience of the Heavenly City or, more characteristically for him, the Heavenly society of relationships. Donne's definition of hell, for example, is eternal absence from a loving God ("To fall out of the hands of the living God. . . .")—a relationship of deprivation rather than a place of physical torment.

One senses that Donne's own intense individualism was an important factor in making this life a battleground for the conflict; in personal terms (that find expression primarily in the lyric poems), Donne's major struggle was with the pride that always sat in judgment upon his present context. At the same time, however, his imagination and the microcosmic/macrocosmic vision of seventeenth-century Anglicanism gave him a typology of rich resources with which to counter the prison of self. It was this very pride of self that Donne seems to have at the end of his life overcome, if perhaps only fully after the death of his daughter in 1627, as we shall see later.[16] He discovered at last in his spiritual struggle, perhaps partially through suffering the mortality of those dearest to him, the fundamental need to submit his own will to the authority of the larger community of saints. The "present absence" of the death of loved ones at last brought him to submission. Therein for Donne lay the difficult freedom of a full experience of society.

Donne's justly popular meditation on human and divine communion, "Perchance hee for whom this *Bell* tolls," from the *Devotions Upon Emergent Occasions* published in 1624 and roughly contemporary with the "Hymne to God my God, in my sicknesse," tolls the advent of the paradoxical resolution of a soul that had ever been on the threshold between individualism and community. Throughout the meditation Donne reiterates a theme of unity that focuses upon the bell tolling for the dead that all hear and are linked through. Perhaps the most finely drawn image in the devotion draws all creation into community with its maker through death:

> All *mankinde* is of one *Author,* and is one volume;
> when one Man dies, one *Chapter,* is not torne out of
> the booke, but translated into a better *language;*
> and every *Chapter* must be so *translated;* God
> employs several *translators* . . . but Gods hand is
> in every *translation;* and his hand shall binde up
> all our scattered leaves againe, for that *Librarie*
> where every *booke* shall lie *open* to one another . . .[17]

In his own hard won but joyous sense of belonging to the Christian community, Donne finds in this meditation a moment of profound rest, but such moments are rare in his work. Even this devotion exists within an elaborate context of working gradually through the illness that was its inspiration. Donne is ever a poet of the narrative struggle. The first meditation in the series, for example, is an anguished confrontation with illness and death. Not only are human beings crucified through death, says Donne, but they are crucified through the suffering of illness as well. Biographers and critics, including Walton, have fictionalized a literal chronology by which he journeyed from cynicism and skepticism in his youth to the faith and pious devotion of old age, but even the old Jack Donne—John Donne myth includes the two ends of the spectrum of a nature in dynamic tension throughout his life.

In reality, Donne lived far closer to Turner's state of "liminality" than most of his contemporaries; his sense of suffering and his recognition of the need to be fashioned anew were exceptionally strong. But submission to the final rite of passage was even more difficult than for most in his age. One side of Donne's personality remained individualistic, sometimes arrogant, proud of his intellect. One could say that at any *one* moment he was far from *communitas*. Such a side had certainly found expression early in both his libertine and his satiric voices. One thinks immediately of "the Flea" and "Elegy XIX," as well as of the Satires. Within his paradoxical nature this strain always questioned submission, sometimes stridently, sometimes in subdued tones. Another aspect of Donne, however, always yearned for community and found a voice increasingly strong, especially in paradoxical metaphors of fusion and integration, such as the "leaves of the book." But fully developed homecomings represent rare and brief moments of transcendence. Donne seems only toward the end of his life to have achieved a depth of Christian experience that disciplined his skeptical, restless mind. Even in those years, Donne stands back at times and questions. As Carey with his somewhat neo-Freudian view of Donne has suggested, Donne saw change as full of intellectual potentiality, even when it undermined his most sacred feelings.[18] Nevertheless, the sermons of the last four years suggest some closure; they are structured around themes of resurrection that at last fully represent the resolution of tensions between life and death and herald Donne's preparation for the great rite of passage.

The several voices of Donne owe the sharpness of their articulation both to the vibration of these two sides of his nature and his frequent metaphors of reconciliation through suffering. This is perhaps only another way of asserting Donne's essential debt to Christian paradoxes in the art of dying. More germane to the parallel between Turner's categories and Donne's is the recognition that for Donne the yeastiness of the *communitas* phase operated out of two opposing extremes or, to put it in other terms, moved in two stages never entirely free of one another—one, the personal, impulsive, proud self's skepticism of convention in religion, love, and poetry; the other, the freeing experience of voluntary submission to a long symbolic, theological, and communal tradition of love. The latter provided an ultimate homecoming. At least his last works provide evidence that he eventually grew into a deeper acceptance of the vision of metaphysics that he had espoused earlier in his life. The radical grace he longed for came in incremental stages.

A variety of human, intellectual, and historic experiences lies behind the tension as Donne knew it. The turmoil of English Reformation controversy had brought his contemporaries and himself, both inside and outside the Roman Church, to the necessity for a more fully developed personal theology. On a more private level, the combination in his own life of a love marriage with the frustration of worldly ambition led to his overt submission and (what the sympathetic would term) *maturation* within divine orders by 23 January 1615. But not until he had lived his new life for some years could he come to full reconciliation. Within this period Anglicanism itself suffered tensions within the Church that were brewing with such intensity as to lead eventually to the final explosion of the English Puritan Revolution. Though recent historical scholars suggest that the worst conflicts did not exist until the thirties, the seeds of them were certainly there in the twenties. Whatever the complex autobiographical and cultural interactions, we see in Donne's early poetry a searing anguish over the divisions of the full Church as a whole and therefore an abiding skepticism toward all human structures. Undoubtedly the death of his brother, Henry Donne, from plague, in Newgate prison for harboring a Roman priest, made immediate to him in his younger years major conflicts of the English Reformation of the day.[19]

Donne's own difficult conversion to Anglicanism also had brought him an agonizing passage through such issues, as we see when he poses them in characteristically passionate terms in the early "Satyre III," in which all the characters who represent the different branches of Christendom have severe limitations. Even Graius (the Anglican) is largely motivated through nationalism, not recognition of truth. In his Holy Sonnet 2 from the Westmoreland Manuscript, Donne says, "Show me deare Christ, thy spouse. . . ." Where is the true church: Rome, Germany, England? Is it possible, the sonnet asks, that she has just now emerged after a thousand years? How can this "amorous soule court thy mild Dove"? Donne's longing for a loving intimacy with the churchly bride rises from the imagery with characteristic intensity. It has behind it the experience of absence or loss: primarily of the old reliability of the church as a single structure of faith. Like many seventeenth-century people, he was experiencing the gradual but radical undermining of the authority of the institution, while clinging to the transcendent reality behind it. Finally, he found a measure of equilibrium between personal faith and institutional faith when he took Anglican orders in 1615. His own Anglicanism, as most scholars have agreed, was largely that of Hooker, who spoke for a broadly Catholic Anglicanism that combined conscience and sacrament.

The Early and the Late Donne: Transitions

The most appealing voices in the Divine Poems, the devotions, and the sermons, to my mind, owe their character, however, not to theology but to the personal intensity by which Donne expresses his longing for perfect integration into the ideal *societas:* the ultimate loving communion with the divine. The comfort of that communion, which he embodies in the few funeral sermons that he preaches during the last fifteen years of his life, is strong evidence of his own personal perspective. Conventional as such a comfort is in the art of seventeenth-century preaching, one can hardly read Donne's rhetoric as mere convention. Certainly in the "Sermon of Commemoration" he preached in 1627 for his old friend, Lady Danvers, formerly Magdalen Herbert, the vision of belonging that he projects in the encounter of the soul with the joy of Christ and its acceptance into the joys of Paradise affirms the joy of Christian communion that Donne the private person longed for:

And this good *Soule,* being thus laid downe to
sleepe in his peace, *His* left hand under her *head,*
gathering and composing, and preserving her *dust* for
future Glory, His right hand embracing her, assuming,
and establishing her *soule* in present Glory, in his
name. . . .[20]

Anthropologists suggest that rites of passage demand utter submission to the authority of a structure or a godhead. Donne's devotional voice at such moments is reminiscent of that of Augustine's *Confessions*—of no other text in the contemporary seventeenth-century devotional tradition, either Roman or Anglican. The quality of its expressed internalized longing derives from the bleakness Donne plumbs in the frequent skepticism he exhibits before conventional worldly structures. It is a characteristically seventeenth-century skepticism of reason and the world itself that finally ends in God—a recognition of Donne's need for radical Pauline grace in freeing within himself the power of love: "Batter my heart. . . ." The ancient tradition of images he draws upon finds a model in the Songs of Songs, the mystical biblical allegory in which desire for the divine is expressed through the imagery of human love and sexual fulfillment.

Throughout his life, he had longed to be free from the skepticism that his own temperament and the cultural dissolution of institutional authority made inevitable for one of his intellectual seriousness. In the Divine Poems particularly, one sees the Donne that speaks in the sermons of the last five years of his life. The poems record the emergence of a new commitment to the role of divine lover. Only through perfect love, he recognizes, do all the paradoxes find reconciliation. The powerful ending of Holy Sonnet 10 is only one early example:

> Take mee to you, imprison mee, for I
> Except you enthrall mee, never shall be free
> Nor ever chast, except you ravish mee.
>
> (11.12–14)[21]

He begs through the intensely erotic language of the Christian mystic (which he was not) for full reconciliation with God.[22]

Many critics have noticed the paradoxes through which Donne humanizes the impulse toward the divine by introducing sexual imagery and, conversely, idealizes human love by introducing celestial imagery. Such an impulse is at times Petrarchan, at other times Neoplatonic.[23] Its richness defies categorizing. There is, however, a further link between the sacred and profane poems, as we saw earlier in the essay. Sexual imagery is the most startling but only one infrequent strand among several. The most striking metaphors are those of integration or unity, as the poet moves through *communitas* toward *societas,* the full community only to be realized in oneness with the divine on the deathbed and after death. Sex is one category, but love in a wider sense is the more fertile one, that equally mixed, resurrective phoenix of "The Canonization," or the souls joined in ecstasy that float above the lovers of "The Exstasie." The intensity the reader experiences is evoked especially by Donne's poetic communion with his beloved, human or divine. Only such a personality as Donne's could express so powerful a fulfillment, containing as it does the recognition of the distance it is necessary to come to experience the loss of self.

In one sense, it is deceptive to speak of the "distance he had come," since even in the idealized poems, his feet still touch the ground where he began. However, a few poems lie at either end of the pole. The skepticism and isolation of the libertine poems ("she will be false, ere I come, to two or three") is as far from the strident longing of "Batter my heart, three-personed God" as the "Take me to you, imprison me. . ." is from the sure faith of "I joy, that in these straits, I see my West."

But surely the distance between those poetic statements contains his struggle to submit his pride of intellect to grace. As the editors of his sermons have pointed out, Donne's Christianity is predominantly moral, not mystical, and embodies struggle. Letting go of self is manifestly so difficult for him that when he does achieve it, his verse soars with the freedom he communicates. Self-fashioning for Donne within the Christian tradition means paradoxically losing the self he has struggled so to maintain. It is no wonder that paradox is for him a constant mode. He once reminded a friend that paradoxes were generative. The paradox of individualism (at times a mistaken freedom?) and community reconciled is central to Donne's distinctive voice in the poems and prose that express joy, although the expression of this paradox varies in terms of the strategy and subject matter of individual works.[24]

After his ordination in 1615 and the death of his wife in 1617, we see the focus of Donne's imagination shift increasingly from the "belonging" of personal erotic love to the full sense of submersion in the community of the church—on the metaphysical level, the Communion of Saints, the living and the dead who comprise the church Triumphant. One might speculate that both from the human perspective of psychological need and the religious perspective of orthodoxy Donne found in such a doctrine the possibility of an ongoing personal relationship with her for whom and with whom he shared the suffering brought about by their marriage. Less mystically, however, the literary critic must also see that the prose forms to which he turned both through vocation and inclination, the sermons and the devotions, demanded a metaphor of *societas* that could be more broadly shared. However constant his unique intelligence and ironic skepticism, his mission as a preacher of the "Book of Love" naturally moved him to meditate upon his "involvement in all mankind."[25]

His images in the religious poetry and sermons written after 1615 are those that submerge the individual in a union of love and comfort. In sermon 48, Donne speaks of the mercy of God available to the individual "at midnight alone." More frequently throughout the sermon, he describes the memory of God's mercies as mediated through the Bible and the Church. Particularly vivid is the typology of Exodus as a journey in which God's mercy brought his people out of their sin to redemption—a prefiguration of the rescue of humankind in Christ.[26]

In a sermon written close to his wife's death, Donne asserts the fundamental change from his early emphasis on human love to the longing for divine love:

> So will a voluptuous man, who is turned to God, find plenty and deliciousness enough in him, to feed his soul, as with marrow, and with fatness. . . [Donne cites Solomon whose disposition was amorous and excessive in the love of women]; when he turned to God, he departed not utterly from his old phrase and language, but having put a new, and a spiritual tincture, and form and habit into all his thoughts, and words, he conveys all his loving approaches and applications to God, and all God's precious answers to his amorous soul, into songs and Epithalamions, and meditation upon contracts and marriages between God and his Church, and between God and his Soule.[27]

With the loss of his wife, he seems to have accepted a "remarriage" that draws him closer not only to God but to the divine communion of saints, a union having a common base in the richly erotic language of his experience of human love.

Unfashionable as it is now, even in theological circles, to see suffering as the passage to a loving submission to the Communion of Saints, critics recognize that Donne delineates the movement of the soul into divine society and acceptance as a way of chastisement. Comparatively early in his work, in "Goodfriday, 1613. Riding Westward," he ends with the characteristic colloquy,

> O Saviour, as thou hang'st upon the tree;
> I turne my backe to thee, but to receive
> Corrections, till thy mercies bid thee leave.
> O thinke mee worth thine anger, punish mee,
> Burne off my rusts, and my deformity,
> Restore thine Image, so much, by thy grace,
> That thou my'st know mee, and I'll turne my face.

$$(11.36-42)$$

He plays upon this theme throughout his later sermons and devotions, in which suffering is clearly linked to illness and death. In one of the first devotions, he speaks of facing death as only second to the agony of being crucified upon a bed of pain. It is through the breaking of the worldly heart that Donne sees himself as purified for acceptance. Perhaps his illness of 1623 is a major step in that breaking. Although this rite of passage is less specifically articulated than that in Shakespeare's *Lear,* with its symbolic stripping away of the royal garments, Donne again and again in his sonnets and sermons asserts a similarly deep need for suffering, even violence, as a necessary mode for disciplining pride. It is clear that Donne sees the painful preparation for death, as in illness, involving a struggle with sin equally important to a doctrine of comfort.

The full-length sculpture of John Donne wrapped in his shroud that still stands within hearing distance of the Dean's pulpit in the new St. Paul's remains one of the great examples of early seventeenth-century preparation for dying. Contrary to the modern notion that having an effigy made illustrates a dark, macabre side in the poet-preacher's nature, the sculpture itself with its blissful smile suggests the efficacy and wholeness of Donne's understanding. A little before his death, Dr. Donne seems to have come at last to the full tuning of his soul, to that moment of perfect acceptance of death when, as in "Hymne to God my God, in my sicknesse," he anticipated joining the celestial choir of saints. More, perhaps, the quality of the smile suggests that Donne already had glimpsed the heavenly terrain of his last journey through the straits of death. For a man whose religious poetry and prose reflect struggle and seldom shine forth in single joy, the smile is an arresting hint that the preparation in the art of dying well could transform the deathbed into a place of peaceful anticipation.

In addition to immediate preparation for death, including making his will and his farewell to friends and family, much of Donne's formal preparation for death may be seen in the body of sermons he prepared over the years as Dean of St. Paul's.[28] Obviously, a number of his earlier sermons and religious poems deal with the theme of death and resurrection. However, many of the sermons of 1627, and, in particular, a commemorative one for Lady Magdalen Danvers, the friend of nearly a lifetime, have special place in his work. Within these sermons, Donne achieves a poetics of preparation and comfort.

The interest of John Donne in the subject or *topos* of death has been well documented by scholars, from his ribald, yet conventional, punning upon dying as a metaphor for sexual consummation to his more characteristic Christian treatment of death in his sermons.[29] Readers have long been aware that as a priest he naturally was called to present to his congregation the Christian interpretation of its meaning. Within a culture that saw the deathbed as the culminating moment of a life, the threshold of *societas* in its fullest sense, he was certainly one who made elaborate preparation for dying.

In the inner world of the mind, or perhaps the *soul,* as seventeenth-century persons would have said, there was also a necessity

for meditative structures that would bring about an imaginative reconciliation with this most difficult passage in the human journey. As
mentioned above, the form of the sermon in Anglican preaching was
the most significant channel for such a task, and it functioned in
two major related ways: to prepare the congregation for the issues
surrounding dying and to console those persons ravaged by grief
and absence by remembering the dead. Donne's sermons often answer both those needs, and this chapter will focus upon both especially in his commemorative sermon for Lady Magdalen Danvers,
mother of the poet George Herbert and member of the prominent
Newport family.[30] Published in 1627, along with memorial poems
by George Herbert, that sermon was structured to comfort the living and to reconcile the congregation to the Christian reality that
includes mortality. Its two parts became richly elaborated illumina-
tions of the biblical text.

As this book has emphasized throughout, scholars such as Spencer, Ariès, Martz, Beaty, Koller, and Stein have over the years
pointed out the importance of death to English people living in the
sixteenth and seventeenth centuries. Ariès has chronicled the various means by which the passage from death to eternity was still for
the English Everyman/woman the crucial journey or rite of passage,
even in a world that was rapidly becoming larger and more open to
competing worldviews. Such an anthropological view of reality that
recognizes the centrality of rites of passage, is, of course, an important underpinning to comfort. Within such a context, Donne
may be seen as a case study of a poet and priest to whom the crucial
issues in confronting death formed the body of his life's work. In
addition to his ten volumes of sermons over the years of his ministry
and the *Devotions upon Emergent Occasions* that chronicled his
meditative way through near mortal illness in 1623, a number of his
poems also dealt with death as a central subject. Even if we omit
the secular poems that include frequent occasional imagery of death
and mortality, there remains a body of poems that reflect Donne's
seventeenth-century predilection for the theme: the anniversaries
and the funeral elegy in memory of Elizabeth Drury; seven funeral
elegies, including that for Prince Henry; a number of Donne's Holy
Sonnets; and, finally, his two great hymns: " A Hymne to God the
Father" and "Hymne to God my God, in my sicknesse."

In both poems and prose, he plays upon many of the ideas,
themes, conventions, and even metaphors that were part of the
commonplace store of Renaissance association with death. As mentioned earlier, one could treat two large categories: the materials
that are part of the historical preparation for dying, including the

two symbolic traditions of the dance of death and the *ars moriendi,* and the rituals of mourning and consolation that developed in a culture where sudden death was so frequent and frightening a guest. Plague, war, pestilence, even childbirth kept visible in the seventheenth-century consciousness death and time as recurrent specters, perhaps most shattering within the bonds of the family where an Englishman might well lose two or three wives before he died, not to mention numerous children.[31]

In light of such a rich tapestry for viewing, one might ask why a single sermon for a woman, who, if known widely as a person of some substance and interest, is, after all, not the puzzling and intriguing patroness that Lucy Countess of Bedford was. Although Donne had known Mrs. Herbert since early in the century, probably she had no substantial means of patronage until some years after her marriage to Danvers. Even the poems written to her suggest a relationship somewhat tame and conventional, perhaps mainly interesting to the sympathetic reader of Donne's elegy "The Autumnal." Though well-crafted and logical, the commemorative sermon itself is probably not Donne's most poetically interesting sermon. On the topic of death, among the funeral sermons the one preached for James himself is more arresting. But this is the most personal sermon, the one that records a personal loss. And among Donne's associates Magdalen Danvers was, after all, the closest figure to being an ordinary woman in the Renaissance. There are at least two other good reasons for examining this sermon among Donne's works on death: it is important within the order of Donne's work and also as the relationship with Lady Danvers sheds light on seventeenth-century attitudes and practices in regard to a discourse of comfort.

Sometime between 1599 and 1607 she met Donne. The tradition, begun by Izaak Walton, is that they met at Oxford University, but this testimony is suspect.[32] In the first edition of his *Lives,* Walton made no reference to Magdalen, but before the next edition was issued, the published commemorative sermon for her was brought to his attention. In this sermon Donne refers to her Oxford days and explains that she had met many "reverend" people there who had remained lifelong friends. Walton could easily have assumed that by the word "reverend" the Dean of St. Paul's referred obliquely to himself and that since she had been at Oxford at least until 1600, Donne must have become acquainted with her at that time. Although as a youth he had been a member of Hart Hall, no definite evidence places Donne at Oxford during 1599–1600. The earliest written evidence of his acquaintanceship with her dates from 11

July 1607, when he wrote to her the first of four extant letters, all of which were published by Walton.[33]

Because the tone of these letters strongly indicates that the two were only then becoming acquainted, it seems likely that they had just met and almost certainly not in London. Whatever opportunities they had to become acquainted, the letters he sent her in 1607 clearly indicate that their friendship was just then blossoming.[34] Unquestionably, he sought her assistance, but the mystery remains as to what assistance. In 1607, she still had young children to provide for, and although she had a jointure, she was not wealthy enough to launch a poet's career.[35] The answer to this mystery probably is contained in these letters, the fourth of which he sent her with two poems, "La Corona" and "Address to Mrs. Magdalen Herbert." The letter has never been properly dated, but its text indicates it was the last in this series.[36] The following words from it may hold the key:

> Your favours to me are everywhere; I use them and have them. I enjoy them at *London,* and leave them there; and yet find them at *Micham:* such Riddles as these become things unexpressible; and such is your goodness.[37]

What was it that she could do for him at these two places? Turning to Micham first, one sees that he was living there in poverty with his wife, for the two of them had been disowned by her father, Sir George More. Possibly Magdalen had offered to assist Donne in reconciling with his father-in-law. Even after her son, Edward, reached his majority in early 1603, she kept up the relationship with Sir George and is known to have sent him at least one letter in early 1607. By 1608, he had relented enough to offer some financial assistance to his unwelcome son-in-law.

At about that same time Magdalen married John Danvers, a young man about half her age, who was to become an important figure in the Virginia Company. This union almost certainly brought an end to any hope Donne had for assistance, since Danvers, as a younger son, had minuscule hereditary prospects and undoubtedly looked to his new wife for financial support. Prior to this marriage, in 1607 or 1608, Donne probably wrote the "Autumnal," his only other poem that has indisputably been associated with Magdalen. In it he honors a woman of about fifty years of age, and most conservative estimates would make her forty-five or forty-six when she became Danvers's wife. Donne found other patrons, including the Countess of Bedford and even King James, but he also kept up his contacts with Lady Danvers and her family, visiting them in 1613 at Montgomery, where he would have been able to view the Herbert tomb with its effigy of her first husband in a winding sheet, and giving a copy of his "Biathanatos" to Edward in 1620.[38]

Whatever the continuing relationship between Donne and Lady Danvers and her family, one of his most important contacts with them was through the Virginia Company, for in May 1622, he was made an honorary member and in July one of its Council. These honors were surely the direct result of his November 1621 election as Dean of St. Paul's, but no record remains of who suggested his name. He had kept up his friendship with the Danvers family, as he had written in August 1621, that he was planning to visit them at Chelsea.[39]

In 1627, when Lady Danvers died, she had been in ill health for many years. Despite this illness, she had reacted valiantly, by Donne's account, to the visitation of the plague in 1625. Her efforts during that crisis form an important part of the eulogy of his sermon and will be dealt with later. Before turning to that sermon, however, we need to assess Donne's attitudes toward death in 1627.

Lady Magdalen's death came at a crucial period in his long attempt to come to a Christian understanding of two of the four last things as understood by the seventeenth century: those essential mysteries of death and resurrection.[40] As his editors point out in the introduction to Volume VIII of the sermons, Donne's quotation on the necessity to die daily from Sermon 6 (preached in the same year as the Sermon of Commemoration) was virtually a thematic focus for the sermons beginning with the death of Lady Magdalen on 1 July 1627, (8:1–17). Perhaps more explicitly he later examines the comforting "promises" of that sermon from a more somber perspective. The majority of these later sermons comprise a deep and probing meditation on death and the Christian fears and hopes for resurrection.

Although they are by no means all funeral sermons—most are not—they are linked not only by Donne's increasing age but more immediately by grief from the period of little more than a year during which he lost four of the people closest to him. Early in 1627, he was deeply shaken by the death of his favorite daughter, Lucy. On May 31, again the figure of Death touched a person who had been extremely close to Donne, his daughter's godmother and Donne's old patroness, Lucy, Countess of Bedford. When a few days later, Lady Magdalen, his friend since at least the first decade of the century, died, Donne was already, like most people who experience a major experience of grief, much more highly sensitive to

the questions surrounding death then we allow ourselves to be during most of a lifetime. Because his dear friend Sir Henry Goodyer
was not to go until 18 March 1628, it was probably the death of these
three towering women that triggered the period of Donne's deepest
meditation on death. It was that period of life when the number of
those participating in the Communion of Saints from the other
world seems to shift suddenly to the dominant figure and to raise
numerous feelings that draw the imagination across the barrier of
time.

It is, of course, difficult to compare this period of personal grief
with that time of radical loss when Anne Donne died in 1617 (when
Donne himself was much younger), or that time of close reflection
upon the possibility of his own death in 1623 when he wrote the
Devotions during his near fatal illness. Both earlier times produced
rich insights in his work that prepare the way for the meditation of
1627. An obvious difference in the period following his wife's death
was that he apparently came to see in it something of God's plan to
move the focus of his intensely passionate love from a woman to
God himself. Certainly his new vocation as a preacher became the
center for his energies and emotions as he mastered the form of
the sermon. His second major brush with death—his own illness of
relapsing fever in 1623—brought forth riches of a different, more
personal, sort in the *Devotions upon Emergent Occasions*. Donne's
most poetic prose focuses upon the suffering of illness and its relationship to the world of damnation:

> My thoughts reach all, comprehend all. Inexplicable misery; I their Cre-
> ator am in a close prison, in a sicke bed. (Meditation I)

By then, his profession may have seemed less an answer in itself.
It must have been even more difficult to sustain within six months
in 1627 three major losses of persons inextricably tied to his emotional life: his favorite daughter, emblem of that strong immortality
"through breed" (or generation) that Shakespeare and others have
shown as so vital to the seventeenth-century sense of survival; his
great patroness, Lucy, Countess of Bedford; and finally, Lady Danvers, the old friend at whose home he had sought refuge as recently
as the plague year of 1625.

Inevitably, such a series of deaths would not only lead him to
intensify his preparation (and in his sermons that of his parishio-
ners) for death but also to search out with sad heart and deepening
faith the commonplace comforts of a tradition that had developed
over the past two hundred years. Donne's editors see the year fol-

lowing as one largely of somberness and melancholy for him. This essay, therefore, examines the commemoration sermon as a major turning point in the process of Donne's preparation for death: his deepening Christian faith and its relationship to the major comforts within seventeenth-century culture. The sermon sets forth a concentrated image of the traditional comforts, especially the New Testament promises of the commemorative sermon: the Last Judgment and resurrection for Christian saints that Donne returns to by the end of the year with a renewed sense of joy.

At any rate the form and conventions of the commemorative sermon for Magdalen spoke to the obvious need for general comfort, not only on the part of family and congregation but even, as we have seen, on the part of Donne himself. Donne had been asked to deliver the funeral sermon for his friend but had been prevented, for which he apologized, by responsibilities in the City. His continuing sense of obligation to the family, however, is affirmed by his having come to Chelsea only a few weeks later on 1 July 1627, to preach the commemorative sermon for Lady Magdalen.

As a talented professional preacher of ten-years' experience he could probably have moved through the consolations of a funeral or commemorative sermon without much personal soul-searching. There is, indeed, more than a suggestion of conventionality in the opening prayer and following development of the sermon. Certainly, there is little surprise that the prayer would reiterate the comfort of Psalm 116.5: "Precious in thy sight is the death of thy Saints." The communion of saints with its connection between the living and the dead as comfort for living was a familiar but powerful consolation to seventeenth-century listeners, as we have seen, and may have reflected a new sense of connection on the part of Donne—a new, grief-stricken sense of the need to see the absent as present. Donne's division of the text from 2 Pet. 3.13—"Neverthelesse, we, according to His promises looke for new heavens, and new earth, wherein dwelleth righteousness"—confirmed the reassurance that death was not a final ending.

Even if in a surfeit of romantic feeling we should examine Donne's approach for some startling, spontaneous departure that reveals the depths of his grief for his friend, it is not surprising that we should not be able to find it. The rhetoric of the Anglican sermon of this period plays upon convention as embodying great universal truths of human experience. The humanist rhetorical principle of *creative imitation* was supported in the articulation of religious forms by a deeply rooted typological view of reality, by which all persons, events, images, and forms are manifestations of the sim-

plicity of divine truths—not to mention the old ordering of reality
through corresponding planes. Donne's originality and power derive not from the use of new ideas or unusual biblical passages but
from his highly individualized turning of familiar structures to release their poetic power.

Even within Anglican conventions, Donne's grief for his friend
remains restrained, perhaps because Lady Danvers's death had
been expected—certainly at her age it was in the nature of things
and more easily accepted as such. It also seems to have been a beautiful death, as we shall see later. From a more psychological perspective, the conventional symbols in the sermon may indicate the
way in which Donne is taking refuge from the accumulated grief
that emerges more clearly in the sermons that follow during 1627.
For example, he inappropriately spent the whole wedding sermon
for the Earl of Bridgewater's daughter on the theme developed in
Matt. 22.30 that there is no marriage in heaven. Following Lady
Danvers's death his interest in the nature of resurrection seems to
be greater than his interest in the immediate nature of the relationship between the bride and groom. Parts of this sermon have even
been labeled "morbid." In some sermons that year there is more of
somberness and melancholy—less of joy and the imagery of light
than is characteristic, particularly in the Fifth Prebend Sermon (No.
4), and that preached at St. Paul's on Christmas Day, 1627 (No. 5).
In the Magdalen Herbert sermon, he is more conventional. He
spends most of his time in the division of the text of comfort, but it
contains the seeds of meditation on the greatest of consolations: the
hope and image of resurrection in the translation of Lady Danvers.
As he announces at the beginning, he is pursuing the two ends of
such a purpose: (1) to instruct the living and (2) to commemorate
the dead.

The first section of instruction presents the major traditions and
consolation by reminding the Christian congregation of the Second
Coming, that belief that Donne says was most subject to the scorns
and jests of unbelievers, but was part of God's promise to mankind
for new heavens and a new earth.

There were several chords in the traditional melody of comfort
sung by seventeenth-century preachers and eulogists. It would
seem to most people that the theme of death's inextricable link with
resurrection was the strongest, and in the long run that was most
certainly true. But as everyone rooted in biblical types knew, an
ambiguity and an ambivalence associated with resurrection had to
be taken into account.

The general resurrection, according to orthodox theology, occurred at the time of the Last Judgment and included the damnation of souls as well as their salvation, fear as well as comfort, hell as well as heaven. A rhetoric of sermonizing on the subject had developed so that by the seventeenth century preachers knew well how to articulate the fearful possibilites and finally to move through grief and fear to hope. The rhetorical process or journey through fear to comfort was essential.

At some periods within the Middle Ages and even as late as the latter part of the fifteenth century and early sixteenth century, however, in both verbal and visual representations of the Last Judgment, images of damnation seemed to dominate the visual arts. Marlowe's *Dr. Faustus* played a variation upon that theme in its last powerful scene, as Faustus cries out in his agony:

> See, see where Christ's blood streams in the firmament!
> One drop would save My soul, half a drop. Ah, My
> Christ!
>
> (V. 153–54)[41]

But Faustus, cut off by despair that comes from a life rooted in sin symbolized by Mephistopheles and his old covenant, finds it impossible to seek mercy. Instead he joins the damned, falling down through the hellmouth of a stage trap door.

By the late 1620s, however, when Donne is writing his funeral sermon for the loving family of his friend, it is appropriate both to the day's occasion and the main-line seventeenth-century attitudes within the Anglican Church to stress the comfort over the fear. To some extent he minimizes the fearful aspects, but the mysterious and fundamental ambiquity of the Last Judgment remains. As Donne says near the beginning of the first half of his sermon, he meant "To instruct the Living":

> Though this *day of the Lord* will certainly *come,* and come as a *Theefe,* and as a *Theefe in the night,* and when it comes, the *Heavens shall passe away with a great noise, and the Earth also, and all the Workes that are therein, shall be burnt up.* . . . Though there be such a *scorne* put upon it, by *scoffers* and *jesters,* and though there be such a horror in the truth of the thing it selfe, yet, *neverthelesse* for all that, for all that *scorne,* and for all that *horrour.* . . . We. . . . We that know, that *the Lord is not slacke in his promise* . . . *We looke for new Heavens and new Earth* . . . in which . . . *Righteousnesse,* shall not only *Bee,* but *Dwell* for ever. . . . (63)

This long sentence, much of which is elaborated in those sections represented by three dots, is simply (or not so simply perhaps) a paraphrase of the text. It does include the paradox of the Last Judgment, both the fearful image of the destruction of time as we know it and the vague possibility of damnation, but also the reassurance that those who are "fixed in God," the Church Militant and Triumphant, are promised a homecoming to a newly righteous heaven and earth. In spite of the frightening image of change (and Donne admits that "the best man trembles at it"), the glorious end of a world made new and the insistence that those who belong to God will all together be part of it as event and theology provide the culminating theme of comfort for Donne's congregation. In this early passage in the sermon Donne's elaborate Ciceronian period postpones the punch until the end and displays all the tricks of rhetoric to release the full power of the paradox. The imaginations of his hearers must have bristled at the mysterious sense of the Day of Judgment coming as a *"Theefe in the night",* with the "great noise" and "fervent heat" of heavens, earth and works therein passing away and burning up. Yet the familiarity of the biblical text may have softened the reaction, and certainly the fear aroused becomes little more than intense excitement in the light of the remembered promise of the Lord to his people.

Donne's reassurance becomes even firmer as he sets up a radical opposition between those "Scorners, Jesters, Scoffers, and Mockers of Religion" (those who scoff at the Second Coming) and the constancy of Christians. He reminds his audience of those types outside the faith: the jester against Job, the Philistines who made fun of Samson, even Julian the Apostate, who, Donne says, in a *"Phrase of Scorne,* confessed that his wound came from the power of Christ: *The* day is thine, O Galilean" (Potter and Simpson 8:66). Among the scorners were those who mocked St. Paul for preaching the resurrection of the dead. Such a danger, however—that of mockery—is so clearly marked, says Donne, that "constant" Christians are able to stand against it.

A subtler and more real temptation occupies the next section of Donne's instruction: the fear of damnation as part of the context of the Last Judgment. The passage that follows, one of Donne's most frequently quoted, foreshadows the somber tone of many of his sermon meditations through the rest of this dark year:

> *It is a fearfull thing to fall into the hands of living God,* if I doe but fall into his hands, in a fever in my bed, or in a tempest at Sea, or in a discontent at home; But, to fall into the hands of the living God, so, as

that *living God,* enters into *Judgement,* with mee and passes a final, and irrevocable judgement upon me. (Potter and Simpson 8:67–68)

He goes on to say that the finality of the judgment may take place after a sudden, arbitrary coming. After all, this is the most frightening aspect of the personal judgment. Donne does not dwell, however, upon the general aspect of the Last Judgment. Perhaps characteristically he focuses at the height of his fear upon the personal anxiety one feels in not knowing when Christ will come, at what moment in his own personal circumstances: "In my night of *Ignorance* hee may come; and hee may come in my night of *Wantonnesse.*"

Using a Senecan "loose" technique of expansion, Donne suggests the other unwelcome times: of Melancholy, when he is in a "*suspicion* of his mercy," or sickness, even when all the nights of ignorance, wantonness, desperation, sickness, stupidity, and rage are all upon him at once (68). All these anxieties press toward spiritual preparation: from a renewed awareness of sinfulness comes the need for penance within the context of the fearful judgment. Still the great promise emerges again: that all Christians belong to the "*fellowship* of the Faithfull" (who earlier, he says, have seen the marks of election (70). Such a body as those who have "laid our *foundations in faith*" can face such fears and tribulations. Characteristically, Donne emphasizes that every suffering or correction is a rebaptism, that tribulation is sacramental.

In this first part of the sermon Donne asserts the promises and the comforts more fully to those who belong to the righteous. One is reminded of how in the *Devotions* he contrasts the agonizing solitude of illness with the communal joy of those who find themselves "involved in all mankind," those leaves bound up in the book of life. One of the great comforts is, of course, the endless expectation imprinted upon human souls. Christians look for Christ and for the day of death. Beyond is the expectation of the Second Coming, and the new righteousness, and the celebration of communal joy.

It is this final section that describes the fullness of the great promise. Donne rejects the theology of the Millenarians, who emphasize a perfect temporal state for God's saints for so many years after the date of the end. But when he cites Augustine's vision of the Judgment as inclusive of the perfection of this world as part of the heavens, he emphasizes the making of men and women better by resurrection. The earth has been purified by the last fires as a fitting dwelling for the saints of God. Donne, however, turns to one of his favorite images of maps and cosmography to admit finally that our maps of the new earth must ultimately remain imperfect (81). We can know only a few things, he says as he enumerates the well-worn guideposts. We shall recognize that it is a "Countrey inhabited with *Angells,* with *Archangells,* with *Cherubins,* and *Seraphins,* and that wee can looke no farther into it, with these eyes," however faithful. It is better than earth, says Donne, and there are milk, honey, manna, and gold. The important aspects, however, that we must look for in the New Jerusalem through the human images of desire that we project—gold, music, priesthood, victory, honor, or feasts— are justice and righteousness:

> What would a dejected spirit, a disconsolate soule, opprest with the weight of heavy, and habituall sinne, that stands naked in a frosty Winter of desperation, and cannot compasse one *fig leafe,* one colour, one excuse for any circumstance of any sinne, give for the *garment of Righteousnesse.* (82)

In the last paragraph of Part I of the sermon, Donne asserts that the saints of God shall all recover innocence and put on the garment of righteousness. The mystery of the purification is the way in which the saints will not only *have* Christian righteousness but *be* also a part of it.

> Arise thou, and bee another Commentary to us; and tell us, what this *new* Heaven, and *new* Earth is, in which, now, thou *dwel'st,* with *that Righteousnesse.* But we do not invoke thee, as thou art a *Saint* in Heaven; Appeare to us, as thou didst appeare to us a moneth ageo; At least appeare in thy *history;* Appeare in our *memory.* . . . (85)

In the second part of the sermon, the literal commemoration, Donne moves from the general instruction on the comforts of the Christian theology—especially the ultimate union of all in Christ— to the remembrance of Lady Danvers, particular image of death and resurrection. He says he remembers her not in heaven but in her human history, under time. He is invoking her absent presence. Unlike the Puritans, who tended to generalize throughout the whole of funeral sermons lest they should seem to present saints in the more narrowly Catholic mode of canonization, Donne individualized the characterization of his friend Magdalen in a loving portrait through which finally to affirm Christ's promises. It is characteristic of Donne's Anglican mind and sensibility that he draw together the macrocosm of the Second Coming (with the participation of Christ and all the saints) and the microcosm of the death and resurrection of his old friend, an individual saint to be commemorated.

His ordering has the dual power that sympathetic readers have associated with Donne: analogical reasoning and intuitive discovery. Along with Milton's, Donne's voice provides perhaps one of the last great instances of the genuinely mythic vision of reality. For Donne, theology is the real structure binding up the disparate, shifting elements of creation. His genius as a baroque preacher is to present the concrete, apparent events of experience as a mirror in which the spiritual realities may be perceived. Typically, Donne does best with that tangible reality, that humanized glass. In this sermon the second section, the *remembering* of his friend, is the most moving and reassuring image of comfort in the text.

But as always in seventeenth-century modes, the individual is not viewed primarily in her own right. It is fitting that in the sermon genre, she become representative of saintly virtue; the record not only speaks for her but inspires the listeners and perhaps even the preacher himself. The Puritans especially emphasized the way in which the person represented the ideal virtue of the Christian. As an Anglican, Donne emphasizes these universal virtues, too, but he also includes the more particular virtues, of her own unique personality and of her sex. She is held up as best wife and mother as well as neighbor and friend. The last two of the four roles bind her to all present and help to prepare for Donne's meditation on her as the resurrected fulfillment of God's promise to Christians. The eulogy presents her as a perfect Christian to whom both men and women could look: "That shee govern'd her selfe, *according to his promises:*" (90). In short, Donne says, she received the *promise,* the rare thing she had expected in her faithfulness: a Christian death (91).

The description of Lady Danvers's deathbed is fully within the tradition of the art of dying well. It may even, however, in some measure transcend that tradition by omitting allusions to the temptations of Satan and by emphasizing comfort for everyone. So far along the way to heaven is this particular saint that her dying is utterly peaceful:

> Shee shew'd no feare of his face, in any change of her owne; but died without any change of countenance, or posture; without any struggling, any disorder; but her Death-bed was as quiet, as her Grave. (91)

Devotional writers as different as Erasmus and William Perkins had often warned their readers that the pain of illness and the weakness of the dying inevitably caused the moments before death to suggest something other than the ideal picture of salvation. Those present should not, however, judge the condition of the soul of the dying;

only God could know that inner state. It was clear, however, that when someone slipped out of life in a peaceful and easy way that the ease itself was the type of the ideal death, a sure sign that the person was chosen for salvation. In this sermon Donne makes a good deal of his friend's proper death and even alludes to it in another sermon later that year.

Undeniably the most emotional part of the second section of the sermon comes when Donne provides a flashing glimpse of heavenly joy. He draws out the connotations of Lady Danvers's womanliness in a quotation from Canticles (8.3):

> *His left hand is under my head, and his right embraces mee,* [it] was the *Spouses valediction* and *goodnight* to *Christ* then, when she laid her selfe downe to sleepe in the strength of his *Mandrakes . . .* in the *influence* of his *mercies.* Beloved, every good soule is the *Spouse* of Christ. (92)

Donne had built up to this image of Christ the Bridegroom for Magdalen and all good souls, however, with a meditation on the bodily resurrection of Magdalen herself. Characteristically, he mentions dust and decay, wittily associating the present motion of her body a month after her death only with its crumbling into dust. But Donne does not stay with the realistic, the purely physical. Instead, he moves quickly to the promise of the Pauline "Glorified body in the Resurrection" as embodied in her. The whole world must die first, he says, but then her charity makes her willing to wait for all her friends and family to have the same resurrection (92).

It is in his description of the ultimate transformation of that body (already transformed in human life to an icon of charity) that Donne shows his most moving tenderness toward his friend:

> That *body,* which was the *Tabernacle* of a *holy* Soule, and Temple of the *holy* Ghost, That *body* that was eyes to the blinde, and hands, and feet to the lame, whilst it liv'd, and being dead, is so still, having been so lively an example, to teach others, to be so, That body at last shall have her last expectation satisfied. . . .(92)

A few sentences later Donne again uses the typology of Christ the Bridegroom holding his spouse:

> *His left hand under her head, gathering, and composing. . . . His right hand embracing her,* assuming and establishing her *soule* in present Glory.(92)

Donne then turns to charge the daughters of Jerusalem to wake her not till she please, but if they must wake her, to do so with action by imitating her virtues. At the end, he pictures her as a model for female saints, addresses the larger community of saints male and female and the possibilities of communal joy in the Second Coming that comes one step closer through her death (93).

The fundamental imagery, however, in this tenderest part of the sermon is that of the canticles, imagery that honors her gender, that also suggests the ideal Christian resolution and union of male and female principles through the iconography of Christ and his church. It is characteristic of Donne to express even divine relationships through erotic images. He accepted fully in his imagination the Bible and the *Book of Common Prayer* in their common imagery of correspondence between human marriage and the relationship of Christ and his Church. It is only through this fundamental connection that the Communion of Saints stretches from eternity into time, providing the essential continuity for Christians between the living and the dead, the essential androgynous reconciliation between male and female, the quintessential harmony of all humankind.

When we compare Donne's comfort in this key sermon with the formal and personal poetic paradox of the ending of "Hymne to God my God, in my sicknesse," "Therefore that he may raise the Lord throws down," we are doubly aware that it is Donne's most powerful statement of that theme. Throughout the Hymne, Donne asserts the necessity for submission in imagery that is possibly his most mature experience of the Communion of Saints and the community of love: in his most fully realized example of the *societas* of Turner. In the first lines, he joins himself to that group and that harmony for which he longs:

> Since I am coming to that Holy roome,
> Where with thy Quire of Saints
> for evermore,
> I shall be made thy Musique. . . .

(11.1–3)

In the intervening stanza, as between these lines and the solemn ending, Donne describes himself in images of submission and constraint that prepare for the fully humble offering to God of himself wrapped in purple. The passages through "streights and none but streights" point the way home. It is the only way, says Donne. He explores the straits of fever and illness as he lies "flat on this bed";

he submits himself to his physicians, as though himself a map, and the images that establish integration and foreshadow full union after the rite of passage tumble forth—images in which West and East are one, Calvary and Paradise joined, the first Adam (who brought death) juxtaposed with the "second Adam" who brought life. For Donne, death becomes tamed as the way or passage to life.

In the final stanza, Donne suggests again that the loneliness and suffering of the preparation will prepare him for the union and the joy of the crown, that he will take his place with the saints after passing through the crucifixion of death:

> So, in his purple wrapp'd receive mee Lord,
> By these his thornes give me his other Crowne;
> And as to other soules I preach'd thy word,
> Be this my Text, my Sermon to mine owne,
> Therefore that he may raise the Lord throws down.
>
> (11.26–30)

The imagery throughout the poem is that of the seemingly disparate: Donne in his shroud binding together the two worlds of flesh and spirit. Through the old macrocosm-microcosm principle he makes of himself as he lies on his sickbed a flat map that draws together all the places of the world by subsuming them under his situation. At the same time all of these metaphors of integration are focused upon preparation for death and the last agonizing journey to joy.

Throughout the whole, the tone is devotional and meditative, the sufferings all brought under "the tuning of the soul" that he has referred to in stanza one. But the emphasis on suffering again reminds us of the pilgrimage and Turner's process of change. In these great hymns as well as in the sermons of his last years, Donne submits to the straits because he is about to become one with the great "Quire of Saints," as he tells us. The rest for his proud intellect comes in the joyful oneness with *societas* where all tears will be "wiped forever from his eyes" and where his restless insistent self will both lose and find itself in God's perpetual music.

10

The Angry Voice of Lamentation and Its Place in the Articulation of Comfort

Alas, alas, the joye of our heart is ceased: our
dance is turned into
mourning: The crown is fallen from our head: Woe
unto us. . . .[1]

Although it may seem an interruption of the discussion of the poetics of comfort explored in the images, events, and words of John
Donne, lamentation and grief are major expressive concerns that
deserve special analysis. They are important because they distin-
guish the articulation of mourning and comfort in the seventeenth
century from that in the twentieth. Twentieth-century readers are
inevitably struck by the intensity of some of the language of grief
found in early modern English documents. Although English culture in general leans toward understatement in comparison with
Italian or Spanish culture, on this *topos* expression seems particularly bold and explicit, and one wonders why such language is not
more likely to point toward despair than toward comfort.

The place of lamentation in the lifelong rituals of preparation,
mourning, and comfort by which seventeenth-century English culture faced death can be seen throughout the literature of the period.
It is that aspect of the whole that modern people can understand
least. Upon first glance the lament seems not to belong in the fundamentally Christian process by which the horrifying presence of
death in seventeenth-century life was tamed by poets and priests
alike, as we saw in Donne's last works. The powerful rawness of
expression in Zachary Boyd's source for the "Queens Lamentations," the Lamentations of Jeremiah, strikes the modern imagination as fundamentally pagan, in spite of its place in biblical
canon. From a strictly logical perspective it is inconsistent with
the elaborate series of rites, religious and devotional, that the
seventeenth-century person (writer or even ordinary Christian)

must go through to arrive at the appropriate integration of life and death within the Christian system.

The paradoxical relationship between lament and comfort, however, is of central importance in analyzing the elaborate attitudes governing mourning. This essay will focus therefore upon two examples of the literature of grief: first the more contained instance of the expression of grief by a preacher, William Fuller, in a sermon for Frances Lady Clifton, the wife of a prominent parishioner who died young; and, second, the more radical and poetic expression of grief in the concentrated form of a "Biblical" lament by Zachary Boyd, entitled "The Queenes Lamentations." Both appeared in the last five years of the 1620s, at the end of the period we are examining.

Angry images of a broken body and a broken life suggest that the grief with which one encounters death remains, in spite of all conventional comforts, ultimately unbearable. What modern critics within a society that represses death so radically as ours cannot see is the greater health of the society that fully articulates the myriad emotions that arise from the most mysterious event in human existence. For the products of modern technological society the end seems to deny the whole thrust of life—its many efforts to protect itself and project its progeny into an ongoing and unbroken line. They must, within this context, eat their fear and anger, or, in psychological terms, repress it. In contrast, in the mind of the seventeenth century and in the face of the shock of mortality as it strikes those they love and, more devastatingly, themselves, what becomes necessary is the healing power of reassuring ritual and, for persons in early modern England, the newly framed deeper healing of the full range of emotional language.

As Renaissance humanists and rhetoricians realized, the psychology of healing through language was the psychology of expression. In this view, the full range of emotions must be structured into forms that allowed expression of all the conflicting feelings and thoughts surrounding death and grief. Within the verbal culture of England, at the moment when language was becoming dominant over ritual, the *Book of Common Prayer,* for instance, was just as important (perhaps more so) as the liturgical drama it encompassed. A similar cultural movement was occurring in the Italian Renaissance, according to George McClure in an important modern essay. Perhaps in the largest sense the Reformation itself heralded a privileging of verbal religious forms over the symbolic actions and musical chants of ancient ritual. In the face of the gradual desacralizing of liturgy, it became essential to develop or sustain verbal forms that contained the full power of grief as well as to develop rational forms to embody the elaborate symbolism of Christian attitudes toward death.

In the study of death in seventeenth-century culture, it is useful to remind readers of the paradoxical fit of various facets in the multi-layered response to death of English persons in that period. Attitudes toward death were complex. The key to understanding them is to see them within a process that cultivates and articulates feelings so as to move through fear, anger, grief, and hope to a sense of ultimate harmony—what the seventeenth-century person would have seen as faith, what we saw in the last chapter on Donne as that tuning of the instrument of the soul. Obviously, the ideal was seldom, if ever, realized, but the goal of harmony was often asserted, as we may see from our two examples from different social worlds within English life: first, that of the funeral sermon honoring Frances Clifton; and second, the poem of lamentation for the death of the son of Elizabeth Stuart, briefly Queen of Bohemia.

In Praise of Lady Clifton: "Comfortable Words"

Frances Clifton was unable to speak by the time she arrived at her final hour. William Fuller, the family friend and preacher who delivered her commemorative sermon, reports that he and a second minister present at her deathbed prayed continually in her behalf while she made signs of response until even her memory failed her. She had, however, completed her preparation that morning and, when she died in the midst of one of the prayers, her earlier cry: "Farewell vaine earth, I embrace thee: Heaven" was a little emblem of her good dying. It was also a point of comfort and praise in her eulogy for the articulation of mourning in the sermon.[2] Arnold Stein in *The House of Death* comments on such claims:

> Where doctrine, or the relationship of self to the dead other, is less exacting, the subject remains more open and flexible—as in poems memorializing the death of public or private figures, or even friends. The necessary claims of lament, praise, and consolation must all be satisfied, but . . . lament and consolation tend to be subordinated to the memorializing by praise.[3]

In the early seventeenth-century eulogies within sermons, memorializing praise dominates lament and consolation in an immediate sense. But overarching the funeral sermon as a whole is a meditational purpose that has as its end instruction of the congregation. On the complex level of mourning the aim is transformational. Through a working out of the process of mourning in the sermon, the preacher is shaping a form designed to bring consolation to the mourners; both praise and lament interlace throughout the sermon to bring comfort. Whatever the means by which the preacher articulates these aspects of mourning, he does not achieve his end until the congregation experiences a diminution of grief and an acceptance of the peace of God that release them into the future. How this process works through lament, praise, and comfort in Lady Clifton's sermon is the subject of this section on funeral lamentation because it illustrates the complex process of mourning and the way in which the funeral sermon helps to structure it.

Grief of the mourners is, of course, not at an end after the funeral sermon (for instance, there may be several funeral and commemorative sermons as well as actual continuing grief), but there is a microcosm of the anguish that, having occurred once, recurs in waves, ideally receding a bit further each time until full healing has taken place. As Fuller demonstrates in his commemorative sermon for Francis Clifton, the experience of peace and comfort rises at the end of the sermon, after the eulogy. The culminating focus upon the image of Frances and her death becomes an important instrument for transforming the grief of the mourners over the death itself into a more serene sorrow for her absence. The modern reader senses at this point a need to analyze the articulation of the elements through which the transformation is accomplished: lament, praise, and promise.

Throughout the structure of the sermon the congregation has received the assurance that the promises of Christian reconciliation are satisfied in the memorialized life and death of the beloved. When the preacher moves from the eulogy to the final lines of the commemorative or funeral sermon, he usually reminds the congregation of the peace and comfort that only result from the empathetic process of mourning through the sermon form. Toward the last few lines of the sermon for Lady Clifton, Fuller says: "And thus our cedar is fallen; If such a fall bee not an exaltation rather, for it shall bee my ambition to liue so, that I may die so . . . what remayneth is but a generall sorrow, not for her, but for our selues" (sig.F3). The quotation embodies three effects of the full integration of the elements: through the description of Lady Clifton's release into heaven, the sorrow is gentled; secondly, it is no longer attached to the dead, but distributed among the congregation; thirdly, the life and death portrayed become a model for the mourners as well as for the preacher.

This sermon is one of two commemorative sermons for women preached in 1627 by two major preachers in England, the poet-preacher John Donne and the increasingly well-known preacher William Fuller, who had received a doctorate from Cambridge in 1625. Both were mature members of their profession: Donne was only four years from his death, and Fuller was at that time already forty-seven years old. As we saw earlier in the Donne chapter, Donne was kept from Lady Danvers's funeral by other obligations in London; I have not been able to find the reason Fuller did not preach until a few weeks after Lady Clifton's death. At any rate Sir Gervase asked Fuller to preach the commemorative sermon (he had done one also for Sir Gervase's first wife). Fuller's sermon was entitled "The Mourning of Mt. Lebanon" or "The Temple's Teares" and is the primary focus for the speculation of this section.[4]

There are, however, several parallels between the two sermons that reinforce the examination of Fuller's for Lady Clifton. Donne was then the Dean of St. Paul's and Fuller was later promoted to the deanery of Ely in 1636. Later yet (in the inauspicious year of 1645) he was appointed Dean of Durham Cathedral by Charles I. His sermon was published in 1625, however, well before he found full recognition, and it was dedicated to his local patron Sir Gervase Clifton of Nottingham in honor of his second wife, who had died from complications of childbirth.[5] As we have seen, Donne's sermon was in memory of Lady Danvers, formerly Magdalen Herbert.[6]

One notices expecially the comparable quality of these two sermons preached in the same year by men of considerable talent, learning, and experience. Both were king's men and bishop's men in the range of positions still within Anglicanism. Both stood with Hooker on most theological matters, supporting both the authority of Scripture and of tradition. This of course meant support for a sacramental religion; Fuller praises Lady Clifton for her frequent feeding of the soul with the eucharist.

More specifically for our topic, both sermons belong to a tradition of mourning that found its greatest expression in English prose in the funeral sermons of the seventeenth century. Why this subgenre should have flourished in the first half of the seventeenth century and why especially good examples of it lie among the twenty-three sermons for women published between 1600 and 1630 become a rewarding focus for reflection.[7] The answers to both questions owe much to the importance of death and the articulation of mourning in the seventeenth century through many verbal forms: Christian humanist letters, elegies, devotions, sermons, eulogies—all in a period when an overall shift from ritual to verbal expression of religious feeling was stimulating the best minds among British writers, including Anglican preachers.[8] The power of ritual, however moderated in the Anglican liturgy, found an analogous function in the dogma of the period.[9] Lady Clifton, for instance, is described by Fuller toward the end of her eulogy in a manner that reflects the warring conflict between Satan and his demons and the forces of God for the soul of the dying:

> My selfe and another Minister (that came in that perplexity) continually solliciting his Diuine Maiesty for mercy, vntill in the middest of one of my prayers, in which I desired him to giue his Angels charge ouer her, in that her agonie against sinne and Sathan, she departed. . . . (36)

In the quotation Fuller is at her deathbed with another minister continually praying for Lady Clifton when she no longer has the strength to pray for herself. This is part of the tradition, especially as elaborated by people like Becon in the sixteenth century. Behind this statement is the even older legend of Satan assaulting the soul of the dying in the weakness of the last illness, but the details of the five temptations and the five inspirations from God's angels, saints, and holy ones are largely in the background. Here the shift occurs from an emphasis upon the largely allegorical portrayal of every man's death surrounded by forces of damnation and redemption to an emphasis upon the death of a particular woman. Nevertheless the scene is still layered with suggestions of those large cosmic forces, and the text moves between the mimetic surface and traces of the larger play between judgment and redemption, just as it moves between particular and type.[10]

This duality of style enriches the tradition of the art of dying in the sixteenth and early seventeenth centuries: theological icons interacting with the emergence of greater personality.[11] Set within the conventions of the tradition, at least for those non-Puritan Anglicans within James's church who included in their sermons a eulogy, the mirror of the life was increasingly elaborated as both a narrative of a type of Christian dying and the portrayal of the death of a particular human model.[12] The extreme Puritan response was to omit the eulogy entirely, but most Anglicans between 1600 and 1630 took a middle way and conflated selected details from the individual life with a portrait of the type of ideal Christian dying.

Another reason for the excellence of these two sermons was undoubtedly the more unusual nature of the women for whom the funeral sermons were preached. Since far more sermons for men were published in the period, the ones for women that found a larger audience through publication inevitably came from talented preachers and demonstrably focused upon women with both unusual social connections and unusual spiritual qualities. As we see in the discussion in the Donne chapter, Lady Danvers was a high-born and intelligent woman. Her life as the mother of several distinguished Herberts and finally as wife of the young Danvers who was knighted by James I indicates that she had dimensions that went beyond the distinction of her relationships.[13]

Lady Clifton was less obviously distinguished, but Fuller creates a rich context in the sermon as well as in the eulogy. That she died of the complications of childbirth suggests that she had less in the way of empirical support for her life as a model of spiritual leadership, although Fuller makes a lot of her prayer life and the leadership of her ladies in devotional directions. She was neither as old as Lady Danvers nor was she engaged in encouraging such events of spiritual assertion as the Childewell Riots, behind which contemporaries saw the radically Puritan hand of Katherine Brettergh, a somewhat earlier example of a woman for whom funeral sermons were published.[14] Lady Clifton had not had time to develop a life that would stand out for its achievements, and her piously Anglican life as young wife and mother was unlikely to lead her into the encouragement of any kind of violence, even for the sake of principle.

It is most in her eulogy that Fuller asserts her outstanding characteristics as a woman. Still, a characteristic of the eulogy was that it focused more on the good dying than on the details of the life. In some sense the fact of her early death gives Lady Clifton a more poignant image than a long life of accomplishment would have contributed. It is the death of the young, after all, that moves us most to grief in every age.

In the sermon for Lady Clifton the transformational power of the final consolation has most to do with the tension between lamentation and comfort. The modulation of that tension produced a strong sense of rhetorical movement within the sermon form. Like many paradoxes that came out of medieval orders of experience into the Renaissance sense of reality, lamentation and comfort had the potentiality of becoming disparate and contradictory. As essential parts of the articulation of mourning, they might have become increasingly discrete.

In the funeral sermon particularly, however, there is an inevitable emphasis on bringing the disparate elements of experience, includ-

ing, of course, the paradoxes of religious experience, chief among
them life and death or life out of death, into a final harmony of comfort that reassures the congregation of an ordered and coherent
creation ordained by a loving God. What after all is the final comfort? In addition to the more particular one of heavenly and external
existence for the dying and those who follow, surely equally important is the comforting idea that all the strange and painful parts
of fallen temporal life are capable of being drawn into a coherent
faith in God's providence. Death, after all, was the supreme instance
of that which seemed on the surface to be an unacceptable fact of
existence under a just and loving God. But since the terrifying response to the Black Death and to later recurrences of the plague,
the tradition had developed rational and ritual modes that brought
about containment of fear. In the early seventeenth century particularly, the link between sin and death was experienced with Calvinist
intensity, and ways of containing fear and providing comfort seem
to dominate the devotional tradition.

Lady Clifton's comforting eulogy, for example, needs to be
viewed within the articulation of comfort in the sermon as a whole.
Fuller's sermon is itself the beginning of a long lament that ultimately brings comfort. The powerful text with its allegorizing of the
destruction of the cedar of Lebanon has deep roots in Old Testament lamentation. Seventeenth-century people were especially
fond of the types of lament and grieving that their scriptural tradition brought to them. For instance, we all know the popularity of
the Psalms with their personal lyrical lamentations, but it is not so
commonly known that the Lamentations of Jeremiah were the second most frequently translated book of the Bible.[15] One wonders,
for instance, if the Old Testament stories and language did not find
a ready vacuum in the loss of saints' legends by which people had
found a human bridge to the divine. Fuller makes his sermon work
for him in the context of that resonant grieving by using Old Testament metaphors and narratives thoughout:

"Howle thou firre tree, for the Cedar is fallen" (sig.B) is the text
from Zechariah (11:13), and within the first paragraph he develops
the desolation of Jerusalem over the destruction of the cedar:

> how she that was so great among the nations, the princesse among the
> provinces, was becoming tributary, weeping continually, even in the
> night, and the teares running downe her cheekes . . . all crying the joy
> of our hearts is gone. (sig.B$_r$)

From the beginning of the sermon where he sets the tone of an-

guish with the raw grief of the word *howl* Fuller sets forth three
major questions that foreshadow a way out of the first stage of grief
into a gentler sorrow. Paraphrased, the questions are the following:

1) Why use the word *howl*, a word that suggests grief without
   measure?
2) Why should a child of God mourn so when we are told not to
   sorrow without hope?
3) And finally—why grieve over a tree that is to be part of the
   glorious sanctuary? (2)

The questions suggest the directions by which the preacher will
transform the grieving into comfort. Fuller skillfully begins with the
"howl," the rage of grief, and in the exposure of it releases some of
its power. The basic theological justification is assumed as always
in the period to be the link between sin and its consequences; suffering and death entering the world by human sin and disobedience—
death, of course, the icon of sin's consequences. One of Fuller's
examples is that supreme model of Christ mourning: "And Jesus
wept"(5). He emphasizes that Jesus was not grieving for Lazarus
(whom he knew he would almost immediately raise up) but for the
shattering ways in which death is the sign of sin in the world: "Woe
unto us that we have sinned" (5).

This gloomy focus on the fallen nature of creation shifts with the
second question as Fuller insists that Christians must not mourn
without hope. This is an important biblical text for the period. Literature in England between 1590 and 1610 reflects the controversy
over mourning. Pious Puritans within the Anglican Church were
saying, as Pigman has pointed out, that mourning is merely a selfish
indulgence and that love for the dead should cause one to rejoice in
her having escaped the suffering of temporal life. Hamlet, for example, is chastened by both Claudius and Gertrude for excessive grief
for his father; it is also clear in *Twelfth Night* that Feste sees the
absurdity in Olivia's insistence that she will continue to mourn her
brother's death for eight years. Jonson's epigrams for his small son
and daughter also are said to reflect the rigorist attitudes. Most Anglicans, however, believed with St. Paul that mourning was necessary but should be moderate within Christian assumptions.
Although the promise is most fully revealed in Christ's cross and
resurrection, Fuller integrates grief and hope by stressing the human crosses, human sorrows, as means of tempering the heart.
Tears themselves he praises as a means of evaporating sorrow:

"Sure griefe oftimes is like fire, the more it is covered, the more dangerously it burneth"(9).

After many types of mercy are brought forth to support the Pauline doctrine that Christians must not "sorrow without hope" nor mourn as the Pagans, Fuller moves to the lyrically powerful last question. Here he denies the necessity of the *howl*. Don't lament the death of the body; one should only lament the death of the soul. It is in this section that the sermon moves to affirm spiritual continuity and the joyful anticipation of it in this particular case: "Cedars . . . were to be transplanted from the hill of Lebanon to the Sanctuary of God" (20). This allegory of the Cedars becoming part of the temple and therefore part of the new Jerusalem is the great promise of heaven. Then he moves from the biblical text to apply it to the lady being mourned: he will "relate with griefe how our Cedar is fallen" (23).

Here the eulogy becomes the culmination of the sermon: the glass through which the congregation sees the applied context of the instruction. The mourners have already been prepared through a theological context to see in this life and death a model for the transformation of grief into acceptance. As he says, "Saynts are not to be lamented as lost, but beloved as absent" (19). Love informs sorrow. He praises Lady Clifton's parents and her background as producing great stock, a flourishing branch. The memorializing praise or encomium is very clear in this section. She possessed all the desirable qualities for which women were praised: courtesy, rationality, conversation, charity, a balance of seriousness and humor, some historical and humane education, but primarily knowledge of religion and God's law. Like St. Paul, she suffered from some "long infirmity" (26) from her childhood, and she prepared daily for death: "she never went to her bed but as to her grave" (p. 27).

In her roles as daughter, wife, mother, mistress to servants, neighbor, she was saintly: fair, disciplined, a peacemaker. In her relation to God she was burning with inward zeal but was outwardly calm. Up at five she began her prayers, and later she and her women went to chapel. It is, however, in her dying that Fuller best mingles the arousal of sorrow and the memorializing praise. Notice the *softening* of sorrow—Old Testament images of *grief* have largely disappeared.

What were the differences between the "good death" for this woman and the "good death" for a man? Obviously in the atmosphere of increasing partriarchy encouraged by Protestant influences, the two genders are praised for different qualities. In these sermons published for women, undoubtedly the two virtues that are most gender-based were submissiveness to husband and motherly concern for children. Lip service is usually paid to chastity and obedience, and frequently no mention is made of silence either. In the Fuller sermon none of the three is explicitly mentioned. In fact, as one may see, reason, *discourse,* and judicious mirth are complimented in Lady Clifton:

> She was a woman full of noble curtesies, eyther when shee did visit others, or herself was visited . . . .One that knew her distance in truth of reason . . . judicious in all discourse beyond the degree of her sex yet pleasant to; interlacing Mirth with ernest . . .

Insofar as communal contribution was concerned, her role as woman dictated motherly love and discipline. Secondly, like most of the eulogies for women, this one praises the giving of charity to the poor, but men also were praised for this virtue. At one point in the sermon, biblical types of morality are invoked in her praise.

Having had a dream before she went into labor, she foresaw her death and accepted it, so prepared was she. Although her labor was difficult, there was some hope that she would recover, but that was not to be. She is reported to have followed all the parts of a good death. She called her husband, took leave, prayed for him, and blessed her children. She took her little one in her arms and prayed he might be like his noble grandfather. Then she turned to all surrounding her bed (death was very communal in those days) and prayed for everyone's welfare and comfort.

In the morning before she died Fuller says that she professed her faith and was absolved by the minister. After that she slept; the ministers prayed; she died. At this point, Fuller again expresses sorrow, but he mingles joy for the departed and sorrow for the mourners. The tone has subtly changed.

By now the articulation of the funereal stage of mourning is complete, when the congregation is reassured of the translation of Frances into God's hands. The mourners are sent forth with sorrow no longer for the dead but for themselves. Fuller closes the sermon then with a prayer for those present that shifts the concern to the future: "God in his infinite mercy grant grace in our lives, pardon at our deaths and after both the fruition of his blessed vision. Amen."

What we have seen in the eulogy is the complex articulation of the elements of mourning. The tone has gradually shifted from the heavy rage against death as focused on the dying into the gentler sorrow for the living who miss them. Praise for the life has played a crucial part by giving meaning to existence: "grace in our lives," says Fuller in the prayer. The underlining of pardon promised at our deaths with the "fruition of his blessed vision" is of course the supreme promise in Lady Clifton's mirrored dying. But the subtlest form of comfort comes from having braided shared grief and lament throughout with praise until at last the *howl* of the initial text has been transformed into *benediction*.

When we turn to the second example of lamentation—words put into the mouth of Elizabeth of Bohemia upon the loss of her eldest son—we see a much simpler expression of pure grief. The sermon form of Fuller presented the grievers for Lady Clifton with an interweaving of lament, praise, and the traditional comforts that clearly transforms the grief for the death into an experience of the grace and benediction of the continuing life of Frances. The progressive rhetoric of the sermon, then, provides a microcosm of the process of mourning and softens the place of lament within it. Moderns, although probably moved by the power of the *howl* metaphor, would be able to overlook the grief and move quickly into the comfort. Not so for the more truncated form of the biblical lament in Boyd for the death of a royal child.

The Queenes Lamentations

Boyd's lament, based on both event and word (the document also contains verbal images), was for the historic death of Frederick, son of the daughter of James I, and was published as expressive of the grief of the mother. This lamentation is a vivid instance of one of the bolder stages of response within a fully expressive culture. It also represents the peak of refinement that the art of dying had reached—so as to include not so much the elaborate articulation of fear and comfort embedded in the Lady Clifton sermon but rather to contain the bitter anguish that was appropriate to mourning within the most sophisticated class in Britain. The fundamental preparation of the art of dying that was so strong in the late Middle Ages and through the last half of the sixteenth century was expanding into greater focus on the art of comfort.

The "Queenes Lamentations for *the death of her Son*," part of prefatory materials in Zachary Boyd's 1,200-page *ars moriendi* tract, was published in 1629. It is essentially a psalm of lament from the point of view of a mother, in partial imitation of Chapter 3 of the Book of Lamentations. Little known among scholars and somewhat obscured by the tedious theologizing of Boyd's tract, the inserted lament provides a window into rhetorical and ritual conventions of seventeenth-century mourning and explores a corner of parental grief in the period. In his book on grief Pigman says that the lament in Boyd would have seemed immoderate to sixteenth-century mourners.[16] It seems almost shocking to twentieth-century ones. In spite of radical historical differences between images of childhood and surrounding family structures in the seventeenth and the twentieth centuries, however, at the center of the "Queenes Lamentations" is the profound grief of a queen mother for the death of her child, an experience shared in some degree by both centuries.

Although this lament for the death of an eldest son is particularized by at least the royalty of the actors involved, it evokes on the symbolic level a specter of the universal figure of death and grief nearly omnipresent to European and English families in the Renaissance.[17] Frederick, son of Elizabeth Stuart and her husband, Elector of Palatine and briefly King of Bohemia, was fourteen in 1627 at the time of his death. As historians have told us, infant mortality was extremely high during the period, but parents of any class would perhaps have expected that a child who had reached fourteen would have had a good chance of survival.[18] A son, therefore, on the far edge of childhood, just beginning to display the potentialities of the adult (indeed at the time of his death on a fishing trip with his father) becomes an especially poignant instance of the loss of the young. The context of the boating accident in which Frederick died makes the situation resonate with sadness by its dramatizing of human helplessness in the face of the powers of the sea. Parallel inklings of the overwhelming sense of helplessness experienced by a parent's facing the loss of a child are foregrounded by Ozment in his work *Magdalene and Balthazar,* with its account from the merchant class of the death of the couple's only child in an earlier time.[19]

The Boyd text comes out of a specific historical situation that also underlines the themes of grief and lament. The devotional work, *The Last Battell of the Soule in Death,* was articulated in two volumes, the first of which was dedicated to Queen Henrietta Maria and the second to Elizabeth Stuart, which included the lament for her son put into the mouth of Elizabeth, daughter of James I and briefly Queen of Bohemia. Zachary Boyd was a member of the important family of Scottish intellectuals that included Robert Boyd, chancellor of the University of Edinburgh. Boyd had spent a number of years in France but returned to Glasgow, where he developed as a theologian and writer of devotional literature.[20] Boyd's book belongs to the family of *ars moriendi* tracts we have examined in some detail that were descended from the block-books developed in the late fifteenth century as a tradition of comfort to counter the

"The Inspiration against Despair." No. 4, *Ars moriendi*. Notice the difference in style from the series at both the Huntington and the British Library. There obviously remains a great similarity in iconography in this woodcut #10123. Permission to reprint is from the John Rylands Library, The University of Manchester.

frightening images of the Dance of Death that emerged from the devastation of the Black Death in the fourteenth century.[21] The particular set of circumstances made it an appropriate document for dedication. Elizabeth's own tragic history as a wife and mother belied her romantic wedding to Frederick the Elector of Palatine just before Lent in 1613. Her marriage itself had probably been hastened to provide the English people with an image of a happy future after the death of the Prince of Wales, but now some years later she was facing the same loss that her own parents had suffered.

Another informative context for the structure and content of the "Queenes Lamentations" is the literature of grief referred to in the Lady Clifton section, especially that which focuses upon the death of the young and the response of the parent.[22] *Grief and the English Renaissance Elegy* is the most helpful treatment of this context. Its author Pigman draws several conclusions from the study of grief in the second half of the sixteenth and early seventeenth centuries. He cites a tension in the elegiac form between lament and praise; the most widely accepted idea by critics has been that in the form praise is dominant and that grief should be suppressed.[23] Pigman argues a cultural modulation from the 1570s when many English poets and devotional writers saw grief as a pagan attitude that good Christians would stoically repress. However, Pigman believes that by the end of the century a complex set of attitudes had also emerged that valued mourning as a part of process of comfort.[24] He cites Menander's justication of lament as one of the influences on Renaissance thinking. Menander does not at all think that lament undermines praise in the elegy; indeed he sees the praise as material to the lament and, perhaps more important to my argument in this essay, the lament as preparation for consolation.[25] In the seventeenth century, however, two contrasting attitudes persist: the justification of a moderate grief as part of the full process of comfort and the concurrent rigorism of a Ben Jonson that harks back to the 1570s.

So-called rigorists exaggerated the Christian notion that no really loving survivors should grieve over their loved ones' having celebrated a birthday into the eternity. Most Christians, although disapproving of excessive mourning, seemed to interpret St. Paul's statement that we mourn "not as the pagans" to mean that mourning within the restraints of Christian faith is necessary. In short, the main-line position supported moderate mourning. It was generally recognized, as it is today, that denial of grief can be harmful, as Shakespeare says in *Titus Andronicus:*

Sorrow concealed, like an oven stopped,
Doth burn the heart to cinders where it is.

(II.iv.36–37)

Most positively, Puttenham is the writer who explicitly points out that the elegiac poet, by identifying with the grief of the bereaved, ministers both to others and mysteriously to his own sorrows.[26] It becomes a commonplace to see lament as beneficial to comfort. The function of lament as part of the process of mourning is essential, then, both to the cultural understanding of Renaissance attitudes toward grieving and death and also the literary understanding of the elegy.

What has perhaps caused greatest misunderstanding for modern readers is the exaggerated idealization of the praise of the dead and the resulting exaggeration of the images of sorrow. By now modern critics seem to have overcome their tendency to link the exaggeration with insincerity and to accept the possibility that the eulogists and elegists empathized with the grief of the bereaved even when not personally attached to the deceased. That the empathy seemed to be unfortunately linked to the patronage system was a corruption that did not escape the sharp eyes of seventeenth-century persons as well as our own. The number of elegies addressed to grieving monarchs or other powerful people raised questions of sincerity even then; by 1638 W. Towers speaks scathingly of "You that sell Tears," and Donne was criticized for his own desperate desire for reward in The Anniversaries.[27]

The death of Prince Henry in 1612 is a documented historical event that indicates in some measure how grief was accommodated to culture and to individuals. History has not preserved much personal material on the responses of the royal parents, but the "funerals" or ceremonies that were so frequently offered to the parents by those who also sought their patronage reveal in their number alone the power of the event. They are almost too complex a set of documents for the limits of this essay.[28] In the mass of descriptive material available, however, what is of most interest in this context is the modulation of lament and comfort within the funeral. Such a process supports the parallel that ultimately develops in the poetic tradition, by which lament and comfort become articulated within an embedded narrative of the elegiac structure.

When Joseph Hall in 1612 addressed the grieving Stuart royal family as the last speaker at the *funeralia* (properly in the plural) of Prince Henry, he moved the funeral mood from lamentation to the comfort of solemn joy. That is not to say that his language abandoned the expression of grief. On the contrary, at the beginning of his sermon the words reverberate with appropriate sorrow for the cruel cutting down of the Prince at only eighteen years. Hall reminded the congregation of the special pain attached to the loss of so much earthly promise in the death of the Prince of Wales and future king. For a people whose historical consciousness had been dominated in the sixteenth century by the need of England for a male heir, the loss of James's eldest son, already being compared to Henry V, must have had a special anguish.

As far as grief is concerned, Hall is not one of the so-called rigorists; unlike the poet Jonson, he does not try to suppress the grief of family and friends—not even to contain it carefully in poetic understatement.[29] On the contrary, he affirms the propriety of lament to the grieving family and insists that death must have its due in lamentation:

> O Henry our sweet Prince, our sweet Prince Henry, the second glory of our nation, ornament of mankinde, hope of posterity and life of our life, how do all hearts bleed, and all eies worthily gush out for thy loss . . . Yet I could not but touch our sore (with this light hand) tho yet raw and bleeding: Death *(especially such a death) must have sorrow and teares.* (462, emphasis mine)

Like his contemporary John Donne, who preached a great sermon on the text *And Jesus Wept,* Hall recognized the need for grief and its modes of expression as a stage in the process of comfort. He avoided the conventional stoic arguments for comfort—the pressure to rejoice over the dead one's escape of this life's misery, and he did not try to leap over sorrow into joy. Rather, he carefully articulated several stages of emotion. George Chapman, the poet, in his little book on the funerals of Henry, makes it clear that they moved from the depths of mourning to this consolatory statement.

Chapman supports the sense of somber mourning in his description of the elaborate ritual practice for Henry, still, by the way, part of funeral custom at the death of Mary Stuart in 1694. For instance, he describes the draping of four chambers in black; the bed chamber of his Highness was draped in black velvet, in the midst of which was set up a canopy of black velvet over trestles upon which was set the coffin, itself covered by a large pall of black velvet and adorned with scutcheons of Henry's arms. Such practice points to the extreme way in which royal rituals embody the general attitudes of the culture. In some deep sense in the first third of the seventeenth century, both language and Anglican liturgy were acting together powerfully to articulate mourning. The funeral procession and the funeral sermon became those public statements that were owed to the living if the frequency of death was to be accommodated in seventeenth-century life.[30] Especially in the instances of the deaths of the young, the raw grief of lamentation required every available ritual comfort, including modes to express lamentation itself. Obviously, royalty possessed the means for the most elaborate rituals.

But by the seventeenth century, the private voice, the inner voice of grieving, in contrast to liturgical act and practice, was crucial. The expression of that complex and paradoxical emphasis may be seen in the intensity of grief expressed in "The Queenes Lamentation." The text contains a number of metaphors that present grief in the boldest and harshest way imaginable, largely as physical pain that somehow must be expressed to be dealt with. Addressing God, the Queen as speaker says,

> My flesh and my skinne hath he made olde, hee hath broken my bones: Hee hath builded against mee, and compassed me with gall and travell: He hath set mee in dark places, as they that bee dead of olde: He hath hedged mee about that I cannot get out: Hee hath made my chaine heauie: Hee hath turned aside my wayes, and pulled mee in pieces. (sig. A6–A6$_v$)

In these lines, the images present the initial experience of grief as literal blows to the body. The lamenter speaks of God as having broken her bones and pulled her in pieces—among slightly less vivid pains. Later in the passage, she cites Job 39.14 to separate herself from the ostrich who leaves her eggs on the ground, forgetful of the natural dangers to them. The point she makes with biblical borrowings, of course, is the greater responsibility and deeper understanding of the human mother that create this overwhelming grief for the loss of a child.

In both the rhetorical structure of the lamentation and in the materials within it, Elizabeth Stuart as poetic voice (or Boyd as author) is not original in any modern sense. The "Lamentations" is an "imitation," according to common seventeenth-century practice, of biblical poetic lamentation or elegy, with an overlay of classical allusion. The first major section, from which the lines cited above are taken, is a direct borrowing from the King James version of the Lamentations of Jeremiah, after the Psalms one of the most frequently translated books of the Old Testament.[31] Scholars are well aware of the many translations of the Psalms, parallel in popularity to the translations of Petrarch, but they are less aware of the poetic attempts to adapt other sections of the Bible. Both Donne and Michael Drayton were among those who a decade or so earlier had tried their hand at the verse translation of Lamentations.[32] In the lament, however, there is no attempt at English versifying, only at poetic prose that in its rhythms, repetitions, and metaphor is fundamentally biblical or Hebraic poetry.[33] This section sets the tone for the whole.

Much of the document suggests the way in which Puritans, particularly, conflated or integrated biblical types. The great Protestant preacher William Perkins, for example, in his *Salve for a Sicke Manne* lists the last words spoken at virtually every death in the Bible as part of a discussion of the "last words" of the deathbed.[34] Donne, writing later and more selectively in his Anglicanism, usually limited himself to fewer examples of the biblical typology—examples treated in greater detail.[35] "The Queenes Lamentations" is dominated in the opening section by a literal borrowing from Chapter 3 of Lamentations. Throughout, not only Jeremiah was used but also passages from the Psalms of lament and from Job. The author is obviously pulling together types of grieving from the Old Testament. As one might expect, David's lament for Absalom (adapted to the present situation) becomes the great emotional culmination of the several types or expressions involved.

All the passages here are not simply listed but are integrated into a single point of view. The entire poem is concentrated on grief; the text does not hint at the comfort of resurrection that one finds in Job nor does it conflate the classical elegy with biblical redemptive assumptions, as in Milton's later elegy "Lycidas." In addition to the typological combination of lament materials from the Bible, the piece reflects the particular adaptation of the materials to the current events of the individual life; there are references in the drowning passage to the Daughters of Britain (Like the Daughters of Jerusalem), to Bohemia and the Palatinate, and, of course, to Frederick, the name of the dead son. It is largely through the sectional structuring of the lament and the catalog of pain, however, that all the borrowings are interwoven to form a powerfully affective poetic monologue.

Four sections comprise the "Lamentations," with some biblical parallels in the marginalia that articulate the grief. The first section describes the terrible consequences of having been punished or attacked by an angry God: "O But God is most terrible, when hee is angrie, He hath called as a solemn day my terrors round about . . . " (sig. A6). Rhetorically the first section shocks the reader into the agony of the speaker. The chapter from which it comes functions in the Book of Lamentations as a personal Psalm of Lament that parallels and ultimately flows into the communal framework of the writings of Jeremiah. These writings mourn the destruction of the temple at Jerusalem and thereby by correspondence the city and the people themselves.[36]

After the personal lament with its catalog of images of pain and grief, the "Queenes Lamentations" moves closer to the particular historical situation with an apostrophe to the "Noble Ladies of Britain." In this section, the speaker addresses both the "Ladies of Britain" and "Bohemia and the Palatinate," calling upon Elizabeth's world to mourn, to put on "Robes of dole," as Zachariah describes the mourning for Josiah. After the address to the community, however, the text moves back to a third litany of lament, returning to the physical images that describe the assault of grief upon the body of the mourner:

> My bowels are troubled, my Liuer is powered upon the earth: I was at ease, but hee hath broken mee asunder: Hee hath also taken mee by the necke and shaken mee to pieces . . . (sig. A7ᵥ)

"On my eye-lids is the shadow of death" (sig. A8), the speaker says toward the end of the section, with the foreknowledge of personal mortality that comes so strongly to those who have experienced grief over the sudden death of a beloved. The poem continues with a reference to the loss of glory and the crown and a final plea to friends to have pity. The last few lines of section three show the Queen's pathetic attempt to find support in a community that she probably feels has failed her, and they also remind the reader of the political difficulties of Elizabeth, already exiled from Bohemia and oppressed by what was to be the Thirty Years War.

In the final section of what is essentially a Psalm, the speaker addresses her son directly. In the long history of grief, the address to the absent one—one who no longer answers—must surely be one of the most powerful rhetorical devices for the expression of lament. Modern theorists of mourning suggest that in such rhetorical device the bereaved refuses to accept the death of the beloved—as if he can will its cancellation. In terms of biblical poetics, it most strongly echoes the book of Samuel and David's lament for Absalom. Within the typology of lamentation in the period, David seems to have been the most popular figure, as one may see from the frequency with which his grief over the death of his child by Bathsheba and the death of Absalom are cited in the devotional literature of grief and comfort. At the same time, the lament in this text is personalized and adapted by Boyd through the use of the proper name *Frederick* and the assertion of the feminine viewpoint:

> O my Sonne, my dearest Sonne is gone: Hee is lost, where shall I finde him? O Frederick my son where art thou? Shall I see thee no more? Shall I never kiss thy mouth againe? Once did thou lye in my bellie neere vnto my heart, but now alas, thou lyes sleeping in slime . . . . (sig. A8ᵥ)

The passage is further personalized by allusions to Frederick's death in a storm at sea and by regrets that the speaker, unsuspecting of the imminence of death, did not have a chance to say goodbye. The drawing out of references to the wish that the Queen had kissed the lips, ears, and eyes of her son ten thousand times is appropriate to the hyperbole of the climactic statement. She turns in anger to curse the waters that drowned him, putting in a moving detail that she will never wash her hands without remembering what the water has done to her. In the marginalia she says that if the waters were sensible, her brother Charles would punish them with ships and cannon.

The elegiac statement rises to a high pitch of lamentation with apostrophes to various waters and boats:

> O Seas of sorrowes, O feareful Floods, O tumbling Tempests, O wilfull Waues . . . was there no mercie among you for such an hopefull PRINCE. (sig. B1ᵥ)

In its personification of nature, this section suggests the classical elegiac form, but its wash of classical convention is subordinated almost immediately to the biblical in the final bleak statement that echoes the powerful type of David's own grief. Within the natural order, the parent must always feel the obligation to die instead of the child, a typology of feeling embodied by David's cry of anguish:

> Yee [Seas of sorrowe] shall neuer bee able to repaire my losses: O my Sonne Frederick, my Son, my Sonne FREDERICK, would God I had dyed for Thee, O Frederick my Sonne, my Sonne. (sig. B2)

"The Queenes Lamentations" is a transitional example of the lament before its full integration into the elegy with its more complex movement into closure, as in a poem like "Lycidas." It is, in some sense, crude in its poetic techniques. At several points, the language needs to be reined in; it is perhaps obvious that the writer is more a student of the Bible than a poet. But in spite of its minor place in the elegiac tradition, the "Lamentations" is a powerful expression of grief. Furthermore, as a cultural text it suggests that children in the period had an important place in the heart of mothers, regardless of the differences in family structure that argue otherwise. However attractive it is to think that Elizabeth wrote this herself, it probably belongs to Boyd, who was likely to have followed Puttenham's suggestion for the poet to enter into the grief of the bereaved. Later Boyd, like many in the period, produced a metrical translation of the Psalms.

Whoever the author, "The Queenes Lamentation for *the death of her Son*" is a unique and tantalizing historical document purporting in its form to express the grief of an English royal mother for the death of a royal son. Otherwise, the only mention of her loss is found in a brief answer to a letter of consolation, in which she speaks of her "poor boy." Elizabeth's grief for her husband, who died three years later a military and political failure, finds expression in a much more extended and poignant letter. But the "Lamentations" as a set of poetic conventions movingly underlines the place of grief over the loss of a child in a sophisticated articulation of comfort. If Lear's Cordelia, Prince Henry, and Frederick are seen as rare and precious children in a world where death sweeps away so many, they nevertheless provide a focus for a shaping of griefs that the culture seems to share. "The Queenes Lamentations" reminds modern readers of the responses that sweep all those for whom the continuity of generation seems threatened: the agonizingly physical assault of grief; the largely futile cry to the community to join in mourning; the attack upon the forces of nature that seemed to participate in the death; and finally the near despairing guilt of the parental survivor—"would God I had dyed for Thee."

The overwhelming bleakness of such a form was for seventeenth-century people part of the tradition by which they encountered death: a full exposure of the anguish of mortality from Old Testament sources, always read, however, in the light of unspoken New Testament sources. According to Pigman, such full lament was more allowable theologically in the seventeenth century than in the sixteenth century. The dominance of biblical form and language permitted, paradoxically, the fullness of grief and the absence of comfort. The presence of implicit promise in the tradition allows the redemptive resolution to remain unspoken. Elaborate modes of comfort, however, were expected to follow: in devotional form, as in the rest of Boyd's volume; in seventeenth-century funeral rituals; in funeral sermons. It is not surprising, however, that in his own brilliant forging of the classical-Christian elegy, Milton later used a form (in some real sense, created it) that moved such a devastating encounter into comfort within the single poetic text. But "The Queenes Lamentations for *the death of her Son*" remains a part of the typology of the suffering of grief: "A side piercing sight" that is a necessary stage for early seventeenth-century mourners on the way to comfort. The medieval legend alluded to in the "Mass for the Blessed Virgin Mary according to Salisbury Use" that the mother of Christ felt the sword piercing her own side at the Crucifixion is an iconographical detail expressive of the identification of mother with child. Such painful empathy continued to inform the typology of lament.

The "Lamentations" affirms the depth of the human need for generation and its continuity that shapes the rebirth imagery of all the language of comfort, classical and Christian, in western civilization. Both strands of the need were embedded in seventeenth-century cultural codes. No other time has so valued the expression of feeling. Whatever the theological tendencies to emphasize individual immortality, children were also for seventeenth-century parents an important emblem of ongoing life. The royal child had become more—the very embodiment of the continuity of power and privilege. The death of such a child threatened the stability of all things human beings valued in earthly existence. For Elizabeth Stuart, who had already experienced a number of deaths, particularly her princely brother and her young children, this death was especially difficult. Exiled as she was from both her past happy youth and her ambitions in Bohemia, the death of her son prefigured the death of most of her hopes. But it was generally recognized by Boyd and others that her grief must be expressed in the language of lament for the comforts of the religious context to have meaning.[37]

Afterword

Thou mett'st with things dying, I with things newborn
—*The Winter's Tale,* 3.3.110–11

Recently when confronted with a twentieth-century person who had lost her son while he was traveling in Africa, I was struck dumb. Here it was again, the fact of death the devourer abroad in the world still. I caught my breath and wondered. I had written a whole book on the subject—at that moment the manuscript was waiting in my hotel for final revisions. What was the use after all if I offered only silence to her grief?

Again, I felt the impulse to disclaim meaning in my work for the twentieth century. It simply could not be applied to a predominantly secular culture. Someone with a better sense of natural forces would have to do the sequel and speak. And yet, when I had some time to think, I wondered. However deeply embedded in seventeenth-century culture and language the text of my work was, it had also been written to make some important comments on the ongoing relationships between life and death and the ways that early English modes of expression spoke more tellingly to these issues than our own largely repressive forms of language and symbol. Although none of those conventions could transfer exactly or literally to another time and another place, the links we still have with that tradition make some of the strange messages meaningful.

The tranformation of death as Milton handles the images in *Paradise Lost* is surely what devout Christians of the period were trying to grapple with. The fundamental tension between death as the rape of life and joy (born out of sin as destruction and loss) and death as the gentle release from the sufferings of nature into the fullness of life was within that tradition to have a mysterious reconciliation in the principle of resurrection. In his great epic drama Milton accounts vividly for the presence of death born into the fallen experience out of Sin:

[Sin to Satan]
Thine own begotten, breaking violent away
Tore through my entrails, that with fear and pain
Distorted, all my nether shape thus grew
Transform'd: but he my inbred enemy
Forth issued, brandishing his fatal Dart
Made to destroy: I fled, and cri'd out *Death;*
Hell trembl'd at the hideous Name, and sigh'd
From all her Caves, and back resounded *Death.*

                                    (*Paradise Lost* II.782–89)

Description of the violent incestuous rape of the mother Sin by
Death follows hot upon these lines about Death's origin, for Satan,
who, as we recall, gave birth himself (another Jove) to Sin out of his
head and then begot upon her Death. The ugliness and violence of
the imagery—incest, sin, rape, pain, is, of course, Milton's allegory
of that two who besmear and violate our world so that it can never
be the Eden we long for. Later in the poem we see the even more
frightening entrance of that hungry pair, mother and son, into history, and the image of death the devourer grows even more terrifying in its presence in the vision of history that Michael shows Adam.

It is, however, the transformation of death through all that the
Christian gospel stands for that Milton struggles to communicate—
the healing love of the Son, God-made-flesh, who volunteers out of
total freedom to conquer death and creates a living model of heroic
caring for the Christians of the seventeenth century. Milton seizes
this theme even after the sacramental devotion of the best years of
Anglicanism has begun to fade. Milton's vision, however, is prepared for in the earlier materials of our period. Most significant in
the tradition during the first thirty years of the century is the evident
ability to forge a language of expression that allows for the full confrontation with all the figures and shapes taken by Death, from the
most rapacious grinning skeleton to the gentle figure that carries
the soul to the hands of God.

But however much of that mythic tradition is under threat in the
twentieth century, it is possible that we can look back for "openings." In the preceding chapters I have journeyed among various
kinds of literary texts, from the epics of so-called "high" culture
down to the simplest devotional books, intended for "new" and
largely unschooled readers of the seventeenth century, and including in between both sermons and dramatic representations presented to a spectrum of society and readers in early modern
England. Since most of what we have looked at, including popular

visual texts and symbols, was published or produced in London, it is probably only, in spite of the varied forms, representative of attitudes in that place during the first thirty years of the seventeenth century, with notable exceptions being the ideologically framing epics of Spenser and Milton and also Shakespeare's *Richard III*, a somewhat earlier example of the art of dying. Most of the texts examined appeared during the reign of James I and inevitably bear the stamp of interaction with events and attitudes supporting cultural power during that period; at the same time such texts often show both continuities and contrasts with the reign of Elizabeth, particular emblem of the new England and its place among European powers.

In sum, I have been about the task of "reading" early seventeenth-century culture, with the primary assumption that attitudes toward death and dying tell us as readers much about what it is to be human in such a creatively expressive culture. My method has been to examine contemporary documents with an eye to the interaction of image, event, and word in order to tease out meanings that speak to the attitudes held toward death and life, despair and comfort. Do some of those meanings still resonate, like a chord played that sounds in the ear even in the following silence?

Perhaps still overarching the whole are several questions: Was it possible for a person in Renaissance England to prepare for a good death in such a way that his whole existence became a constant growing into greater life? Concomitantly, was it possible in the process of this preparation for him and his survivors to move through the inevitably spectral and terrifying image of Death as Triumphant to the tamed and gentle notion of Death transformed through the "long day's dying" of the fallen world into the instrument by which a loving God gently wafts the soul to heaven? Finally, could the rawness of grief expressed in the lamentations chapter ever be disciplined or actually transformed into the calm acceptance or benediction of the devotional tradition? Answers embedded in the texts remain, like answers in the midst of life, qualified, but perhaps, most importantly, tease us into framing some of our own answers.

Tentative answers to all three of these questions must inevitably seem to many twentieth-century readers not qualified at all, but a resounding *no*. My own experience of deaths in the midst of life— particularly deaths of the young—brings me to question meaning. Suicide, murder, accident, even illness when it snatches off those who have not led a full life into ripe old age inevitably seem representative of the iron power of death over life—not death disciplined and tamed by a kindly nature into the tilt toward life and love that all the great mythic visions of civilization suggest as final meaning. Even tragic form with its waste and darkness that nevertheless shows meaningful sacrifice to the reordering of the future has come to be profoundly a matter of question in twentieth-century minds.

But then our world is different, I hear my readers or my students say. We have in the twentieth century repressed death and somehow raced to replace the vacuum left from the dying, filling our lives with business and pleasure so that we can deny our own ultimate demise—until finally the shattering experience of mortality comes home to us in our own mortality or in that of those closest to us. Early modern England with its rudimentary medicine could not repress (or suppress) so pervasive a fact of human experience to the same degree that our culture denies its presence. So the documentation of this book proves in its sheer quantity. Late sixteenth- and early seventeenth-century writers, preachers, dramatists all had to struggle with death-in-life and did in more variations than I have chronicled.

The questions and the struggle itself, then, are what most informs the English literature of death and dying. That movement between despair and hope remains both a paradoxical and an ambivalent motion in most of the writing, certainly for most audiences and readers. It is characteristic of a still fundamentally religious culture that it does not deny doubt and suffering; anyone who reads the Psalms recognizes that a major component of spiritual growth is embodied in facing and working through those things in experience that are most unacceptable: the presence of hatred in every experience, violence and cruelty, betrayal and rejection by those we love—worst of all, our own betrayals and failures—in sum, mortality and all its manifestations. At the end (those last moments) in a religious culture, these imperfections must be faced, the personal ones as well as the larger ones of context. According to the art of dying, they ought to be faced daily, but as English persons recognized, the deathbed was the representative last moment for fully facing those aspects of life. Ideally, by relying upon the positive resources of the Christian myth, one might overcome despair with faith and hope. The cross and the resurrection, says Donne again and again; the paradox fused only by love, though the firmness of the resolution appears most obviously in seventeenth century didactic religious literature. Popular forms stated the answer most strongly because of their unspoken dialogue with all the restless search for certainty within seventeenth century epistemology that other forms—especially that of tragic drama—reflect.

It is perhaps in *Hamlet* (1600–1601) that we find the most charac-

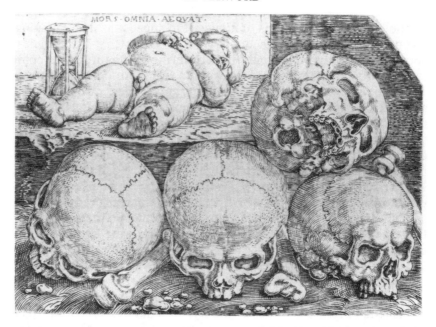

"Mors omnia aequat." **Woodcut by B. Beham in Bartsch for this touching icon of Death's lack of pity for youth. Permission to reprint is from the Warburg Institute, The University of London.**

teristic early voice of the time in terms of those questions asked above. I left out the chapter on *Hamlet* because I believed that the play had less to do with the temptation to Despair than with a world in which angry grief was frustrated from expression—not allowed its full ritual resolution. Cole's *The Absent One* perhaps chronicles this best in psychoanalytical, anthropological, and ritual terms. Hamlet's society and world—largely because of the power of the politics in Denmark that cover up the murder of Hamlet Senior— do not allow for the full ritual of mourning that places the absent one at the center. Without those rituals the Ghost is caught between earth and heaven on one level, but, most importantly, cannot be released from Hamlet's grieving imagination. The court does not allow for grief, and the free-floating anger of grief is ultimately exaggerated to near madness by the need for concealment and revenge and the frustrating difficulties of carrying the latter out. One cannot help wondering whether *Hamlet* was written partly out of Shakespeare's experience of the death of his son in a time when antique rituals of mourning were changing within the new church and when, in general, there was an abandonment of prayers for the dead, surely an important primitive reassurance of survival that allowed surcease to the grieving. The substitution of verbal forms of expression for liturgical ones to a dramatist, himself a master of secular liturgy, may well have seemed inadequate.

In the play itself, of course, the grief and anger against Claudius cannot be focused in open attack and ultimately, in spite of careful plans, find expression in another unjust death of a father, that of Polonius. That act brings upon Hamlet exile. When he returns, the graveyard scene becomes a *memento mori* focus for the whole play and for the audience as well.

But the exposure of Ophelia's suicide is, of course, an instance of the worst kind of death—the undeserved suicide of one who has not been allowed the full ritual of grief for her father under the particular political circumstances. Madness becomes a destructive substitute for ritualized grieving. More importantly, she is not allowed in her own death a fully celebrated funeral, and, whatever Hamlet's protests, the suicide itself brings with it the fear of spiritual death. Her "maimed rites" become another instance of the symbolically destructive lack of ritual that has its most ancient model in *Antigone,* where Antigone sacrifices her life to fulfill that necessary ritual burial for her rebel brother. That such a ritual is in less "enlightened" times a necessity for the welfare of the dead does not mean that it is not also—and *predominantly* for twentieth-century readers—a nagging necessity for the grieving, who must maintain their relationship with the dead, as Hamlet does when he leaps into Ophelia's grave or even earlier when he brutally chastises his mother and, mistaking Polonius for Claudius, stabs him through the arras. At the same time that psychological necessity to hold on to the dead and take their absent part must inevitably require some culturally defined ritual process of mourning, through which the griever must move and eventually find release from the dead. Hamlet, therefore, clings to both his father and Ophelia but, at the same time, acts within his own existence to move on from their deaths.

At last in the play (the most ambivalent and puzzling of Shakespeare's plays) Hamlet himself lies dying, poisoned in the duel. His attempt to deal with grief by avenging his father's murder and, in some sense, by becoming his father has brought him also to the inexorable fact of mortality. The difference in his own death on the tragic stage (V.vii) is that it allows for the ritualizing of the rite of passage and its actual passing. Hamlet counters the violence of Horatio's grieving desire to join his friend in death with his plea:

> If thou didst ever hold me in thy heart
> Absent thee from felicity a while,
> And in this harsh world draw thy breath in pain
> To tell my story.
>
> (V.ii.346–50)

Here the lament is replaced by the opportunity for the grieving to remember in a way that assures the classical immortality of fame. Across the whole play echoes and resonates Hamlet Senior's words near the beginning: *Remember me.* Submerged of course is the suggestion of Christ at the Last Supper.

In terms of dramatic irony the audiences join in the ongoing survival of Hamlet, knowing that they themselves have been present in the unfolding of the story. And then at last the stoic Christian symbolism frames the ending with the promise of a loving and provident God, as Horatio says a benediction upon the passing of the soul of the Prince:

> Good night, sweet prince,
> And flights of angels sing thee to thy rest!
>
> (V.ii.359–60)

There is in the death itself no hint of the conventional *ars moriendi* deathbed; but the earlier meditation on Yorick's skull and the *memento mori* foreshadowing of Ophelia's funeral have prepared the way for the concentration of ritual elements in the last scene, set in tragic mode upon a stage littered with the bodies of Death Triumphant. Yet the establishment of continuity with the Horatian mourner establishes the full context of hope. The mourner himself is comforted by the continuity provided in his memorial task and by his own "angelic" blessing, followed by the ritual funereal dignity of Hamlet's being carried from the stage as Fortinbras waits to hear from Horatio the story.

Survival, rebirth, "things newborn"—it is in hints and possibilities both literal and metaphorical that people in the seventeenth century found comfort. Especially the language of death and rebirth brought openings. "Death, thou too shalt die," says John Donne firmly, but both the experiences of people in actual life and on the tragic stage remain qualified and various. Certainly now we cannot echo such certainty. But "openings" are possible, perhaps given a nudge by observing closely human expression in another age. The variety of human communities, even in a time less pluralistic than our own, brought about a variety of expressive forms on the subject that make us wonder and dream.

In that time and place they all pointed toward the light—still the tilt of a world toward love, the incredible tenacity of hope, the reenactment of human efforts to care for each other, the force of memory to return to them those they love, the connective power of the metaphor of the Communion of Saints, an undefined presence in themselves that affirms life. Most of all, we might learn from that time the possibility that out of lamentation and mourning can come comfort. Fully realized rebirth remains a question and a mystery. Death itself often seems rawly triumphant, but the emblem of the lily growing out of the skull is at least an assurance of the power that moves the heart and transforms the memories of the dead. "Appeare to us as thou didst appeare to us a month ago," says Donne of his friend. After the haunting images of the dead, a healing process of mourning speaks out of these materials to bring them to us alive—like a glimpse of "things new-born," recovered selves. Only through such a process can we minister to the rooted sorrow of our own mortality.

Notes

Introduction: Cultural Poetics

1. Svetlana Alpers, "Is Art History?" *Daedalus* 106, no. 3 (1977): 1–13.

2. See Clifford Geertz, *Interpretation of Cultures* (New York: Basic Books, 1973), and Jonathan Z. Smith, "Myth, Story, and History," Interpretation of Culture Lecture, Arizona State University (1981).

3. Joan Webber, *The Eloquent I: Style and Self in Seventeenth-Century Prose* (Madison: University of Wisconsin Press, 1968); Stephen J. Greenblatt, *Renaissance Self-Fashioning* (Chicago: University of Chicago Press, 1980).

4. David Bevington, *Action is Eloquence: Shakespeare's Language of Gesture* (Cambridge, Mass., and London: Harvard University Press, 1984).

5. Stanley Fish, *Is There a Text in This Class?: The Authority of Interpretive Communities* (Cambridge, Mass.: Harvard University Press, 1980). Fish asserts a historical community to militate against the wholly subjective theory of audience response. C. S. Lewis, *English Literature in the Sixeenth Century excluding Drama* (Oxford: Oxford University Press, 1954). Jonathan Dollimore, *Radical Tragedy: Religion, Ideology, and Power in the Drama of Shakespeare and His Contemporaries* (Brighton: Harvester, 1984); Jonathan Goldberg, *James I and the Politics of Literature: Jonson, Donne, and Their Contemporaries* (Baltimore: Johns Hopkins University Press, 1983). I am closest to the New History here and in the works of Leah S. Marcus, such as *Childhood and Cultural Despair: A Theme and Variations in Seventeenth-Century Literature* (Pittsburgh: University of Pittsburgh Press, 1978).

6. Erwin Panofsky, *Idea: A Concept in Art Theory,* trans. Joseph J. S. Peake (Columbia: University of South Carolina Press, 1968); see also Don Cameron Allen, *Mysteriously Meant: The Rediscovery of Pagan Symbolism and Allegorical Interpretation in the Renaissance* (Baltimore: Johns Hopkins University Press, 1970), for the transformation of biblical typology to include humanist texts and symbols as prefiguration.

7. See Ann Jennalie Cook, *The Privileged Playgoer of Shakespeare's London 1576–1642* (Princeton: Princeton University Press, 1981), for a "revised" argument for the aristocratic nature of Shakespeare's audience.

8. See Stephen G. Nichols, Jr., "The Poetics of Historicism: Recent Trends in Medieval Literary Study," in *Medievalia et Humanistica: Studies in Medieval and Renaissance Culture* 8 (1977): 77–101, for a perceptive discussion of the psychology of the Christian deathbed.

9. See *The Ars Moriendi,* Editio Princeps, ca. 1450 [probably closer to 1465], ed. W. Harry Rylands, Holbein Society (London, 1881), for facsimiles of the first woodcut series. Other editions appeared throughout Europe: e.g., Editiones Torculum, *Art de bene morir* (Edition Catalana, 1493; Barcelona, 1951); Guido

de Monte Rocher, *Ars moriendi* (Cologne, 1476), which chronicles elaborate temptations.

10. Greenblatt, *Renaissance Self-Fashioning*.

Chapter 1. The Visual Text As Mirror of Feeling: Skull, Skeleton, and Deathbed

1. *The Last Battell of the Soule in Death,* II (Edinburgh, 1629).

2. Allan H. Gilbert, *The Symbolic Personages in the Masques of Ben Jonson* (New York: AMS Press, 1965); see for this Aristotelian idea *The Poetics,* ed. D. W. Lucas (Oxford: Clarendon Press, 1968).

3. The three images of the skull, skeleton, and the deathbed are so pervasive in the period's iconography of death that one would think they might become almost devoid of resonance had they not so often been given new associations of horror by plagues and pestilences. Peter de Luca, author of *The Dialogue of Dying Wel* trans. Richard Verstegan (Antwerp, 1603), sig. C3, is aware of this irony and suggests meditating on one's skull only every several days to avoid overfamiliarity and therefore loss of meaning. Skull and skeleton are constant reminders of the presence of Death, the mighty emperor who broods over life: "To the most puissant Emperor, and Conqueror of all the World, Death, greeting," in Samuel Garey, "Death's Welcome," in *Two Treatises* (London, 1605); he emphasizes the notion of the "triumph of death" as in Petrarch. See also Petrarcke, *The Trymphes of Fraunces Petrarcke,* trans. Henrye Parker (London, 1555): "Death dyd take my love and ioye awaye," 16$_v$. The frequent image of the skull as a *memento mori* is picked up by the printer John Day in his popular devotional book falsely attributed to Augustine, *Certaine Select Prayers* (London, 1574), in which he places numerous skulls and mottoes at the bottom of the pages. The first page carries the reminder of shared mortality: "As you are, so were we." The deathbed becomes, of course, a more specifically pointed emblem for the actual deathbed experience and the instruction for the last phase of the *ars moriendi*.

4. See the fifteenth-century block-book *ars* series: five temptations, five inspirations, and the Happy Death, in *The Ars Moriendi,* Editio Princeps, ca. 1450, ed. W. Harry Rylands, Holbein Society (London, 1881); see also Lionel Cust, *The Master E. S. and the 'Ars Moriendi'* (Oxford: Clarendon Press, 1898), 11–15; for later reproduction of single European woodblocks in English books, see Caxton's *The Boke named the Royall* (London: Wynkyn de Worde, 1506). There is a complete set of the *ars* by the Master E. S. in the Douce Collection, now in the University Galleries at Oxford; Cust argues that these are prior to those in the Editio Princeps.

5. The iconographical implications of Shakespeare's staging have continued to be an important interest for scholars who view Shakespeare's plays as *script* rather than reader's *text* and yet also as rich interaction between audience and culture, drama and ritual. See John Doebler, Shakespeare's *Speaking Pictures: Studies in Iconic Imagery* (Albuquerque: University of New Mexico Press, 1974); Alan C. Dessen, *Elizabethan Stage Conventions and Modern Interpreters* (Cambridge: Cambridge University Press, 1984); David Bevington, *Action Is Eloquence: Shakespeare's Language of Gesture* (Cambridge, Mass.: Harvard University Press, 1984). Most useful for the exploration of links between royal iconography and drama remain the studies of Roy C. Strong, i.e., *The Tudor Icon: Elizabethan and Jacobean Portraiture* (London: Routledge & Kegan Paul, 1969) and the later Ste-

phen Orgel and Strong, *Inigo Jones: The Theatre of the Stuart Court,* 2 vols. (London: Sotheby-Parke Bernet, 1973).

6. See Philippe Ariès, *The Hour of Our Death,* trans. Helen Weaver (New York: Knopf, 1981) for the long tradition; for history of the plague see Philip Ziegler, *The Black Death* (New York: John Day, 1969); Frank Percy Wilson, *The Plague in Shakespeare's London* (Oxford: Clarendon, 1927); John F. D. Shrewsbury, *A History of Bubonic Plague in the British Isles* (Cambridge: Cambridge University Press, 1970). Frequent occurrences of the plague from 1340 on made pestilence very much a part of the English perspective on death and its suddenness. "The Communion of the Sicke," in *The Booke of Common Prayer* (London, 1590), contains special instructions for solitary communion:

> At the time of plague, sweat, or such other like contagious times of sickness or disease, when none of the parish or neighbors can be gotten to communicate with the sicke in their houses, for feare of the infection, upon speciall request of the diseased, the Minister may alonely communicate with him (sig. P_{vii}).

Thomas Dekker's *The Wonderfull Year 1603. Wherein is shewed the picture of London, lying sicke of the Plague* (London, 1603) provides an account of the plague episode during the year of Elizabeth's death and James's accession, the coronation for which was delayed and blighted by the visitation. For the Dance of Death, see "The Dance of Death," in *Mss. Ellesmere 26/A.13 and B. M. Lansdowne 699, Collated with the Other Extant Mss.,* ed. Florence Warren, Early English Text Society OS, no. 181 (London: Oxford University Press for EETS, 1931); and *The Dance of Death,* by Hans Holbein, with intro. and notes by James M. Clark (London: Phaidon Press, 1947). *A Booke of Christian Prayers* printed by Richard Day, sometimes called "Queen Elizabeth's Prayerbook" (London, 1590), has *memento mori* engravings as border designs. Many editions followed.

7. London Company of Parish Clerks, *A True Report of All the Burials and Christenings . . . .* (London, 1603); also 37,717 dead are recorded for the 1603 visitation of the plague in *London's Mourning Garment* (London, 1603), E2.

8. I am grateful to Carol Livingston for bringing several ballads and their illustrations to my attention at the Huntington Library one summer; for "The Daunce and Song of Death" see BL (British Library) Huth 50 (32), 1568–69 (AI 480).

9. There is no reason to associate every open grave with *Hamlet,* but Shakespeare's scene makes such vivid use of that image that it is difficult not to do so. The lively dance surrounding the minstrel "Sycknes" in the ballad woodcut illustration is clearly a theatrically shaped image of performance. The presence of the musical instrument, the joining of hands of the living and the dead, the circle around the minstrel all contribute to that effect.

10. See Hans Holbein, *The Dance of Death,* Facsimile of Woodcuts in First Complete Edition (Lyons, 1547; London, 1916); also Natalie Zemon Davis, "Holbein's *Pictures of Death* and the Reformation at Lyons," *Studies in the Renaissance* 3 (1956), 97–130; also Ernest B. Gilman, *The Curious Perspective: Literary and Pictorial Wit in the Seventeenth Century* (New Haven: Yale University Press, 1978), 89–104, for discussion of Holbein's *Ambassadors.*

11. In *Petrarca* (Venice, 1497); Jacobus de Voragine, *Legendario* (Venice, 1499); and Natalibus, *Catalogus Sanctorum* (Venice: B. de Zani, 1506). See also Peter Thon, "Bruegel's *Triumph of Death* Reconsidered," *Renaissance Quarterly,* 21, no. 3 (Autumn 1968): 289–99.

12. BL Huth 50 (#63), L25. The relationship between image, poem, and moral apostrophe is almost that of the emblematic tradition. See Rosemary Freeman,

English Emblem Books (New York: Octagon Books, 1966) for a full discussion. Under such frequent and intensely realized visual warning it is no wonder that those devotional writers who were concerned with shoring up the faith of the Christian in dark times should have published numerous treatises that focused upon practical means of comfort. *The Booke of Common Prayer,* in "The Communion of the Sicke," called the faithful to prepare:

> Forasmuch as all mortal men be subject to many sudden perils, diseases, and sicknesses, and ever uncertaine what time they shal depart out of this life: there to the intent they may be alwayes in a readinesse to dye whensoever it shall please Almightie God to call them, the Curates shall . . . specially in the plague time exhort their Parishioners, to the oft recyving . . . *Communion* (P$_{vkv}$).

See also I. Guillemand, *A Combat betwixt Man and Death or A Discurse against the immoderate apprehension and feare of Death* (London, 1629). Though Guillemard is a little later in our period, there are indications of earlier efforts to maintain the balance between a healthy fear and a desire to comfort people in danger of being drawn into despair: for instance, one example of many, *The Maner to Dye Well,* by Petrus de Soto, trans. B. S. (London, 1578), is a meditation on the Four Last Things that rises to a peroration on heavenly joys. In terms of the difficulty of facing one's inadequacies, the books of the devotional tradition constantly pointed to Christ's mercy. B.S., sigs. A4$_v$–A5$_r$ points to Christ's offering his sorrow for mankind.

13. "Ladies, Gentlemen, and Skulls: *Hamlet* and the Iconographic Traditions," *Shakespeare Quarterly,* 30 (1970) 1: 15–28.

14. *Book of Common Prayer* (London, 1848).

15. Sister Mary Catharine O'Connor, *The Art of Dying Well: The Development of the Ars Moriendi,* Columbia University Studies in English and Comparative Literature (New York: Columbia University Press, 1942); Nancy Lee Beaty, *The Craft of Dying: A Study in the Ars Moriendi in England* (New Haven: Yale University Press, 1970).

16. David Atkinson, "The English *ars moriendi:* Its Protestant Transformation," *Renaissance and Reformation* 6, no. 1 (1982): 1–10. See also for Protestant attitudes and themes Barbara Kiefer Lewalski, *Protestant Poetics and the Seventeenth Century Religious Lyric* (Princeton: Princeton University Press, 1979).

17. *The Grimani Breviary,* reprod. from the illuminated manuscript at the Biblioteca Marciana, Venice, trans. Simon Pleasance, Linda Packer, and Geoffrey Webb; pref. Giorgio Ferrari; intro. Mario Salmi; comment. Lorenzo Mellini (Woodstock, N.Y.: Overlook Press, 1974), plates 57 and 48.

18. Jacobus de Voragine, *The Golden Legend* (Westminster, 1483). The visual motifs of the good and bad angels are, of course, the veriest commonplaces throughout the late Middle Ages and the sixteenth century; Shakespeare alludes to the opposing angels in his sonnet, "Two loves I have of comfort and despair," *Shakespeare's Sonnets,* ed. Stephen Booth (New Haven: Yale University Press, 1977), 123.

19. *The Book of Common Prayer,* as well as virtually every *ars* book of the period, urges such preparation, but the details of it tend to be extended in the more radically Protestant tracts. Nevertheless, the making of the will was part of the Catholic tradition from the beginning, as the Breviary indicates. For a late instance of such practical considerations see I. B. D. D., *A Sermon Preached at Flitton at the Funerall of the Right Honourable Henrie Earle of Kent, the sixteenth of March,*

1614 (London, 1615), particularly the section concerned with the responsibility of the dying one toward others.

20. In one edition of Thomas Laurent's *Royal Book* (Westminster, 1486), instead of the woodcut of the happy dying, Christ is placed beside a woodcut of someone in a winding sheet praying. The ideal, of course, is always that the moriens will model his death upon the death of Christ. The crucifix is said to be the most efficacious symbol against the devil. In Bosch's early sixteenth-century painting "The Death of the Miser," The National Gallery, Washington, D.C., there is a crucifix at the window through which the beam of the light of grace shines.

21. Juxtaposition of opposites is frequent in the visual tradition. On the first page of John More, *A Lively Anatomie of Death* (London, 1596), which was dedicated to Thomas South on his father's death, there is an emblem with the poem "Omnia mors aequate." The upper circle encloses the shrouded body lying on a mattock and shovel resting over a dug grave. The lower ellipse shows a fierce skull with bone between teeth surrounded by snakes, mattock, crossbones, sceptre, and hipbones with motto: *mors septra ligonibus equat.*

22. Family and friends were particularly important when the moriens was too ill to speak or communicate; hence one reason for the popularity of the dialogue form. Thomas Becon in the popular *The Sicke Mans Salue* constructs a dialogue between the dying and his friends (London, 1582). Sometimes the dying is urged to request his friends to speak for him in answer to the crucial questions. I refer to a number of different printings of this text because of its popularity.

23. The number of Puritan *ars* books (Perkins and others) attest to this absorption.

24. The Rohan Master in a beautiful painting in T. S. R. Boase, *Death in the Middle Ages: Mortality, Judgement, and Remembrance* (New York: McGraw-Hill, 1972), shows St. Michael as a good angel flying down to retrieve a soul snatched by a bad angel, while God looks on beneficently. The City of God and the City of Man are frequently part of the allegorical landscape even by the end of the sixteenth century; see the printer Daye's device at the end of Becon's *Salue,* which shows on the left the two cities.

25. (Paris, 1492; the English trans. 1503). This text emphasizes the sacramental, with the necessity of the seven sacraments received by civil authority, especially to combat the devil (when dying) and human nature (when living) GG1–GG1v.

26. BL Huth 50 (#56).

27. In sum, the popular secular tradition in the ballads stresses living well over dying well, or living well in order to die well.

28. In *The Illustrated Bartsch,* 11, 1723. (Munich [?], 1823).

29. *The Doctrynall of Dethe* (London, 1523), prefatory section.

30. See Chapter Three for discussion of the two major texts, the one illustrated, the other not. English books that have the woodcuts usually have only one or two: See Voragine, *The Golden Legend.*

31. Cook, *The Privileged Playgoer of Shakespeare's London 1576–1642.*

Chapter 2. Execution and Ritual Dying: Lord Essex as Cultural Event

1. William Barlow, *A Sermon Preached at Paul's Crosse* (London, 1601). See also Francis Bacon, *Declaration of Practices and Treasons of . . . Essex* (London, 1601); Bacon was the ideal person to summarize the complete chain of events from

the point of view of the crown. Essex's own earlier *An Apologie, against those which jealously, and maliciously, tax him to be the hinderer of the peace and quiet of his country* (London, 1603) was written in 1598. Not until 1624 was a sympathetic treatise published by Thomas Scott, *Robert Earle of Essex, His Ghost sent from Elizian* (London, 1624), which emphasized all the services of Essex to the crown through the fiction of Essex speaking from heaven.

2. John Ernest Neale, *Queen Elizabeth I* (Garden City, N.Y.: Anchor ed., 1957; originally published 1934). I am indebted to this definitive biography for interpretation of Essex's long and complex conflict with the queen, which culminated in the execution. Cf. the contemporary biography of Elizabeth: William Camden, *The Historie of the Most Renowned and Victorious Princesse Elizabeth Late Queen of England . . .* (London, 1630); see also *The Letters of Queen Elizabeth I,* ed. G. B. Harrison (New York: Funk and Wagnalls, 1935), and G. B. Harrison, *The Life and Death of Robert Devereux, Earl of Essex* (London: Cassel, 1937), especially the final chapter; also Lytton Strachey, *Elizabeth and Essex in Tragic History* (New York: Harcourt, 1928) for the most literary and romantic account. See also Samuel Y. Edgerton, Jr. "Maniera and the Mannaia: Decorum and Decapitation in the Sixteenth Century," in *The Meaning of Mannerism,* eds. Franklin W. Robinson and Stephen G. Nichols, Jr. (Hanover, N.H.: University Press of New England, 1972), 69–103.

3. The job of the historian is to speak indirectly about the great body of commonplace associations, to bring alive the atmosphere of a time and place. As Jonathan Z. Smith suggests in "The Influence of Symbols upon Social Change," in *Map Is No Territory* (Zurich: Brill, 1974), 129:

> The historian's task is to complicate, not to clarify. He strives to celebrate the diversity of manners, the opacity of things, the variety of species. He is barred, thereby, from making a frontal assault on his topic. Like the pilgrim, the historian is obligated to approach his subject obliquely. He must circumambulate the spot several times before making even the most fleeting contact. His method, like that of Tristram Shandy, Gentlemen, is that of the digression.

He might have added "or like the writer of fiction, like indeed the poet, he must speak indirectly to create for the reader an illusion of participation in historical reality." For general assumptions about history and culture that underlie the kind of historic construction attempted in this study, see Geertz, *Interpretation of Cultures,* particularly the assumption of cultural anthropology that man is in a fundamental sense completed by the various symbolic systems of his culture. The variety of results of such interaction even in a single culture provides a fascinating spectrum: cf., for example, Essex in his final religious position with Donne in his. The separation of a generation is one of the factors, but the genetics of personality as it interacts with different aspects of culture is another.

4. *Letters and Papers, Foreign and Domestic, of the Reign of Henry VIII,* eds. J. S. Brewer, J. Gardner, and R. H. Brodie, 21 vols. in 33 (London, 1862–1910), VIII, no. 996.

5. "English Treason Trials," *Journal of the History of Ideas,* 15, no. 4 (October 1954): 471–98.

6. Smith argues the sacrosanct nature of the crown. Although there was no theory of divine right, there was a tremendous sense of the king as God's agent, to whom one owed absolute obedience. Such an attitude makes explicable Ann Boleyn's strange words that she had "come hither only to die and thus yield herself to the will of the King, my lord." Perhaps it is easier for moderns to understand the

emphasis English people put upon the buttressing power of the law and the corporate state. See Smith's further discussion of this aspect. My own further argument tends to see these assumptions as articulated within larger cultural and religious values that can be seen only within the immediate encounter with death. L. B. Smith, "English Treason Trials," 488, 491–94.

7. *The Hour of Our Death,* trans. Helen Weaver (New York: Knopf, 1981), 28. Many saw the "good deaths" of others as a comfort; for example, Guillemand's little treatise *A Combat betwixt Man and Death or A Discourse against the immoderate apprehension and feare of Death,* trans. Edward Grimeston (London, 1621), 460–61, among others, lists Socrates and St. Paul as supreme types of dying. An example, however, of the ambivalence of sixteenth- and seventeenth-century attitudes toward the tameness of death appears in Don Peter de Luca's *A Dialogue of Dying Wel,* trans. Richard Verstegan (Antwerp, 1603) in the following quotation from the dedication to Joan Berkley, Abbess of the Engish Monastery of Nuns of the order of St. Benedict, in Brussels:

> There are sundry serpents and monsters that out of filth and corruption do take their originals, and so in lyke manner was that ugly monster, called death; out of the filth and sin of our first auncestor, first engendred. The agillitie & arte of this moste mercilesse tyrant consisteth in the continual casting of deadly dartes and infynit hee throweth out, even in euery moment, neuer ayming but neuer missing those hee aymeth at. (A2–A3)

8. *The Sermons of John Donne,* eds. Evelyn Simpson and George Potter (Berkeley: University of California Press, 1957), III, 188. Examples of the *contemptus mundi* theme abound in the devotional tradition; it is in more devotional works than those in the *ars* tradition, but it is always part of the setting for the *ars* treatises. For examples, see such different authors as Erasmus, *A Comfortable Exhortacion against the Chaunces of Death* (London, 1553) and William Loe, *Songs of Sion* (Hamborough, 1620) especially the preface to the congregation at Hamborough.

9. Johan Huizinga, *The Waning of the Middle Ages* (London: E. Arnold, 1924). See also Greenblatt, *Renaissance Self-Fashioning,* for an interpretation the vitality of which depends in many ways upon the present questions and concerns of the author and thereby in some fundamental way represents an integration of present human needs with the symbols of the earlier culture.

10. *The Hour of Our Death,* 129.

11. Some devotional works isolated the theme for special treatment, for example: Arthur Dent, *The Plaine Mans Path-way to Heauen* (London, 1601); Lewis Bayley, *The Practice of Dying Well,* 2d ed. (London, 1622); de Luca, *A Dialogue of Dying Wel.* Numerous other devotional texts include the attitude within a larger meditative framework. Augustine was the Father most often quoted during the period. *The City of God,* with commentary by Lodovico Vives, was translated by Healey (London, 1610); the 1522 edition of *The City of God* included an introduction by Erasmus. The iconography of Augustine's two cities of God and Man was pervasive in the sixteenth and early seventeenth centuries. The very intensity of the *contemptus mundi* attitude was probably increased by political tensions and a general sense of melancholy disillusionment; see Bridget Gellert-Lyons, *Voices of Melancholy: Studies in Literary Treatments of Melancholy in Renaissance England* (London: Routledge, 1971); also more practical efforts to assuage economic problems or by developing commerce within emerging expedient attitudes, in R. H. Tawney, *Business and Politics under James I* (Cambridge: Cambridge University Press, 1958). Out of an increasing sense on the part of conservatives that the

moral values of England were somehow being depreciated arose a cult of nostalgia for the reign of Elizabeth. See Roy C. Strong, *The Cult of Elizabeth: Elizabethan Portraiture and Pageantry* (London: Thames and Hudson, 1977).

12. See Louis L. Martz, *The Poetry of Meditation* (New Haven: Yale University Press, 1954) 136; also Lewalski, *Protestant Poetics and the Seventeenth-Century Religious Lyric.* Both Catholics and Protestants alike in the devotional tradition continued to emphasize the importance of preparing for death, upon which hung an eternity:

> According to the judgement of Aristotle, man of all mortal creatures is moste prudent, for that hee alone foreseeith thinges to come, and therefore differeth from the brute beast, which regardeth only things that bee present. (*A Dialogue of Dying Wel,* sig. A4)

That this little manual was translated from Italian into French by Frison and then into English suggests the pattern of the dissemination of the conventions of the tradition in early modern England throughout European countries. Even as late as 1634, the conventions of the *ars moriendi* and preparation for death as the culminating experience of life are sounded in the preface of *The Carnall Professor A Little Posthumous Volume brought out by I. T. as Meditation Preparing the Reader for a Good Death* (London, 1634):

> Our life is nothing but a daily warfare, every moment wee are more or lesse to encounter with adversaries, Satan alwaies labours for the destruction of the Saints. . . . Thy time is short, the art of well doing long: on this moment depends eternity of blessednesse if it be well, of misery if it be ill employed.

13. Dekker, *Wherein is schewed the picture of London, lying sicke of the Plague.* Published accounts of deaths of prominent persons throughout the sixteenth century are too numerous to mention; one famous example, done in verse, is that of Thomas Wolsey: Thomas Storer, *The Life and Death of Thomas Wolsey Cardinall* (London, 1599).

14. Neale, 397.

15. Stephen Greenblatt, *Sir Walter Ralegh: The Renaissance Man and His Roles* (New Haven: Yale University Press, 1973), 1–21.

16. Ralegh and Essex were rival courtiers and the point of view toward each depends in part (for Elizabethans, at least) on the one to whom one owed most for patronage. My own viewpoint is in part colored by Donne's admiration for Essex; in part by the ultimate difference between the deaths of Ralegh and Essex. For discussion of relevant political manipulation of symbolism, see Roy C. Strong, *Portraits of Queen Elizabeth I* (Oxford: Clarendon Press, 1963). See also for the imperial image dominant during Elizabeth's reign, Frances Yates, *Astraea: The Imperial Theme in the Sixteenth Century* (London: Routledge & Kegan Paul, 1975). Cf. the political climate with that of the Stuarts: see Stephen Orgel, *The Illusion of Power: Political Theater in the English Renaissance* (Berkeley: University of California Press, 1975).

17. C. S. Lewis, *Preface to Paradise Lost* (New York: Oxford University Press, 1961), 21. It is in relation to this tradition that I wish to qualify Greenblatt's interesting discussion in *Renaissance Self-Fashioning* of the importance of the individual. Modern attitudes toward shaping the self are profoundly different from those of the Renaissance.

18. "The Communion of the Sicke," in *The Booke of Common Prayer, and administration of the sacraments and other Rites and ceremonies in the Church of*

England (London, 1590), sig. Pii–Qi, is a ritual way of bringing about the oneness between the one about to die and Christ himself.

19. See William Roper, *The Life of Sir Thomas More,* in *Two Early Tudor Lives: The Life and Death of Cardinal Wolsey, by George Cavendish* and *The Life of Sir Thomas More by William Roper,* eds. Richard Sylvester and David Harding (New Haven: Yale University Press, 1962). See also Thomas More, "The Four Last Things," in *The Workes* (London, 1557); 38ff. More records the death scene of King Edward, trying to reconcile his friends. From the other major religious perspective, see John Foxe, *Acts and Monuments,* ed. Josiah Pratt, 8 vols. (London: George Seely, 1870). The tremendous reverence for the last words of the dying has a model in the last words of Christ; see *The Betraying of Christ: Iudas in despaire* (London, 1598), which includes poems on the last words. See also Ernst H. Kantorowicz, *The King's Two Bodies: A Study in Medieval Political Theology* (Princeton: Princeton University Press, 1957), for discussion of the divinely anointed aspect of kingship—the foundation in great measure for the demands of loyalty from the subject. The final reconciliation with both God and prince was recognized by all to involve a complex and sophisticated spiritual process. Peter Moulin, *The Comfort of a Communicant* (London, 1623), 34–37, suggests the general attitude throughout the period:

> Some will say, this peace is to be wished for, and I aspire to it euen with all my heart, but the way to come thereto is very hard to find out, the passage to death is dolorous and fearefull and Sathan lyeth in Ambush euen in the way; and all the feare, and feeblenesse, and sorrow that is there, is purposely placed to intrap. . . . Some say the Diuell appeared to a dying man, and showed him a Parchment . . . wherein was written . . . the sinnes of the poore sicke man.

20. David Bergeron, *English Civic Pageantry, 1558–1642* (London: Edward Arnold, 1971); see also *The Progresses and Public Processions of Queen Elizabeth,* ed. John Nichols, 3 vols. (London: J. Nichols, 1823); Roy C. Strong, *The English Icon, Elizabethan and Jacobean Portraiture* (London: Routledge, 1969). Shakespeare's death of Buckingham in *Henry VIII* integrates these aspects of the civic and the religious.

21. *A Sermon Preached at Paul's Crosse with a short Discourse of the late Earle of Essex, his confession, and penitence, before and at the time of his death.*

22. See also the antirebellion tract, *The most true reporte of James Fitz Morrice death, and others the like offenders; with a brief discourse of Rebellion* (London, 1579).

23. This preference is attested to in the period not only by explicit statements from devotional treatises but also by the visual tradition, particularly the popularity of deathbed scenes in the *ars* tradition and also in the frequency of more particularized deathbed scenes. Death of the Virgin paintings proliferated in the late Middle Ages, e.g., in the *Hours of Catherine of Cleves,* intro. John Plummer (New York: George Braziller, 1966), no. 14, but by the seventeenth century more different subjects were being portrayed in their final moments: e.g., Rembrandt's "Death of Dives."

24. The thief on the cross became in the symbolism the most vivid type of the inspiration against despair, the clear emblem of last minute repentance and redemption. As such he is the central figure in the "Inspiration against Despair" from the old woodcuts.

25. See her letters concerning the 1591 expedition to Normandy, *The Letters,*

211–18. The ambivalence of her feelings is clear; her irritation with Essex's rash behavior also shows through the diplomatic surface.

26. Harrison, see "Dangerous Courses," in *The Life and Death*, 183–210.

27. Neale, *Queen Elizabeth I*, 376–77; see letter in *Letters* of 17 September 1599, 274–78, from Elizabeth to Essex, written in response to a letter from Essex about the parley with Tyrone.

28. Robert Devereux, *An Apologie*. The *Apologie* was written earlier, but was published first in 1600.

29. Neale, *Queen Elizabeth I*, 369.

30. Ibid., 370.

31. After writing secretly to James about the succession, Essex had received a reply that he put into a little bag for safe-keeping and wore around his neck.

32. Neale, *Queen Elizabeth I*, 374; Harrison, *The Life and Death*, 294–314. Barlow in *A Sermon*, sig. B₅, gives the official line toward any form of rebellion:

> . . . they who thinke that they may eyther *Occidere* or *Excidere*, kill their liege, or fall from him, *Aut deponere a throno, aut exponere periculo*, depose and thrust them out of their seate, or expose them to danger or feare, are guiltie not onely of rebellion but of irreligion.

33. Barlow records this change of heart, and numerous historians have speculated upon it. Apparently the respected Ashton's sharp denunciation of Essex brought about a sudden change in the convicted lord. Although he argued vigorously against Ashton's accusations, when he saw that he had not prevailed, he began to counter Ashton with the confession of his aim to settle the succession; see Harrison, *The Life and Death*, 316–18. On a psychological level, the suddenness of change may be attributed to Essex's tendency toward depression and religious melancholia, as well as a parallel but opposite tendency toward arrogance and elation—in short, a difficult and intense personality that could shift perspectives violently.

34. Barlow, sig. C8

35. Barlow, sigs. C8–D.

36. Barlow, sigs. E3–E4.

37. Barlow, sigs. Eᵥ–E6.

38. Barlow, sig. E6.

39. Barlow, sig. E7.

40. Barlow, Ibid. After Essex's death the crowd would have fallen upon the headsman and killed him if the sheriffs had not provided protection. Essex's popularity continued, even after his death; see "A Lamentable Dittie composed upon the death of Robert Lord Devereaux late Earl of Essex" (London, ca. 1603).

41. *Ibid.*

42. I would agree with Jackson I. Cope, *The Theater and the Dream: From Metaphor to Form in Renaissance Drama* (Baltimore: Johns Hopkins University Press, 1973) especially chaps. 4–6, that Renaissance drama moves through a reality that is apparently random finally to touch the eternal forms. The *ars* is one of the means by which conventions and experience meet to expose the principles of renewal, transformation, integration, and resurrection.

Chapter 3. The Popular Word: Two Case Studies in Devotion

1. Samuel Garey, *Two Treatises, the first entitled The Food of the Faithfull. The Second Death's Welcome* (London, 1605).

2. Particularly popular sources throughout the late Middle Ages were the *Biblia Pauperum* and de Voragine, *The Golden Legend.*

3. For examples, the stained glass windows (early seventeenth century) at Lincoln's Inn chapel, where Donne was reader, show Old Testament prophets.

4. The sixteenth-century devotional literature, both Roman and Anglican, shows near-constant allusions to figures from the biblical system of typology (Job-Christ; Aaron-Christ), with frequent quotations from Old and New Testaments interlarded in the texts; for examples, see B. W., *The Maner to Dye Well* (London, 1578), Latin by Petrus de Soto; Innocent III, *Mirror of Man's Lyfe,* trans. H. K. (London, 1576).

5. *A Salve for a Sicke Man* (Cambridge, 1595).

6. *The Following of Christ,* trans. B. F.; also Epistle of St. Bernard and *Certaine Rules of A Christian Life* by Picus the Elder, Earle of Mirandula (n.p., 1615).

7. *Seven Helpes to Heaven* (n.p., 1620), 360.

8. In some sense the full bibliography of this chapter (or even of the entire book) is the proper footnote, for such a list includes numerous books of devotion, Shakespeare's plays, the *Faerie Queene, Paradise Lost,* and numerous lyric poems, particularly elegies of the period, but they are not limited to that form.

9. See the article by David W. Atkinson that analyzes what he calls "The English *ars moriendi:* its Protestant Transformation," *Renaissance and Reformation/Renaissance et Reforme,* new ser., vol. VI, no. 1; old ser., vol. XVIII, no. 1 (1982), 1–10.

10. *Ars moriendi,* that is to say, the craft for to deye for the helthe of mannes soule, 1491 (Oxford: Clarendon Press, 1891). Other fifteenth-century early *ars* texts and facsimiles at the Huntington Library include *Ars moriendi* (Kachelhofen, 1494); *Livre de bien vivre* (1492); *Ars moriendi,* (1465); *Ars moriendi* (ca. 1740); *Ars moriendi* (Augsberg, before 1472); *Art de bene Mour,* Ediciones Torculum (Catalana, 1493; Barcelona, 1951); *The Ars Moriendi,* Editio Princeps, ca. 1450, ed. W. Harry Rylands, Holbein Society (London, 1881); Cardinale de Fermos, *Ars moriendi: Questa operecta tracta dellarte del ben morire . . .,* 1787; *Ars moriendi* (Cologne, ca. 1474).

11. (Antwerp, 1603), sig. C1ᵥ. Page numbers to this book will hereafter be included in the text.

12. Perkins, "A Salve," sig. A1. Later references to this book will be included in the text.

13. Dying ones are often comforted by example, both in woodcuts and/or in texts. John Foxe in *A Brief Exhortation to the Sicke* (London, 1563), 13, counsels the sick not to fear and sin; to remember the example of the thief on the cross.

14. See Helen C. White, *English Devotional Literature 1600–1640,* University of Wisconsin Studies in Language and Literature, no. 29 (Madison: University of Wisconsin Press, 1931), 204–05.

15. Becon, sig. B1. I am told that a very elaborate instance of Job's patience is embodied in one of the portals at Chartres.

16. Becon, sig. B1.

17. Petrus de Soto, the Latin author of The *Maner to Dye Well,* which includes vivid descriptions of the death of a good man and the death of an evil man, sig. D4ᵥ–Dᵥ; for example, the canonization of Plato:

And by this old Doctours Hierome and Augustine do write, that Plato (that excellent and moste noble Philosopher) dyd forgoe the delicate and beautifull Cittie of Athens, with certayne of his Schollers, choosing rathr to dwell in an olde ruinous vyllage, being often with Earthquakes and Tempestes wel neare ouer-turned, so that by the feare of dangers and death, they myght in them selues mortifie the vices of the flesh. . . . And that by this (the premeditation of death) there might growe in vs such an healthful feare.

18. *Ars Moriendi,* Editio Principio; see other *ars* editions that include woodcuts: *Ars moriendi* (Kachelhofen, 1494), that includes in addition to the usual series an image of the weighing of souls at the end; *Ars moriendi,* ca. 1470, that includes several additional woodcuts: creation, fall, and a woodcut of God sending forth Christ to the cross.

19. See Shirley Ann Felt, "Ars Moriendi and Donne," diss., Riverside, 1975. See also *The Doctrine of Dying Well. Or the godly man's Guide to Glory. Wherein is briefly comprised a short view of the glorious estate of Gods Saints in the Kingdome of Heaven. Together with the Meanes to obtaine, the Markes to know and the Motiues to vrge vs to prepare our selues for Christ, before our soules be vnbodied, lest Heauens gate be shut against vs.* (London, 1628); "The Cure of the Feare of Death" found in *The Marrow of the Oracles of God. Or Divers Treatises,* 2d ed. (London, 1629; 14th ed. London, 1623). The first edition was 1612.

20. Frontispiece, *A Salue for a Sicke Manne.*

21. In *Hooker's Works,* ed. John Keble, 7th ed., rev. R. W. Church and Paget (Oxford, 1888), I. Henry Cuffe, *The Differences of the Ages of Man's Life* (London, 1607), 72.

22. (1553), trans. from *De morte declamatio.*

23. Zachary Boyd, *The Last Battell of the Soule in Death,* II (Edinburgh, 1629), Preface.

24. Foxe, 10.

25. (London, 1620); (London, 1548).

26. (London, 1606); Potter and Simpson, *The Sermons of John Donne,* X (Los Angeles and San Francisco: University of California Press, 1962).

27. Ariès, *The Hour of Our Death,* 5–92.

28. See, among other historical scholars, Roy C. Strong, *The Cult of Elizabeth* (London: Thames and Hudson, 1977).

29. See O'Connor, *The Art of Dying Well* for the history of the *ars* tradition; also Beaty, *The Craft of Dying; A Study in the Literary Tradition of the Ars Moriendi in England.*

30. In Martz, *The Poetry of Meditation,* Intro. For the greater ironies and ambiguities of More's *Utopia,* see Elizabeth McCutcheon, "Denying tthe Contrary: More's use of Litotes in the *Utopia,*" in *Essential Articles for the Study of Thomas More,* eds. R. S. Sylvester and G. Marc'hadour (Hamden, Conn.: Creton Books, 1977), 271–72.

31. George W. McClure, "The Art of Mourning: Autobiographical Writing on the Loss of a Son in Italian Humanist Thought 1400–1461," *Renaissance Quarterly* 39.3 (1983): 473. See the second plate in *Ars moriendi* (Kachelhofen, 1494) and also *Le Livre de bien vivre* (Paris, 1492); English trans., 1503; see also the deathbed painting in the Grimani breviary, *Fac.-Simile Delle Minature Contenute nel Brevario Grimani,* E. Sequito in *Fotografia Da Antonio Perini* (1480–1490; Venezia: A. Perini, 1862), fol. 168.

32. There was always a sense of the special needs of those who did not die in the course of nature, as Foxe in his *Exhortation* contains a prayer to be "sayd over children, visited by Gods hand with sicknesse, in this sorowful tyme of Gods visitation," title page.

33. For discussion of the new middle class see Louis B. Wright, *Middle-Class Culture in Elizabethan England* (Chapel Hill: University of North Carolina Press, 1935). See also Boyd's Preface.

34. Boyd, 99.

35. See Lewalski, *Protestant Poetics and the Seventeenth-Century Religious Lyric* and William H. Halewood, *The Poetry of Grace* (New Haven: Yale University Press, 1970).

36. See also for a more modern perspective Greenblatt, *Renaissance Self-Fashioning,* for discussion of Renaissance attitudes toward the uniqueness of self.

37. See White, *English Devotional Literature 1600–1640,* 167ff.

38. G. W. Pigman, *Grief and the English Renaissance Elegy* (Cambridge, Mass.: Harvard University Press, 1985), 36–37.

39. Nigel Llewellyn, *The Art of Death: Visual Culture in the English Death Ritual* ca. 1500–ca. 1800 (London: Reaktion Books, 1991). This helpful book was published in relation to an exhibit of death symbolism and artifacts held at the Victoria and Albert Museum during 1992.

Chapter 4. "A Long Day's Dying": Spenser and Milton on Despair (1590–1667)

1. See Augustine, "Sermo de Disciplina Christiana," Migne, *Omnia Opera, Cursus Completus Patrologiae Latinae,* 40, XII, col. 676; Richard Hooker, *Of the Laws of Ecclesiastical Polity,* Everyman, II (London, 1907), Bk. V; William Perkins, *A Salve for a Sicke Man* (London, 1592), Ch. 55; John Donne, *The Sermons,* eds. Potter, Simpson, and Gardner, I–X (Berkeley and Los Angeles: University of California Press, 1953–62), throughout; Lancelot Andrews, *Ninety-Six Sermons,* ed. J. W., Library of Anglo-Catholic Theology, II (Oxford, 1841), throughout.

2. Edmund Spenser, *The Faerie Queene,* ed. Thomas Roche, Jr., Assis. C. Patrick O'Donnell, Jr. (New Haven and London: Yale University Press, 1978); John Milton, "Paradise Lost," *Complete Poems and Major Prose,* ed. Milton Y. Hughes (New York: Odyssey Press/Bobbs-Merrill, 1973). All quotations will be from these texts.

3. See especially exponents of the New Historicism: Greenblatt, *Renaissance Self-Fashioning;* also Marcus, *Childhood and Cultural Despair; A Theme and Variations in Seventeenth-Century Literature;* Leah S. Marcus, *The Politics of Mirth: Jonson, Herrick, Milton, Marvell, and the Defense of Old Holiday Pastimes* (Chicago and London: University of Chicago Press, 1986).

4. Rosalie Colie, *The Resources of Kind: Genre Theory in the Renaissance,* ed. Barbara K. Lewalski (Berkeley: University of California Press, 1973); John M. Steadman, *Epic and Tragic Structure in Paradise Lost* (Chicago: University of Chicago Press, 1976).

5. Douglas Peterson, *Time, Tide, and Tempest: A Study of Shakespeare's Romances* (San Marino, Calif.: The Huntington Library, 1973).

6. Douglas Bush, *Prefaces to Renaissance Literature* (New York: W. W. Norton & Co., 1965), 65–90.

7. The popularity of sermons and devotional literature attests to this point. As in the twentieth century, far more religious works were sold than secular ones. As Louis B. Wright pointed out many years ago in *Middle-Class Culture in Elizabethan England,* the vast majority of books sold for a penny a piece on the streets of London every day were religious tracts. See Susan B. Snyder for her article on "The Left Hand of God: Despair in Medieval and Renaissance Tradition," *Renaissance Studies* 12 (1965): 18–59.

8. See the essay in this book on Essex, emblem of the discontent that threatened England during this period sometimes called "Recessional."

9. "The Sicke Mans Salve," *The Second Part of the Bokes, which Thomas Becon hath made and published* (n.p., 1560). Numerous editions of this book were published—a fact that suggests the pervasiveness of Christian Stoicism.

10. See the early history of the *ars* as it came into England in Beaty, *The Craft of Dying: A Study in the Literary Tradition of the Ars Moriendi in England;* also the more general history in Mary Catharine O'Connor, *The Art of Dying Well: The Development of the Ars Moriendi.*

11. See the *Ars Moriendi* (Editio Princeps, ca. 1450), facsimile edition, ed. W. Harry Rylands (London, 1881). A later English example is Wynkyn de Worde, ed. of Caxton's *Book Named the Royall* (London, 1506). Both explore the spiritual temptations and comforts for the dying. Especially vivid are the woodcuts. According to Rosamund Tuve, in *Allegorical Imagery* (Princeton: Princeton University Press, 1966), 57, *The Boke Named the Royall* is one of the most important sources for the iconography of death in the Renaissance.

12. Practitioners of the New History assume in most instances the modern Marxist view of monarch and hierarchy and therefore an attitude toward the Renaissance that has much in common with what we used to call "whig history," which includes the underlying assumption that the Renaissance was the great beginning of liberalism and individualism. If E. M. W. Tillyard was too idealistic in his view of hierarchal continuities in the Renaissance, the New History perhaps emphasizes power politics as too dominant over other modes of valuing. See Joseph Anthony Wittreich, Jr., *Visionary Poetics: Milton's Tradition and His Legacy* for the Platonic tradition that lies behind the belief in hierarchy (San Marino, Calif.: Henry E. Huntington Library, 1979), 3–78.

13. Kathrine Koller, "Art, Rhetoric, and Holy Dying in the *Faerie Queene,* with special reference to the /Despair Canto," *Studies in Philology* 61 (1964): 128–39.

14. See for general studies John M. Steadman, *Milton and the Renaissance Hero* (Oxford: Clarendon Press, 2967); Northrop Frye, *The Return of Eden* (Toronto: University of Toronto Press, 1967): Joseph Summers, *The Muses's Method: An Introduction to Paradise Lost* (Cambridge, Mass.: Harvard University Press, 1962); Barbara K. Lewalski, *Paradise Lost and the Rhetoric of Literary Forms* (Princeton: Princeton University Press, 1985). For elements of tragedy closely related to the theme of despair, see Steadman, *Epic and Tragic Structure in Paradise Lost;* Helen Gardner, "Milton's Satan and the Theme of Damnation in Elizabethan Tragedy," *E&S* 1 (1948), 46–66), rpt. of *A Reading of Paradise Lost* (Oxford: Clarendon Press, 1965); Marshall Grossman, "Dramatic Structure and Emotive Pattern in the Fall, *Paradise Lost,* IX," *Milton Studies* 13 (1979): 201–19; Richard S. Ide. "On the Uses of Elizabethan Drama: The Revaluation of Epic in *Paradise Lost,*" *Milton Studies* 17 (1983); 121–40.

15. "Psalms and the Representation of Death in *Paradise Lost,*" *Milton Studies,* 23 (1987): 133–44. See Patrick Cullen, *The Infernal Triad: The Flesh, the World and the Devil in Spenser and Milton* (Princeton: Princeton University Press, 1974). See also Mary Ann Radzinowicz, "The Politics of *Paradise Lost,*" in *The Politics of Discourse,* eds. Kevin Sharpe and Stephen N. Zwicker (Berkeley and Los Angeles: University of California Press, 1987).

16. Snyder, "The Left Hand of God," 18–59.

17. Martz, *The Poetry of Meditation.*

18. "Hell," *The Comedy of Dante Alighieri The Florentine,* trans. Dorothy L. Sayers (Middlesex, England: Penguin Books, 1949), Canto XXXIV, 28–60.

19. John Milton, *Complete Poems and Major Prose,* ed. Merritt Y. Hughes, (New York: Odyssey Press/Bobbs-Merrill, 1973).

20. Bernard Spivack, *Shakespeare and The Allegory of Evil: The History of Metaphor in Relation to His Major Villains* (New York: Columbia University Press, 1958); see also Edward Weismiller, "Materials Dark and Crude: A Partial Genealogy for Milton's Satan," *Huntington Library Quarterly* 31 (1967): 75–93.

Chapter 5. "Despair and Die": The Ultimate Temptation of Richard III

1. *The Variorum Shakespeare,* (New York: Columbia University Press, 1958); ed. Howard Furness, XVI (Philadelphia and London: Lippincott, 1908); also *The Riverside Shakespeare,* ed. G. Blakemore Evans (Boston: Houghton Mifflin Co., 1974). All quotations from the play will be taken from this edition.

2. For the origin of the great tradition behind the Renaissance devotional attitudes, see the *Ars Moriendi* (Editio Princeps, ca. 1450), facsimile edition, ed. W. Harry Rylands (London: Holbein Society, 1881). The importance of death in the graphic tradition is most well known through Holbein's *Les Simulacres et historiées faces de la mort,* (Lyons: Trechsel fratres, 1538, Facs. Rep.: *Hans Holbein's Todtentanz,* Munich: G. Hirth, 1903). There are other series that use the conventions by Dürer and others. In A. M. Hind, "The Tudor Period," *Engraving in England in the Sixteenth and Seventeenth Centuries* (Cambridge: Cambridge University Press, 1952), Pt. 1, Pl. 59, Theodor de Bry is shown in self-portrait with compass and skull. He is known also for a rare engraving of Sidney's funeral procession. See notes on *ars* in earlier chapters.

3. It is interesting to compare an illumination of "Psychomachia," from the eleventh-century manuscript of Prudentius at the British Museum. This is not Shakespeare's source, but it is an early ancestor of one of the most common oppositions of Renaissance iconography, an opposition that was essential to the structure of most of the morality plays. See also Erwin Panofsky, *Early Netherlandish Painting: Its Origins and Character,* I & II (Cambridge, Mass.: Harvard University Press, 1953).

4. One needs only to recall the importance of death in popular Renaissance theology. Dying was seen as the supreme moment of a man's life and the last opportunity for the Devil (The Bad Angel) to ensnare the soul. Likewise, as we have seen, an eternity of bliss or damnation hung upon the outcome of the final battle between the Devil and the Guardian Angel (The Good Angel). See White, *English Devotional Literature 1600–1640; Tudor Books of Devotion* (Madison: University of Wisconsin Press, 1951) for discussion of the popularity and influence of devotional tracts.

5. See Kathrine Koller, "Falstaff and the Art of Dying," *MLN* 60 (June 1945): 383–86.

6. The descriptions of the deaths of great men (to be remembered) were one strain within the *ars moriendi.* See the traditional account by Isaak Walton of the death of John Donne first published in the *LXXX Sermons* of Donne in 1640 (*Life of John Donne* (London, 1658). Even as late as the middle of the seventeenth century, the traditional interest in the way a man faced his death survived in such a form as William Somner's *The Frontispiece of the Kings Book,* which opened with a poem annexed "The In-security of Princes. Considered in an occasional Meditation upon the King's late Sufferings and Death 1650."

7. See Bernard Spivak, *Shakespeare and the Allegory of Evil* for a discussion of the morality play ancestors of Richard. See also Wolfgang Clemen, *A Commentary on Shakespeare's Richard III,* trans. Jean Bonheim (London: Methuen Press, 1968), 202–4, 216. For the more historical argument for the fall of vice, see Tom F. Driver, *The Sense of History in Greek and Shakespearean Drama* (New York: Columbia University Press, 1960), 87–105. An article by psychologist Donald S. Shupe, "The Wooing of Lady Anne: A Psychological Inquiry," *Shakespeare Quarterly* 29 (1978): 28–36, argues on modern grounds the acceptability of change in relation to the high "Machiavellian type" of Richard.

8. See *Hercules am Scheidewege und andere antike Bildstoffe in der neueren Kunst* (Leipzig: B. G. Teubner, 1930). See also "Dream of Hercules," Plate 19, in Doebler, *Shakespeare's Speaking Pictures: Studies in Iconic Imagery.*

9. Robert and Oliver Steele, "Introduction," Edmund Spenser, *The Faerie Queene,* Books One and Two (New York: Odyssey Press, 1952), for discussion of Spenser's relationship to the painterly tradition *via* St. George and the dragon. See the *Christian Knight Map of the World,* engraving by Jodocus Hondius, 1596, for the continuing popularity of the themes, British Museum reprod. in Roy C. Strong, *The English Icon: Elizabeth and Jacobean Portraiture* (London: Routledge & Kegan Paul, 1969), 41.

10. Desiderius Erasmus, replenished with most wholesome precepts made by the famous clerk Erasmus of Rotterdam to which is added a new and marvelous preface, Orig. pub. 1518 (Methuen Edition, London, 1905), opp. 1.

11. See O'Connor, *The Art of Dying Well: The Development of the Ars Moriendi,* and the history of the *ars* tradition; also Beaty, *The Craft of Dying: A Study in the Ars Moriendi in England.* For an understanding of the relation between continental books and popular devotion in England during the sixteenth and seventeenth centuries, see Martz, *The Poetry of Meditation.*

12. *The Ars Moriendi,* fig. 11.

13. Ed. John Plummer (New York: Pierpont Morgan Library, 1964), illum. 102.

14. In T. H. R. Boase, *Death in the Middle Ages: Mortality, Judgment, and Remembrance* (New York: McGraw-Hill, 1972).

15. I have obtained photographs of the Beham engravings from the print collection in the Warburg Institute, London, but the notes on them are from Adam von Bartsch, *Le peintre-graveur* (Vienne: D. V. Degen, 1808), VIII, 113. The Dürer is "Coat of Arms with Skull" from *The Intaglio Prints of Albrecht Dürer,* ed. Walter L. Strauss (New York: Kennedy Galleries and Abaris Books, Inc., 1976–77), 40.

16. Richard's bravery in the final battle would have been qualified by theological implications. In act 5, scene 3, he encourages his forces by speaking of being "hand in hand with hell," a coalition which would make his actions seem obviously malevolent and desperate to an Elizabethan rather than heroic, as they probably seem to a modern audience.

17. (Cambridge, 1595).

Chapter 6. Othello's Angels

1. See L. J. Ross, "The Use of a 'Fit-Up' Booth in Othello," *Shakespeare Quarterly,* 22, no. 4 (1961): 359–70, for an interesting discussion of the staging of *Othello.* Although I am not entirely convinced that a booth was used, I should agree that it seems highly unlikely that the bed was originally in the inner stage. In the sixteenth century the four-poster was the bed *par excellence* with a paneled tester on four

posts—the most important piece of furniture in the private rooms of the house and as a valuable inheritance passed on from one generation to another. See *The Tudor Period: 1500–1603,* eds. Ralph Edwards and L. G. G. Ramsey (London: Rainbird, McLean, 1956), 37. For the iconographic distinction between the "family" bed, the childbirth bed or the deathbed, and the bed of luxury, see Gabriel Chappuys, *Figures de la Bible* (Lyon: E. Michel, 1582). In this illustrated Bible there is only one bed of luxury, curved and voluptuous, belonging to Potiphar's wife, while there are numerous representations of the massive, rectilinear deathbeds, or, upon occasions, beds of birth. The bed in *Othello* is ironically both a marriage and a deathbed.

2. These images belong both to the early medieval drama of the Psychomachia and to the nondramatic and visual tradition of the *ars.* I should contend, however, that the popularity and pervasiveness of the *ars* instruction would make associations with the tradition more immediate to the Shakespearean audience.

3. E. K. Chambers, *The Elizabethan Stage,* III (Oxford: Clarendon Press, 1923), 487. All references to the play will be from the following edition: William Shakespeare, "Othello," ed. G. Blakemore Evans, *The Riverside Shakespeare.*

4. Paul N. Siegel, "The Damnation of Othello," *PMLA* 68 (December 1953): 1068–79. Cf. Kenneth O. Myrick, "The Theme of Damnation in Shakespearean Tragedy," *Studies in Philology* 38 (April 1941): 221–45, who does not see Othello as damned. An example of the third point of view may be seen in Irving Ribner, *Patterns in Shakespearian Tragedy* (New York: Barnes and Noble, 1960).

5. *The ars moriendi* (Editio Princeps, ca. 1450), facs. ed., ed. W. Harry Rylands (London: Holbein Society, 1881). The book contains twelve leaves without signatures with illustrations scattered throughout. Dr. William Thomas has described one of the stained glass windows at the great church at Malvern as representing this one of the *ars* scenes in the fifteenth century. In the top part of the window a monk was kneeling with demons behind him, and in the lower part a man lay on his deathbed with demons trying to seize his soul as it issued from his mouth in the shape of a child, while the Good Angel tried to protect it. G. McN. Rushforth, *Medieval Christian Imagery* (Oxford, 1937), 307.

6. See Launcelot Andrews, *The Private Devotions and Manual for the Sick* (London, 1839). No translator is given.

7. Robert Bellarmine, *The Art of Dying Well,* trans. C.E. of the Society of Jesus, sec. ed. (St. Omer: St. Omer College Press, 1622); a popular extension of the *ars* tradition is suggested by the practice of recording the deaths of the great or popular men of the day; this little book contains an account of Bellarmine's sickness, death, and burial in Rome. See also Christopher Sutton, *Disce Mori, Learne to Dye,* eds. Edward H. Dewar and Charles Daman (London, 1858).

8. Roland Mushat Frye, *Shakespeare and Christian Doctrine* (Princeton: Princeton University Press, 1963), 25. In Thomas Becon, "The Sicke Mannes Salve," *Works,* ed. Rev. John Ayre, IV (Cambridge, 1844), 165, we see the traditional use of Cain as an illustration of one who fell into desperation, believing his sin was too great to be forgiven, and was damned.

9. Christopher Sutton, *Disce Mori,* 6. This book was published first in 1600 and was frequently reprinted. Sutton's family was in high favor with Queen Elizabeth. See also *King Lear,* ed. Alfred Harbage (Baltimore: Penguin, 1958), I.i.292–93: "yet he hath ever but / slenderly known himself."

10. Richard Hooker, "The Laws of Ecclesiastical Polity," *Works,* ed. the Rev. John Keble, 7th ed., rev. by the Very Rev. R. W. Church, and the Rev. F. Paget (Oxford, 1888), I, Bk. V, ch. xlvi, 195–97.

11. Desiderius Erasmus, *Preparation to Death,* (n.p., 1535), sig. D2ᵥ.

12. The *ars moriendi,* Rylands.

13. Frances M. M. Comper, ed., "The Craft to know Well to Die," *The Book of the Craft of Dying* (London, 1917), 77–78. Réau also notes in *Iconographie de L'Art Chrètien* (Paris: Presses Universitaires de France, 1957), II, 2, 657, the continuing popularity of the injunction to model one's death on that of Christ: he mentions the thirty-nine stamps attributed to Romeyn de Hooghe (late seventeenth century) that illustrate the death of the Franciscan David de la Vigne. Each scene in the process of dying is paralleled by an episode from the Passion of Christ.

14. Erasmus, *Preparation,* sig. F3v.

15. The text of this work also appears in Latin in a book by Erasmus and George Aemylius, *Imagines mortis* (Cologne, 1555 [?]), in which the text accompanies some of the plates of the *danse macabre.*

16. A Latin letter given in an article by Geoffrey Tillotson, in "Othello and the Alchemist at Oxford in 1610," *The Times Literary Supplement* (20 July 1933), 494, describes the way in which the audience was moved, especially by Desdemona's pitiful aspect in the death scene: "cum in lecto decumbens spectantium misericordiam ipso vultu imploraret."

17. In "The Lamentation of the Creature," Miss Comper's modern printing of one of the *ars* texts in the *Book of the Craft of Dying,* 139, we may see a characteristic use of the opposition:

> The Complaint of the Dying Creature to the Good angel O my GOOD ANGEL, to whom our Lord took me to keep, where be thee now? Me thinketh ye should be here, and answer for me; for the dread of death distroubleth me, so that I cannot answer for myself. Here is my bad angel and is one of my chief accursers, with regions of friends with him. I have no creature to answer for me. Alas it is a heavy case!

18. *The Oxford English Dictionary,* VII (reprinted 1961), 488. The dictionary gives as one of its illustrations the following quotation from Sir Thomas More, "Confutation Tindale," *Works,* 815: "To fall in Despicions upon God's eleccion, . . . and eternall sentence of reprobation." The term was used often in opposition to *election.*

19. Traditional advice against suicide is given by the popular preacher, Christopher Sutton, in *Disce Mori,* in a section entitled: "An admonition for all such as find themselves troubled with evil motions, to commit faithless and fearful attempts against themselves." In the third paragraph of the section Sutton makes explicit the connection between despair and suicide:

> Abridge the time we may not, we must not, for all the disgraces, and injuries, and obliquies, the crosses and losses this world can lay upon us: fie upon that discontentment that should make any cowardly to run away, or distrustfully to give over his standing, before he be called by the general of the field: fie upon that despair that should make any cast away themselves, and forget they have souls to save. (252)

20. Martin Luther, *Every Dayes Sacrifice* (London, 1607).

21. In Bayley's *The Practice of Pietie,* 694, the strategy of the devil is commented upon:

> It is found by continuall experience, that neere the time of death, (when the Children of God are weakest) then Sathan makes the greatest flourish of his strength: and assailes them with his strongest temptations. . . . And therefore he will now bestirre himselfe as much as he can, and labour to set before their eyes all the grosse sins which ever they

committed, and the *Judgements* of God which are due unto them: thereby, to drive them if hee can, to despaire; which is a grievouser sinne then all the sinnes that they committed.

22. John E. Hankins, "The Pains of the Afterworld: Fire, Wind, and Ice in Milton and Shakespeare," *PMLA* 71 (June 1956): 482–95. This article, on the basis of some sound background materials, distinguishes between purgatorial and hell imagery, but my own reading indicates that in the sixteenth and seventeenth centuries sometimes the distinction is not made.

23. Siegel, "The Damnation of Othello," 1068–79. Ribner in *Patterns in Shakespearian Tragedy* is, I think, recognizing this dramatic redemption in his argument that though Othello dies expecting damnation, Desdemona as a symbol of mercy has prepared the audience for his salvation.

24. Frye, *Shakespeare and the Christian Doctrine,* 63.

25. Erasmus, *Preparation to Deathe,* sig. A4v.

Chapter 7. Lear, Gloucester, and Dread Despair

1. William Shakespeare, *King Lear,* ed. G. Blakemore Evans, The Riverside Edition (Boston: Houghton Mifflin Co., 1974), I.i.41. Further references to the text will be to this edition.

2. See introduction to William Shakespeare, *King Lear,* ed. Alfred Harbage (Baltimore: The Penguin Shakespeare, 1958), xviii; Frank Kermode, "Introduction," Riverside Edition, *King Lear,* 1254. Kermode, though deeply aware of the darkness in *Lear,* mentions the importance of the rich interaction between the characters and the religious perspective of the audience.

3. Norman Rabkin, *Shakespeare and the Common Understanding* (New York: Free Press, 1967); also "Meaning and Shakespeare," in *Shakespeare 1971, Proceedings of the World Shakespeare Congress, Vancouver, August, 1971,* eds. Clifford Leech and J. M. R. Margeson (Toronto: University of Toronto Press, 1972), 89–106.

4. *The Age of Humanism: Europe, 1480–1530,* trans. Katherine M. Delvenay and E. M. Gwyer (London: Thames and Hudson, 1963), 17.

5. See, for example, William Elton (San Marino, Calif.: Huntington Library, 1966); also Russell A. Fraser, *Shakespeare's Poetic in Relation to King Lear* (London: Routledge & Kegan Paul, 1962).

6. See the major work that links Lear to Renaissance self-knowledge: Paul A. Jorgensen, *Lear's Self Discovery* (Berkeley: University of California Press,1967).

7. See *The Essays of Montaigne,* trans. John Florio, ed. George Saintsbury (Re 1892–93; New York: AMS Press, Inc., 1967), vols. I, II, III. Throughout Montaigne's essays there is a continual stripping away of both rational and worldly values, finally to expose the self to God and grace.

8. Sonnet 4, "Holy Sonnets," *The Divine Poems,* ed. Helen Gardner (Oxford: Clarendon Press, 1952).

9. Douglas L. Peterson, "John Donne's Holy Sonnets and the Anglican Doctrine of Contrition," in *Essential Articles for the Study of John Donne's Poetry,* ed. John R. Roberts (Hamden, Conn.: Archon Books, 1975), 313–23.

10. See *Speculum bonae mortis* (1694). I examined this series in the photograph collection of the Warburg Institute.

11. For the paradoxical balance involved see especially Adolf Katzenellenbogen, *Allegories of the Virtues and Vices in Medieval Art, from Early Christian*

Times to the Thirteenth Century, trans. Alan J. Crick (1939; reprint, New York: W. W. Norton, 1964). See end notes for list of scenes.

12. St. Thomas, "Summa Theologica," *The Basic Writings of St. Thomas Aquinas,* ed. Anton Pegis, II–III (New York: Random House, 1945) 14, 2.

13. Desiderius Erasmus, *Preparation to Deathe,* no trans. (n.p., 1534), sig. F. Luther in "A Sermon on Preparing to Die," written in 1519, in Luther's *Works,* ed. Martin O. Dietrick (Philadelphia: Fortress Press, 1969), I, 99–115, warns strongly against facing one's sins at the actual moment of death. He suggests as proper focuses for meditation not only Christ but also the saints, who are examples of God's mercy and the hope of salvation.

14. *Elizabethan and Metaphysical Imagery: Renaissance Poetic and Twentieth-Century Critics* (Chicago: University of Chicago Press, 1947).

15. (Madison: University of Wisconsin Press, 1976), 92–119.

16. Doran, 110.

Chapter 8. "Rooted Sorrow": The Metaphor

1. Bernard of Clairvaux refers to such a rooted sorrow when he says in his *De Consideratio:* "This is the worm that dieth not: the memory of things past." See also Bridget Gellert-Lyons, *The Voices of Melancholy: Studies in Literary Treatments of Melancholy in Renaissance England* (London: Routledge & Kegan Paul, 1971) for a study of related ideas in the early seventeenth century.

2. William Shakespeare, "Macbeth," *The Riverside Shakespeare,* ed. G. Blakemore Evans (Boston: Houghton Mifflin Co., 1974).

3. Within the widespread tradition, most pertinent here is the *ars moriendi* pattern. Among numerous examples, Catholic and Protestant, see Robert Bellarmine, *The Art of Dying Well,* trans. E. Coffin of the Society of Jesus, sec. ed. (St. Omer, 1622) and Christopher Sutton, *Disce Mori: Learne to Dye* (London, 1600); Thomas Becon, *The Sycke Man's Salve* (London, 1561?); Henry Thorne, *Phisicke for the Soule* (London, 1568); Sir Thomas Elyot, *A Preseruatiue Agaynste Deth* (London, 1545); Desiderius Erasmus, *Preparation to Deathe, A Boke as Deuout as Eloquent,* (n.p., 1534); Lewis Bayly, *The Practice of Pietie,* 12th ed. (London, 1620). These are selected sixteenth- and seventeenth-century heirs of the medieval tract.

4. Susan Snyder, "'The Left-Hand of God': Despair in Medieval and Renaissance Tradition," *Studies in the Renaissance,* 12 (1965):18–59. I am much indebted to Snyder's article. The major way in which this essay differs is in literary application and focusing of the commonplaces more firmly within the visual tradition.

5. Aquinas, *Summa Theologica,* II–III, 14, 2.

6. *The Sermons of John Donne,* ed. George R. Potter and Evelyn Simpson, II (Los Angeles: University of California Press, 1955), 72–94.

7. "The Faerie Queene," *Works of Edmund Spenser,* A Variorum Edition, eds. Greenlaw, et al (Baltimore: Johns Hopkins University Press, 1932), I, IX, 40–49. See also Kathrine Koller, "Art, Rhetoric, and Holy Dying in the *Faerie Queene* with Special Reference to the Despair Canto," *Studies in Philology* 61 (1964): 126–39.

8. Andrea Alciati, *Emblematum liber* (Augsburg, 1531). Visual reminders of the macabre Dance of Death motifs abound throughout the sixteenth century; one instance is the popular *A Booke of Christian Prayers* by Richard Day (London, 1578), which contains engravings by Holbein and Dürer of *memento moris* as page

borders. Another earlier example is that of Erasmus and George Aemylius, *Imagines Mortis* (Cologne, 1555 [1557?]), which contains plates of the danse macabre plus epigrams.

9. *Works*, ed. Martin O. Dietrich (Philadelphia: Fortress Press, 1969), I, 99–115.

10. In the Bosch painting (National Gallery, Washington, D.C.) the head of the *moriens* is turned toward a high window which focuses a beam of light on which rests a crucifix. Obviously both light and crucifix are the images of redemptive mercy upon which the *moriens* is being encouraged to meditate as a corrective to the temptation to avarice represented in the rest of the painting.

11. Samuel Schoenbaum, *William Shakespeare: A Compact Documentary Life* (New York: Oxford University Press, 1977), 251.

12. An example of such a work is the Platonic dialogue written by Thomas Becon (chaplain to Archbishop Cranmer), "The Sicke Mans Salve," in which friends take the part of the sick person and give the proper responses to carry him through the temptation of the last struggle. Becon's treatment is a variation on the simpler advice given in the *ars moriendi Here begynneth a lytell treatyse* (London, 1532), in which Section 1 advises the presence of a friend who counsels the *moriens* to remember the blessings of God, keep the crucifix in his sight and use holy water. The friend is also told to encourage the *moriens* to cry for mercy and to remind him of Jesus and His suffering.

13. Samuel Chew, *The Virtues Reconciled: An Iconographic Study* (Toronto: University of Toronto Press, 1947).

14. According to Aquinas, penitence must be a mean between fear and hope. For example, Judas, who seems to repent, was said to be damned because his remorse was excessive. The Aristotelian doctrine of the mean continued to be part of Renaissance thinking.

15. See Beach Langston, "Marlowe's Faustus and the *Ars Moriendi* Tradition," in *A Tribute to George Coffin Taylor*, ed. Arnold Williams (Chapel Hill: University of North Carolina Press, 1952), 148–67, for a fuller discussion of the issue. Faustus's conscious pact with the devil underlines his sense that he is not personally worthy of mercy.

Chapter 9.   A Case Study in Dying: Donne's Poetics of Preparation and Comfort

1. 2 vols. (Edinburgh, 1629).

2. See David Bevington, ed., *Homo, Memento Finis: The Iconography of Just Judgment in Medieval Art and Drama* (Kalamazoo: Western Michigan University, 1985). These essays are especially important for understanding the continuity of the *ars* with much of the medieval theology of the Last Judgment.

3. Jonathan Dollimore, *Radical Tragedy: Religion, Ideology, and Power in the Drama of Shakespeare and His Contemporaries* (Brighton: East Anglia Press, 1984); Jonathan Goldberg, *James I and the Politics of Literature: Jonson, Shakespeare, Donne, and Their Contemporaries* (Baltimore: Johns Hopkins University Press, 1983).

4. Arnold Stein, *The House of Death: Messages from the Renaissance* (Baltimore and London: Johns Hopkins University Press, 1986), 3–16.

5. See R. Tuve, *A Reading of George Herbert* (London: Faber & Faber, 1952). Goldberg, 230.

6. See *Renaissance Self-Fashioning* (Chicago: University of Chicago Press, 1980), Intro. See also Introduction to *The Forms of Power and the Power of Forms in the Renaissance* (Norman, Okla.: Pilgrim Books, 1982). Greenblatt, 3–6.

7. Although it is not fashionable among many critics today to see connections between the arts, the sense that there were some major ideas in the Baroque Age that shaped both literature and the visual arts lingers. See especially Joan Webber, *The Eloquent I: Style and Self in Seventeenth-Century Prose* (Madison: University of Wisconsin Press, 1968) and also Frank M. Warnke, *Versions of Baroque: European Literature in the Seventeenth Century* (New Haven and London: Yale University Press, 1972).

8. See Roy C. Strong, *The English Icon: Elizabethan and Jacobean Portraiture* (London: Routledge & Kegan Paul, 1969); also "The Popular Celebration of the Accession Day of Queen Elizabeth," *Journal of the Warburg and Courtauld Institutes* 21 (1958): 86 ff.; and Stephen Orgel and Roy Strong, *Inigo Jones: The Theatre of the Stuart Court,* 2 vols. (London: Sotheby-Parke Bernet, 1973).

9. Goldberg, 239.

10. See Meditation 17, *Devotions upon Emergent Occasions,* ed. J. Sparrow (Cambridge: Cambridge University Press, 1923), 98. I have also used the more recent edition, ed. with commentary by Anthony Raspa (Montreal: McGill-Queen's University Press, 1975). The introduction was especially helpful in its analysis of the nature of Donne's illness, probably a relapsing spotted fever, which was epidemic at the time, and preceded by a bout with a less severe fever.

11. See Victor Turner, *Schism and Continuity in African Society* (Ithaca and London: Cornell University Press, 1974). In chap. 1, "Social Drama and Ritual Metaphors," 25–59, Turner explores relationships between "root metaphors" and change. See also Isaak Walton, *Walton's Lives of Dr. John Donne, Sir Henry Wotton, Mr. Richard Hooker, Mr. George Herbert, and Dr. Robert Sanderson,* rev. ed. by A. H. Bullen (London: George Bell, 1884), 5–81, for the 1639 origin of the familiar romantic opposition between John Donne the Lover and Jack Donne the Priest, a construction modeled upon the Augustinian spiritual journey and essentially based upon Donne's frequent reading and citation of Augustine. The modern editors of Donne's sermons have shown us that Donne cites Augustine more frequently than any of the Fathers.

12. See also Victor Turner, *The Ritual Process* (Chicago: Aldine Press, 1969) and "Passages, Margins, and Poverty: Religious Symbols of *Communitas,* Dramas, and Metaphor" in *Symbolic Action in Human Society* (Ithaca and London: Cornell University Press, 1974), 231–17.

13. *De civitate Dei* (London, 1610), 291.

14. (London, 1612). Other contemporary devotional works that stress the comforting image of existence in the heavenly city include William Bulleyn, *A dialogue bothe pleasainte with pietifull, wherein a goodly regimente againste the fever Pestilence with a consolation and comfort against death* (London, 1594); Urbanus Regius, *The Solace of Sin and Joy of Jerusalem* (London, 1594); Petrus Luccensis, *A Dialogue of Dying Wel* (Antwerp, 1603); John Bradford, *Meditation of Death and A Fruitefull Treatise . . . full of Heavenly Consolation Against the Feare of Death* (n.p., 156?). The above brief list is not meant to be comprehensive, but rather a selected one from the many works within the contemporary devotional books that focus death as the bridge to eternal life.

15. See Rosalie Colie, *Paradoxica Epidemica: The Renaissance Tradition of Paradox* (Princeton: Princeton University Press, 1966) for discussion of Donne's place within the tradition. Donne's own sense of self-conscious, intellectual, para-

doxical, and symbolic vision is probably best described in the first essay of Joan Webber's *The Eloquent I: Style and Self in the Seventeenth Century* cited above. For an overall view of Donne's imagery in his sermons see Winfried Schleiner, *The Imagery of John Donne's Sermons* (Providence, R.I.: Brown University Press, 1970).

16. See Stanley E. Fish, in *Self-Consuming Artifacts* (Chicago: University of Chicago Press, 1966), who argues throughout that Donne, like Augustine, is dialectical rather than merely rhetorical in his approach to poetry. See my essay "Donne's Incarnate Venus," *South Atlantic Quarterly,* Festschrift for Allan H. Gilbert, 71 (October 1972): 504–12, for a discussion of the iconographical theme of the marriage of Mars and Venus, by which Florentine Neoplatonists had understood the reconciliation of aggression and concupiscence. Among the many critical studies of Donne I have found the following most helpful for the poetic questions discussed in this essay: Helen C. White, *The Metaphysical Poets; A Study in Religious Experience* (New York: Macmillan, 1936); Clay Hunt, *Donne's Poetry: Essays in Literary Analysis* (New Haven: Yale University Press, 1954); Richard E. Hughes, *The Progress of the Soul: The Interior Career of John Donne* (New York: William Morrow, 1968). His sermons reflect this shift. It is difficult to argue such a case from sermons with their formal and external demands, but internal evidence is convincing.

17. Meditation 17, *Devotions upon Emergent Occasions,* ed. Raspa, 97.

18. John Carey, *John Donne: Life Mind and Art* (New York: Oxford University Press, 1980), 167–97.

19. R. C. Bald, *John Donne: A Life* (New York and Oxford: Oxford University Press, 1970), 302; Carey, 88, sees Donne's ordination as a capitulation to necessity, not a point of real spiritual commitment. See also Bridget Gellert-Lyons, *Voices of Melancholy: Studies in Literary Treatments of Melancholy in Renaissance England* (New York: Norton, 1975), for suggestions of the rather gloomy atmosphere of the early seventeenth century. Roy C. Strong in *Portraits of Queen Elizabeth* (Oxford Oxford University Press, 1963) also underlines the common view of the disillusionment and increasing corruption of the early seventeenth century; nostalgia finds expression in the posthumous portrait of "Elizabeth and Time and Death."

20. *The Sermons of John Donne,* eds. George Potter and Evelyn Simpson, VIII (Los Angeles: University of California Press, 1955), 92.

21. *Divine Poems,* ed. Helen Gardner (Oxford: Oxford University Press, 1952). All quotations from the *Divine Poems* are from this edition.

22. It is interesting to know that next to Augustine, Donne most frequently cites Bernard of Clairvaux in his sermons. Bernard is responsible for the most widely known interpretation of the erotic imagery of the Song of Songs as an allegory of the love between Christ and his church. See Migne, *Patrologiae Latinae,* CLXXXIII, 794–96, for three spiritual stages of mystical ascent of the soul to God: humility, love, and contemplation, described in the metaphor of kissing the foot, hand, and mouth of God.

23. See Donald L. Guss, *John Donne Petrarchist* (Detroit: Wayne State University Press, 1966) for the definitive discussion of Donne's Petrarchism. Donne's particular brand of Neoplatonism with its rare incarnate focus is also discussed by Helen Gardner in an appendix to her edition of *The Elegies and Songs and Sonnets* (Oxford: Oxford University Press, 1965), 259–65. All quotations from the elegies and songs and sonnets are from this edition. See also, more recently, David Novarr, *The Disinterred Muse* (Ithaca: Cornell Unviersity Press, 1980).

24. Colie, 299.

25. See Dennis Quinn, "Donne's Christian Eloquence," *ELH* 27 (1960), in Stanley E. Fish, *Seventeenth-Century Prose* (New York: Oxford University Press, 1971), 353–74; and Achsah Guibbory, "John Donne and Memory as 'The Art of Salvation,'" *Huntington Library Quarterly* 43 (Autumn 1980): 261–74.

26. John Donne, *The Sermons,* II (Los Angeles and Berkeley: University of California Press, 1955), 73.

27. *The Sermons,* I (1953), 237.

28. For all the published sermons, see *The Sermons of John Donne,* ed. E. M. Simpson and G. R. Potter, 10 vols. (Berkeley: University of California Press, 1953–62); Edward, Lord Herbert of Cherbury, *Autobiography of Edward, Lord Herbert of Cherbury and the History of England Under Henry VIII* (London: Ward, 1970), 6.

29. Arnold Stein, 94–110, organizes his own discussion of Donne around "imagined dyings."

30. See Amy Charles, *A Life of George Herbert* (Ithaca: Cornell University Press, 1977).

31. Bettie Anne Doebler and Retha M. Warnicke, "Sex Discrimination after Death," *Omega The Journal of Death and Dying* 17, no. 4 (1986–87): 313. I am grateful to Professor Warnicke for much of the biographical material in this chapter.

32. Herbert, *Autobiography,* 15, 29, says he moved to London when he was about eighteen; A. Charles, "Mrs. Herbert's Kitchin Booke," *English Literary Renaissance* 4 (1974): 164–73.

33. H. W. Garrod, "Donne and Mrs. Herbert," *The Review of English Studies* 21 (1945): 161–73; and D. Novarr, *The Making of Walton's Lives* (Ithaca: Cornell University Press, 1958), 67.

34. Magdalen Herbert, who moved to Oxford in February, 1599, probably did not meet Donne at Oxford while Wolley was a student (Charles, *Life,* 34), for he earned his B.A. in December 1598. Clark, *Register,* 2–i: 13–18; II 3:211. Professors G. R. Elton, Cambridge University, and J. McConica, University of Toronto, kindly offered comments to Retha Warnicke about the custom of witnessing university rituals and ceremonies; I. Walton, *The Lives of John Donne, Sir Henry Wotton, Richard Hooker, George Herbert, and Robert Sanderson,* Intro. G. Saintsbury (London: Oxford University Press, 1927. Reprt., 1966), 265–67; 335–37.

35. Walton, *Life of John Donne,* 265–67.

36. In Charles, *Life,* 55.

37. Edmund Gosse, *The Life and Letters of John Donne* (London, 1899); see also *Letters to Severall Persons of Honour* (facsimile of original ed., 1651).

38. *The Divine Poems; The Complete Poetry of John Donne,* ed. J. Shawcross (New York: New York University Press, 1968), 113–15; Donne probably did not address "The Primrose" to her. See Shawcross, 140 and 401. This presentation copy of the *"Biathanatos"* is at the Bodleian.

39. S. Johnson, "John Donne and the Virginia Company," *A Journal of English Literary History* 4, (1947): 128; J. E. Jackson, ed., *The Topographical Collections of John Abrey* (London: Devizes, 1862), 226; for the age at marriage, R. Finlay, *Population and Metropolis* (Cambridge: Cambridge University Press, 1981), 139; for his residence in 1617, *Calendar to the Sessions Records; County of Middlesex,* ed. W. Lee Hardy, N. S. (London: C. Radcliffe, 1941), 4: 133–34.

40. Johnson, "John Donne," 131–38.

41. Christopher Marlowe, *Dr. Faustus,* ed. Sylvan Barnet (New York: Signet, 1969). See also Thomas More, "The Four Last Things," *The Works* (London, 1557).

Chapter 10. The Angry Voice of Lamentation and Its Place in the Articulation of Comfort

1. "The Queens Lamentation for *the death of her Son,*" in Zachary Boyd, *The Last Battell of the Soule in Death,* Vol. II (Edinburgh, 1629), sig. A6ᵥ.

2. William Fuller, "The Mourning of Mount Libanon" or the "Temples Teares," London, 1628. Citations to this sermon will be included in the text.

3. Arnold Stein, *The House of Death* (Baltimore and London: Johns Hopkins University Press, 1986), 143.

4. See Barbara Keifer Lewalski, "The Funeral Sermon: The Deceased as Symbol," *Donne's Anniversaries and the Poetry of Praise: The Creation of A Symbolic Mode* (Princeton: Princeton University Press, 1973), 174–215, for discussion of the seventeenth-century funeral sermon with its two-part structure: instruction for the living and praise of the dead. G. W. Pigman III, "Suppressed Grief in Jonson's Funeral Poetry," *English Literary Renaissance* 13, no. 1 (1983), 203–20; also "On My First Son," Ben Jonson: *The Complete Poems,* ed. George Parfit (New Haven: Yale University Press, 1952), 48. Rigorists were generally a small group of those who believed that one should not grieve for the dead because they were now in bliss. For a fuller study see Pigman, *Grief and the English Elegy* (Cambridge: Cambridge University Press, 1985).

5. I am indebted to the *DNB* and my colleague in history Retha M. Warnicke for most of the biographical information on the preachers and their families as well as for research on the relationship between the preachers and women who died.

6. *The Sermons of John Donne,* eds. George Potter and Evelyn Simpson, VIII (Berkeley and Los Angeles: University of California Press, 1956), 61–93, also intro., 39. For a highly poetic and moving structuring of contemporary attitudes toward salvation as the art of memory, see Donne's sermon 2, *The Sermons,* II, 27–94.

7. See for background on twenty-odd funeral sermons published in England for women between 1600 and 1630 the following: "Sex Discrimination after Death: A Seventeenth-Century English Study," *Omega: The Journal of Death and Dying,* 309–20, co-authored with Retha M. Warnicke (Winter 1987). (Supported by ASU grant.)

8. G. W. McClure, Jr., "The Humanist Art of Mourning: Autobiographical Writings on the Loss of a Son in Italian Humanist Thought (1400–1461)," *Renaissance Quarterly* 39 (1986): 440–75.

9. Duncan Harriss, "Tombs, Guide-books and Shakespearean Drama: Death in the Renaissance," *Mosaic* 15, no. 1 (1982) 13–28; Anne Laurence, "Godly Grief: 2nd Responses to" in *Death, Ritual, and Bereavement* (London and New York: Routledge, 1989), 62. See also Ralph Houlbrooke, "Death, Church, and Family in England between the Late Fifteenth and the Early Eighteenth Centuries" in *Death, Ritual, and Bereavement,* ed. Ralph Houlbrooke (London and New York: Routledge, 1989), 34 (25–42).

10. *Ars moriendi* series, Rylands Library, ca. 1450.

11. See also the woodcuts in *ars moriendi* published in Augsburg, 1465, in the Pierpont Morgan Library. Visual reminders of the dance of death abound; see *A Booke of Christian Prayers* (London, 1578), which has engravings by Holbein and Dürer of *memento moris* as page borders for sermon analysis; see W. F. Mitchell, *English Pulpit Oratory from Andrewes to Tillotson:. Study of Its Literary Aspects* (New York: Macmillan, 1932); for Donne's sermons, see Barbara Kiefer Lewalski, "The Funeral Sermon: The Deceased as Symbol," *Donne's Anniversaries and the*

Poetry of Praise: The Creation of A Symbolic Mode (Princeton: Princeton University Press, 1973); Janel Mueller, ed. *Donne's Prebend Sermons* (Cambridge, Mass.: Harvard University Press, 1971); William Mueller, *John Donne Preacher* (Princeton: Princeton University Press, 1962); Winfried Schleiner, *The Imagery of John Donne's Sermons* (Providence, R.I.: Brown University Press, 1970); Lawrence Stapleton, "John Donne: The Moment of the Sermon," *The Elected Circle* (Princeton: Princeton University Press, 1973); and Bettie Anne Doebler, *The Quickening Seed: Death in the Sermons of John Donne* (Salzburg: Institut für Englishe Sprache und Literatur Universität Salzburg, 1974).

12. For various views about death as the major rite of passage, see Philippe Ariès, *The Hour of Our Death*, trans. Helen Weaver (New York: Knopf, 1981); Louis L. Martz, *The Poetry of Meditation* (New Haven: Yale University Press, 1954); Theodore Spencer, *Death in Elizabethan Tragedy* (Cambridge, Mass.: Harvard University Press, 1936); Clare Gittings, *Death, Burial and the Individual in Early Modern England* (London: Croom Helm, 1984);

13. "Magdalen Herbert Danvers and Donne's Vision of Comfort," *George Herbert Journal*, Memorial Volume for Amy Charles (Winter 1988) vol. 10, no. 1: 5–22, co-authored with Retha M. Warnicke. (Supported by ASU grant.)

14. See her life in William Harrison and William Leigh, *Death Advantag'd . . . including "A Brief Discourse,"* intro and eds. Retha M. Warnicke and Bettie Anne Doebler (Delmar, N.Y.: Scholars' Facsimiles & Reprints, 1993), 250.

15. See especially Dame Gardner's Notes on Donne's "Lamentations of Jeremy," *Divine Poems* (Oxford: Clarendon, 1952), and Barbara Kiefer Lewalski, *Protestant Poetics and the Seventeenth-Century Religious Lyric* (Princeton: Princeton University Press, 1979), 69–70.

16. G. W. Pigman, III, *Grief and the English Renaissance Elegy* (Cambridge, Mass.: Harvard University Press, 1985), 36–37.

17. Linda Pollock, *Forgotten Children* (Cambridge, Mass.: Harvard University Press, 1983), chap. 1.

18. Peter Laslett, *The World We Have Lost*, 3d ed.; with added materials (New York: Charles Scribner's Sons, 1984), chap. 4.

19. Steven Ozment, *Magdalene and Balthazar: An Intimate Portrait of Life in 16th-century Europe Revealed in the Letters of a Nuremberg Husband and His Wife* (New York, 1986). The letters are unusually warm and human in their commentary upon their only child, exploring particularly the grief upon his loss.

20. "Boyd," *Dictionary of National Biography*, 1917 ed. Reprint 1921–22.

21. Philip Ziegler, *The Black Death* (New York: Harper & Row, 1969), 230. Anna Montgomery Campbell, *The Black Death and Men of Learning* (New York: AMS Press, 1966). *The Black Death: The Impact of the Fourteenth-Century Plague*, ed. Daniel Williman (Binghamton, N.Y.: Center for Medieval and Early Renaissance Studies, 1982).

22. The important sixteenth- and seventeenth-century descendants of the *ars* tradition include, among many others, the following: Desiderius Erasmus, *Preparation to Deathe* (n.p., 1538); William Perkins, *A Salve for a Sicke Man: or a Treatise Containing the Nature, Differences and Kinds of Death; as also the right manner of dying well, in The Works of that Famous and Worthy Minister of Christ in the University of Cambridge Mr. William Perkins* (London, 1612); Cardinal Bellarmine, *The Art of Dying Well*, trans. Thomas E. Coffin, S.J., 2d ed. (n.p., 1622); Arthur Dent, *The Plaine Mans Path-way to Heaven* (London, 1601); Christopher Sutton, *Disce Mori: Learne to Dye* (London, 1600). The heirs are obviously both Catholic and Protestant (Anglican and Puritan), but the books themselves are re-

markably common in important themes, all emphasizing in some measure the temptations to be overcome on the deathbed and to be prepared for in the devotional life. Philippe Ariès has chronicled the history of childhood in his earlier book, *Centuries of Childhood: A Social History of Family Life*, trans. Robert Baldick (New York: Vintage Books, 1962). He sees little indication of the kind of childhood we know until its very beginnings in the Puritan family of the seventeenth century. Lawrence Stone in *The Family, Sex, and Marriage in England, 1500–1800* (New York: Harper, 1977), who emphasizes the pervasiveness of death and infant mortality in the seventeenth century, nevertheless argues a kind of self-protective lack of feeling on the part of parents. Both Steven Ozment, however, and also G. W. Pigman III see grief over the death of children as a major sorrow in the European Renaissance. For an especially moving essay on mourning a child in Italy, see McClure, Jr., "The Humanist Art of Mourning," 440–74.

23. See also O. B. Hardison, *The Enduring Monument: A Study of the Idea of Praise in Renaissance Literary Theory and Practice* (Chapel Hill: University of North Carolina Press, 1962).

24. Pigman, *Grief and The English Renaissance Elegy*, especially chapters entitled "The Angry Consoler," 11–26; "The Emergence of Compassionate Moderations," 27–39; "Praise and Mourning," 40–51; "The Shift from Anxious Elegy," 52–67.

25. Pigman, *Grief*, 40–46.

26. George Puttenham, *The Arte of English Poesie*, ed. Gladys D. Willcock and Alice Walker (Cambridge: Cambridge University Press, 1936), 47.

27. The *Poems of John Donne*, ed. Herbert J. G. Grierson (Oxford: Clarendon Press, 1912), II, Intro.

28. See, for only one example, *Lachrymae Lacrymarum* (3d ed.), in which Donne published an elegy for Prince Henry.

29. *A Farewell Sermon Preached to the Familie of Prince Henry* (London, 1624).

30. *The Funerals of the High and Mighty Prince Henry* (London, 1613).

31. Barbara Kiefer Lewalski, *Protestant Poetics and the Seventeenth Century Religious Lyric* (Princeton: Princeton University Press, 1979), 8.

32. Among the numerous elegists were Donne and William Campion; examples of the sermons of lamentation are *Lamentations for the Death of the Late Illustrious Prince Henry, Two Sermons*, preached on November 10 and 15, 1612, by his chaplain, Daniel Prince; and such a memorial biography as Robert Alleyn, *The Laudable Life, and Deplorable Death, of our late peerless Prince Henry, 1612*. Other important works are Philip Edmond, "Elegies and other Tracts Issued on the Death of Henry, Prince of Wales. 1612," *Publications of the Edinburgh Bibliographical Society* 6 (1906), 141–58; Elkin Calhoun Wilson, *Prince Henry and English Literature* (Ithaca: Cornell University Press, 1946). See also Ruth C. Wallerstein, *Studies in Seventeenth-Century Poetic* (Madison: University of Wisconsin Press, 1950) for a discussion of elegiac form and major themes.

33. See especially Dame Helen Gardner's Notes on Donne's "Lamentations of Jeremy," *Divine Poems* (Oxford: At the Clarendon Press, 1952), and Lewalski's *Protestant Poetics*, 69–70.

34. William Perkins, *A Salve for a Sicke Man* (Cambridge, 1597), 90–95.

35. See especially his commemorative sermon for Lady Magdalen Danvers, No. 2, *The Sermons of John Donne*, eds. George Potter and Evelyn Simpson (Berkeley and Los Angeles: University of California Press, 1954) VII, 61–93.

36. Gordis, Robert, *Introduction to Song of Songs and Lamentations,* rev. and augm. ed. (New York: KTAV Pub., 1974), 139–40.

37. *Letters,* 77, 86. The one mentioning Frederick was written to Robert Earl of Essex, 13 March 1629; the one concerning her husband to Charles I, 29 December 1632.

38. See also Peter M. Sacks, *The English Elegy* (Baltimore: Johns Hopkins University Press, 1985), 1–37, for discussion of elegiac expression.

Bibliography

Primary Sources

A Booke of Christian Prayers. London: John Daye, 1569. STC 6428.

"A Lamentable Dittie composed upon the death of Robert Lord Devereaux late Earl of Essex." London, ca. 1603.

A Dialogue of Dying Wel. Translated by Richard Verstegen. Antwerp, 1603.

Aemylius, George. *Imagines Mortis.* Cologne, 1555 [1557?].

Alciati, Andrea. *Emblematum liber.* Augsburg, 1531.

Andrews, Launcelot. *The Private Devotions and Manual for the Sick.* London, 1839.

Aquinas, Thomas. "Summa Theologica, *The Basic Writings of St. Thomas Aquinas.* Edited by Anton Pegis. New York: Random, 1945. II-II, 14, 2.

Ars Moriendi. Munich, 1623.

Ars moriendi. Kachelhofen, 1494.

Ars moriendi: the craft for to deye for the helthe of mannes soule. 1491. Oxford, 1891.

Ars Moriendi. Editio Princeps, circa 1450 facsimile edition. Edited by W. Harry Rylands London, 1881.

Ars moriendi. Augsburg, before 1472.

Ars moriendi. Cologne, ca. 1474.

Ars moriendi Here begynneth a lytell treatyse. Westminster: W. Caxton, 1490. STC 789.

Ars moriendi. N.p., ca. 1470.

Ars moriendi. N.p., 1465.

Ars moriendi. N.p., ca. 1740.

Art de bene Mour. Ediciones Torculum Catalana, 1493; Barcelona, 1951.

B. W. *The Maner to Dye Well.* Latin trans. Petrus de Soto. London: R. Jones, 1578. STC 1075.

Bacon, Francis. *Declaration of Practices and Treasons of . . . Essex.* London, 1601. STC 1133.

Barlowe, William. *Sermon Preached at Paules Crosse.* London, 1601. STC 22237.

Bayley, Lewis. *The Practice of Pietie.* 12th ed. London, 1620. STC 1604.

Becon, Thomas. "The Sicke Mannes Salve." *Works.* Edited by Rev. John Ayre IV. Cambridge, 1844.

Becon, Thomas. *The Syke Man's Salve.* London: for John Day, 1561? STC 1757.

Bellarmine, Robert. *The Art of Dying Well.* Translated by E. Coffin of the Society of Jesus, sec. ed. St. Omer, 1622. STC 1838.5.

278

The Betraying of Christ: Iudas in despaire. London, 1598.

Boke named the Royall. London: Wynken de Worde, 1506.

Bosch, Hieronimus. "The Death of the Miser." The National Gallery of Art, Washington, D.C.

Boyd, Zachary. *Four Poems from "Zion's Flowers"; or "Christian Poems for Spiritual Education."* Edited by Gabriel Neil. Glasgow, 1855.

————. *The Last Battell of the Soule in Death.* 2 vols. Edinburgh, 1629. STC 3447.

Camden, William. *The true and royal historie of Elizabeth Queene of England.* London: B. Fisher, 1625. STC 4497.

The Carnall Professor A Little Posthumos Volume brought out by I. T. as a Meditation Preparing the Reader for a Good Death. London, 1634.

Chapman, George. *An epicede or funerall song; on the death of Henry Prince of Wales with the Funeralls, ect.* 2 pts. T.S. [nodham] for J. Budge, 1612, 1613. STC 4974.

The charterhouse with the last will and testament of T. Sutton. 2 pts. G. Eld for T. Thorp, 1614. STC 5056.

Cheke, Sir John. *A royal elegie briefly describing the vertuous reign and happy death of King Edward the sixth.* for H. Holland, 1610. STC 5112.

Chettle, Henry. *Englandes mourning garment: worne here by plaine shepheardes; in memorie of their mistress Elizabeth.* V. S[ims] for T. Millington, [1603]. STC 5121.

Chetwind, Edward. *Votive lachrymae; teares for the loss of prince Henry; a sermon.* W. H[all] for W. Welby, [1612]. STC 5128.

Churchyard, Thomas. *The fortunate farewel to the most forward and noble Earle of Essex, etc.* London: E. Bollifant for W. Wood, 1599. STC 5234.

Clapham, Henoch. *An epixtle discoursing upon the pestilence.* London, 1603. STC 5339.

Cowper, William Bp. *A defiance to death.* London, 1610. STC 5917.

"The Communion of the Sicke," in *The Booke of Common Prayer, and administration of the sacraments and other Rites and ceremonies in the Church of England.* London, 1559. STC 16291.

Cuffe, Henry. *The Differences of the Ages of Man's Life.* London: A. Hatfield, 1607. STC 6103.

Cust, Lionel. *The Master E. S. and the 'Ars Moriendi.'* Oxford, 1898.

"The Daunce and Song of Death," BL Huth 50: 32. 1568–69 AI #480.

Davies, John of Hereford. *Humours heav'n on earth; with the civile warres of death and fortune, etc.* A. I[slip], 1605. STC 6331.

————. *The muses-teares for the losse of Henry Prince of Wales.* G. Eld for J. Wright, 1613. STC 6339.

Day, Richard. *A Booke of Christian Prayers:* Sometimes called "Queen Elizabeth's Prayerbook." London, 1578. STC 6429.

de Fermo, Cardinale. *Ars moriendi: Questa operecta tracta. dellarte del ben morire,* 1787.

Dekker, Thomas. *The Wonderfull Yeare 1603. Wherein is schewed the picture of London, lying sicke of the Plague.* London, 1603. STC 6535.

de Luca, Don Peter. *A Dialogue of Dying Wel.* Translated by Richard Verstegan, from the dedication to Joan Berkley, Abbess of the English Monastery of Nuns of the Order of St. Benedict, in Brussels. Antwerp, 1603. STC 6802.

de Monte Rocher, Guido. *Ars moriendi.* Cologne, 1476.

De morte declamatio. Translated by T. Berthelet. London, 1553.

Dent, Arthur. *The Plaine Mans Path-way to Heaven.* London, 1601. STC 6626.

Devereux, Robert, Earl of Essex. *An Apologie, against those which jealously, and. maliciously, tax him to be the hinderer of the peace and quiet of his country.* London, 1603. STC 6788.

de Voragine, Jacobus. *The Golden Legend.* English translator William Caxton. Westminster: W. Caxton, 1483. STC 24873.

The Doctrynall of Dethe. Westminster: Wynkyn de Worde, 1532. STC 6931.

Donne, John. "Holy Sonnets" in *The Divine Poems,* edited by Helen Gardner. Oxford: Clarendon Press, 1952.

Drouet, Pierre. *A new counsell against the pestilence.* Translated by T. T. J. Charlewood. London: A. Maunsell, [1578]. STC 7241.

Dudley, Lady Jane. *The life, death and actions of the Lady Jane Gray.* London: G. Eld for J. Wright, 1615. STC 7281.

Elyot, Sir Thomas. *A Preseruative Agaynste Deth.* London: T. Bertheleti, 1545. STC 7674.

Erasmus, Desiderius. *Preparation to Deathe, A Boke as Deuout as Eloquent.* No trans. N.p., T. Bertheleti, 1538. STC 10505.

———. *Preparation.* The text of this work also appears in Latin in a book by Erasmus and George Aemylius, *Imagines mortis.* Cologne: A Birckmanni, 155[?]; orig. pub., 1518. Methuen Edition, London, 1905.

———. *A Comfortable Exhortacion against the Chaunces of Death.* London, 1553. STC 10476.7.

Foxe, John. *Acts and Monuments.* Edited by Josiah Pratt, 8 vols. London, 1870.

Foxe, John. *A Brief Exhortation to the Sicke.* London, 1563. STC 11230.

Fuller, William. *The Mourning of Mount Libanon* or *The Temples Teares.* London: T. Harper for R. Bostocke, 1628. STC 11468.

Gardner, J. ed. *Letters and Papers, Foreign and Domestic, of the Reign of Henry VIII.* 1862–1910. Vol. 8 of 21 vols. Vaduz: Kraus, 1965.

Garey, Samuel. *Two Treatises, the first entitled The Food of the Faithfull. The Second Deaths Welcome.* London: Jefferie Chorlton, 1605. STC 11600.

The Grimani Breviary. Reproduced from the illuminated manuscript at the Biblioteca Marciana, Venice. Translated Simon Pleasance, Linda Packer, and Geoffrey Webb; preface Giorgio Ferrari; intro. Mario Salmi; comment. Lorenzo Mellini Woodstock, N.Y.: Overlook Press, 1974. ca. 1972, plates 57 and 58.

Grimani. *Fac.-Simile Delle Minature Contenute nel Brevario Grimani.* E. Sequito in *Fotografia Da Antonio Perini.* 1480–1490; Venezia, 1862, fol. 168.

Guillemand, J. *A Combat betwixt Man and Death or A Discourse against the immoderate apprehension and feare of Death.* London: N. Okes to J. Okes, 1630. STC 12495.

Harrison, William and William Leigh. *Deaths Advantage Little Regarded.* London, 1601. [Includes] Anon., *A Brief Discourse of the Christian Life and Death of Katherin Brettergh.* Intro. and facsimile edition by Retha M. Warnicke and Bettie Anne Doebler; Delmar, N.Y.: Scholars' Facsimiles and Reprints, 1993.

Hastler, Thomas. *An Antidote against the plague. A sermon.* M. Flesher, 1625. STC 12930.

Heale, William. *An apologie for women.* [lmt. W. H.] Oxford: Jos. Barnes, 1609. STC 13014.

Holbein, Hans. *The Dance of Death.* Introduction and notes by James M. Clark. London: Phaidon Press, 1947.

———. *The Dance of Death.* Facs. of woodcuts from the first complete edition: Lyons: [Trechsel fratres?], 1549; London, 1916.

———. *Les Simulacres at historiées faces de la mort.* Lyons: Trechsel fratres, 1538, Facs. Rep.: *Hans Holbein's Todtentanz.* Munich: G. Hirth, 1903.

Hooker, Richard. "The laws of Ecclesiastical Polity." *Works.* Edited by the Rev. John Keble, 7th ed., rev. by the Very Rev. R. W. Church, and the Rev. F. Paget. Oxford, 1888.

The Illustrated Bartsch. Edited by Walter L. Strauss. New York.: Abaris Books, 1978. 80 vols.

Innocent III, *Mirror of Mans Lyfe.* Translated by H. K. London: H. Bynneman, 1576. STC 14092.

Joceline, Elizabeth. *The mothers legacie to her unborn child.* London: J. Haviland for H. Barret, 1624. STC 14624.

Johnson, Richard. *Anglorum lacrimae.* London: for T. Pauier, 1603.

Laurent, Thomas. *Royal Book.* Westminster: Caxton, 1486.

Leighton, Sir William. *The teares or lamentations of a sorrowfull soule.* London: R. Blower, 1613. STC 15433.

Le Livre de bien vivre. Paris: Verard, 1492. English trans., 1503.

Lodge, Thomas. *A treatise of the plague.* London: [V. Sims] for E. White and N.L[ing], 1603. STC 16676.

Loe, Wiliam. *Songs of Sion.* Hamborough, 1620. STC 16690.

Longueval, Charles Bonaventure de, Count de Bucquot. *The lamentable death of the Earle of Bucguoy.* Paris: P. Rocolet, 1621. STC 16798.

London Company of Parish Clerks. *A True Copy of All the Burials and Christenings.* London: for J. Windet, 1603. STC 16739.

London's Mourning Garment. London, 1603. STC 16757.

Luther, Martin. *Every Dayes Sacrifice.* London, 1607. STC 16978.

Montaigne. *The Essays of Montaigne.* 3 vols. Translated by John Florio. Edited by George Saintsbury Rep. 1892–93. New York: AMS Press, Inc., 1967.

More, John. *A Lively Anatomie of Death.* London: G. Simpson for W. Jones, 1596. STC 18073.

More, Thomas. "The Confutation of Tindale." *The Workes of Sir Thomas More—1557.* London: Scholar Press, 1978. 1: 339–852.

———. "The Four Last Things." *The Workes of Sir Thomas More—1557.* London: Scholar Press, 1978. 1: 1–34.

The most true reporte of James Fitz Morrice death, and others the like offenders; with a brief discourse of Rebellion. London, 1579.

Moulin, Peter. *The Comfort of a Communicant.* London, 1623.

Natalibus, *Catalogus Sanctorum.* Venice, 1506.

Ozment, Steven. *Magdalena and Balthazar: An Intimate Portrait of Life in 16th*

Century Europe Revealed in the Letters of a Nuremberg Husband and Wife. New York: Simon and Schuster, 1986.

Perkins, William. *A Salve for a Sicke Man.* Cambridge, 1595. "A Salve for a Sicke Man. Or a Treatise Containing the Nature, Differences and Kinds of Death; as also the right manner of dying well." *The Workes of that Famous and Worthy Minister of Christ in the University of Cambridge M. W. Perkins.* London: J. Legatt, 1603. STC 19647.

Petrarca. Venice, 1497.

Petrarcke, Fraunces. "Death dyd take my love and ioye awaye." *The Tryumphes of Fraunces Petrarcke.* Translated by Henrye Parker. London: J. Cawood, 1565. STC 19811.

Picus the Elder, Earle of Mirandula. *Epistle of St. Bernard* and *Certaine Rules of A Christian Life.* N.p., 1615.

Pricke, Robert. *A verie godlie and learned sermon, treating of mans mortalitie.* [Ed.] (R. Allen.) London: T. Creede, 1608. STC 20338.

Raleigh, Sir Walter. *History of the World.* Vol. 5 of 7 vols. *The Works of Sir Walter Raleigh.* 1829. New York: Bart Franklin, 1964.

Roper, William. *The Life of Sir Thomas More.* In *Two Early Tudor Lives: The Life and Death of Cardinal Wolsey, by George Cavendish and The Life of Sir Thomas More by William Roper,* edited by Richard Sylvester and David P. Harding. New Haven: Yale University Press, 1962.

Scott, Thomas. *Robert Earle of Essex, His Ghost sent from Elizian.* London, 1624.

A Sermon Preached at Flitton at the Funerall of the Right Honourable Henrie Earle of Kent, the sixteenth of March, 1614. London, 1615.

Shakespeare, William. *The Riverside Shakespeare.* Edited by G. Blakemore Evans. Boston: Houghton Mifflin Co., 1974.

———. *King Lear.* Edited by Alfred Harbage. Baltimore: Penguin, 1958.

———. *Shakespeare's Sonnets.* Edited by Stephen Booth. New Haven: Yale University Press, 1977.

Simpson, Evelyn, and George Potter, eds. *The Sermons of John Donne.* 10 vols. Berkeley: University of Califoria Press, 1957.

Somner, William. *The Frontispiece of the Kings Book.* "The In-security of Princes. Considered in an occasional Meditation upon the King's late Sufferings and Death, 1650."

Speculum bonae mortis. N.p., 1694.

Spenser, Edmund. "The Faerie Queene." *Works of Edmund Spenser.* Vol. 1 of 9 vols. A Variorum Edition, eds. Greenlaw et al. Baltimore: Johns Hopkins University Press, 1932.

Sutton, Christopher. *Disce Mori: Learne to Dye.* London: J. Wolfe, 1600. STC 23474.

Thorne, Henry. *Phisicke for the Soule.* London: H. Denham, 1568.

Threnoikos. Hpnvolkos. *The house of mourning. Delivered in XLVII sermons, preached at funeralls* by D. Teatly M. Day R. Sibbs T. Taylor. And other revered divines. [Ed.] (H.W.). London: for J. Davson for R.M.(abb.); sold by P. Nevill, 1640 (1638.) STC 24048.

Tourneur, Cyril. *A funeral poeme. Upon the death of sir Francis Vere.* London: [J. Windet] for E. Edgar, 1609. STC 24148.

The Veil. Or the godly man's Guide to Glory. Wherein is briefly comprised a short view of the glorious estate of Gods Saints in the Kingdome of Heaven. Together with the Meanes to obtaine, the Markes to know, and the Motiues to vrge vs to prepare our selues for Christ, before our soules be vnbodied, lest Heauens gate be shut against vs. London, 1628.

Voragine, Jacobus. *Legendario.* Venice, 1499.

Walton, Isaak. *Life of John Donne.* London, 1658.

Warren, Florence ed. "The Dance of Death." In ed. *Mss. Ellesmere 26/A.13. And B. M. Lansdowne 699, Collated with the Other Extant Mss.* Early English Text Society OS, no. 181, London, 1931.

Secondary Sources

Allen, Don Cameron. *Mysteriously Meant: The Rediscovery of Pagan Symbolism and Allegorical Interpretation in the Renaissance.* Baltimore: Johns Hopkins Press, 1970.

Alpers, Svetlana "Is Art History?" *Daedalus* 106, no. 3 (1977): 1–13.

Altick, Richard. "Hamlet and the Odor of Mortality." *Shakespeare Quarterly* 5 (1954).

Ariès, Philippe. *Centuries of Childhood.* Translated by Robert Baldick. New York: Vantage, 1962.

———. *The Hour of Our Death.* Translated by Helen Weaver. New York: Knopf, 1981.

Atkinson. David W. "The English *ars moriendi:* Its Protestant Transformation." *Renaissance and Reformation/Renaissance et Re'forme* 6 (n.s.), VI, no. 1; 18 (o.s.), no. 1 (1982).

Bald, R. C. *John Donne, A Life.* New York: Oxford University Press, 1970.

Banker, J. "Mourning a Son: Childhood and Paternal Love in the Consolateria of Giannozzo Manetti." *History of Childhood Quarterly: The Journal of Psychohistory* 3 (1976): 351 – 62.

Beaty, Nancy Lee. *The Craft of Dying: A Study in the Ars Moriendi in England.* New Haven: Yale University Press, 1970.

Bergeron, David. *English Civic Pageantry.* London: Edward Arnold, 1971.

Bevington, David M. S. *Action Is Eloquence: Language of Gesture.* Cambridge, Mass.: Harvard University Press, 1984.

———, ed. *Homo, Memento Finis: the Iconography of the Just Judgment in Medieval Art and Drama.* Kalamazoo: Western Michigan University Press, 1980.

Bloomfield, Morton W. "The Elegy and the Elegaic Mode: Praise and Alienation." In *Renaissance Genres,* edited by Barbara Kiefer Lewalski. Cambridge, Mass.: Harvard University Press, 1986.

Boase, T. S. R. *Death in the Middle Ages: Mortality, Judgement, and Remembrance.* New York: McGraw-Hill, 1972.

Bush, Douglas. *Prefaces to Renaissance Literature.* New York: Norton, 1965.

Carey, John. *John Donne: Life, Mind, and Art.* New York: Oxford University Press, 1980.

Cavell, Stanley. *Must We Mean What We Say?* Cambridge: Cambridge University Press, 1976.

Chambers, K. *The Elizabethan Stage*. Oxford: Clarendon Press, 1923.

Chappuys, Gabriel. *Figures de la Bible*. Lyon, 1582.

Chastel, Andre. *The Age of Humanism: Europe, 1480–1530*. Translated by Katherine M. Delavenay and E. M. Gwyer. London: Thames and Hudson, 1963.

Chew. *The Virtues Reconciled: An Iconographic Study*. Toronto: University of Toronto Press, 1947.

Clark, James M. *The Dance of Death in the Middle Ages and the Renaissance*. Publications 86. Glasgow: Glasgow University Press, 1950.

Clemens, Wolfgang. *A Commentary on Shakespeare's Richard III*. Translated by Jean Bonheim. London: Methuen, 1968.

Cole, Susan Letzer. *The Absent One: Mourning Ritual, Tragedy, and the Performance of Ambivalence*. University Park: Pennsylvania State University Press, 1985.

Colie, Rosalie L. *Paradoxica Epidemica: The Renaissance Tradition of Paradox*. Princeton: Princeton University Press, 1966.

Comper, Frances M. M., ed. "The Craft to Know Well to Die." In *The Book of the Craft of Dying*. 1917; New York: Arno, 1977.

Cook, Ann Jennalie. *The Privileged Playgoer of Shakespeare's London 1576–1642*. Princeton: Princeton University Press, 1981.

Cope, Jackson I. *The Theater and the Dream: From Metaphor to Form in Renaissance Drama*. Baltimore: Johns Hopkins University Press, 1973.

Davis, Natalie Zemon. "Holbein's *Pictures of Death* and the Reformation at Lyons." *Studies in the Renaissance* 3 (1956): 97–130.

Doebler, Bettie Anne. *The Quickening Seed: Death in the Sermons of John Donne*. Edited by James Hogg. Salzburg Studies in English Literature, no. 30. Salzburg, Austria: Institut für Englische Sprauche und Literatur, 1974.

Doebler, John. *Shakespeare's Speaking Pictures: Studies in Iconic Imagery*. Albuquerque: University of New Mexico Press, 1974.

Driver, Tom F. *The Sense of History in Greek and Shakespearean Drama*. New York: Columbia University Press, 1960.

Edgerton, Samuel Y., Jr. "Maniera and the Mannaia: Decorum and Decapitation in the Sixteenth Century." In *The Meaning of Mannerism,* edited by Franklin W. Robinson and Stephen G. Nichols, Jr. Hanover, N.H.: University Press of New England, 1972.

Edwards, Ralph and L. G. G. Ramsey, eds. *The Tudor Period: 1500–1603*. London: Rainbird, McLean, 1956.

Elton, William. *Lear and the Gods*. San Marino, Calif.: Huntington Library, 1966.

Fallon, Stephen M. "Milton's Sin and Death: The Ontology of Sin and Death in *Paradise Lost*," *ELR* 17 (1987): 329–50.

Felt, Shirley Ann. "Ars Moriendi and Donne." Diss. Riverside, 1975.

Fineman, Joel. "The Structure of Allegorical Desire." In *Allegory and Representation,* selected papers from the English Institute, 1979–80, edited by Stephen J. Greenblatt. Baltimore and London: Johns Hopkins University Press, 1981.

Fish, Stanley, *Is There A Text In This Class?: The Authority of Interpretive Communities*. Cambridge, Mass.: Harvard University Press, 1980.

———. *Surpris'd by Sin: The Reader in Paradise Lost*. Berkeley: University of California Press, 1967.

Fraser, Russell A. *Shakespeare's Poetics in Relation to King Lear.* London: Routledge & Kegan Paul, 1962.

Freeman, Rosemary. *English Emblem Books.* New York: Octagon Books, 1966.

Frye, Roland Mushat. "Ladies, Gentlemen, and Skulls: *Hamlet* and the Iconographic Traditions." *Shakespeare Quarterly* 30, no. 1 (1979): 15–28.

————. *The Renaissance Hamlet: Issues and Responses in the Sixteenth-Century.* Princeton: Princeton University Press, 1984.

————. *Shakespeare and Christian Doctrine.* Princeton: Princeton University Press, 1963.

Gallagher Philip J., "'Real or Allegorie': The Ontology of Sin and Death in *Paradise Lost*," *ELR* 17 (1987): 317–35.

Geertz, Clifford. *The Interpretation of Cultures.* New York: Basic Books, 1973.

Gellert-Lyons, Bridget. "The Iconography of Melancholy in the Graveyard scene of *Hamlet*." *Studies in Philology* 57, no. 1, 1970.

————. *The Voices of Melancholy: Studies in Literary Treatments of Melancholy in Renaissance England.* London: Routledge & Kegan Paul, 1971.

Gilman, Ernest B. *The Curious Perspective: Literary and Pictorial Wit in the Seventeenth Century.* New Haven: Yale University Press, 1978.

Gittings, Clare. *Death, Burial, and the Individual in Early Modern England.* London: Croom Helm, 1984.

Goldberg, Jonathan. *James I and the Politics of Literature: Jonson, Shakespeare, Donne, and their Contemporaries.* Baltimore: Johns Hopkins University Press, 1983.

Greenblatt, Stephen. *The Forms of Power and the Power of Forms in the English Renaissance.* Norman, Okla.: Pilgrim Books, 1982.

————. *Sir Walter Ralegh: The Renaissance Man and His Roles.* New Haven: Yale University Press, 1973.

————. *Renaissance Self-Fashioning.* Chicago: University of Chicago Press, 1980.

Halewood, William H. *The Poetry of Grace: Reformation Themes and Structures in English Seventeenth-Century Poetry.* New Haven: Yale University Press, 1970.

Hallstead, R. N. "Idolatrous Love: A New Approach to Othello." *Shakespeare Quarterly* 19: 107–24.

Hankins, John E. "The Pains of the Afterworld: Fire, Wind, and Ice in Milton and Shakespeare." *PMLA* 71 June (1956).

Hardison, O. B. *The Enduring Monument: A Study of the Idea of Praise in Renaissance Theory and Practice.* Chapel Hill: University of North Carolina Press, 1962.

Harrison, G. B., ed. *The Letters of Queen Elizabeth I.* New York: Funk and Wagnalls, 1935.

————. *The Life and Death of Robert Devereux, Earl of Essex.* London: Cassel, 1937.

Hercules an Scheidewege und andere antike Bildstoffe in der neuren Kunst. Leipzig: B. G. Teubner, 1930.

Here begynneth a lityll tretise spekynge of the arte and crafte to knowe well to dye. Westminster: Caxton 1490.

Hind, A. M. "The Tudor Period." *Engraving in England in the Sixteenth and Seventeenth Centuries*. Cambridge: Cambridge University Press, 1952.

Howard, D. R. "Hamlet and the Contempt of the World." *South Atlantic Quarterly* 18 (1959): 167–75.

Huizinga, Johan. *The Waning of the Middle Ages*. London: E. Arnold, 1924.

James, Mervyn. "At a Crossroads of the Political Culture: The Essex Revolt, 1601." In *Society, Politics, and Culture,* edited by Mervyn James. Cambridge: Cambridge University Press, 1986.

Jorgensen, Paul A. *Lear's Self Discovery*. Berkeley: University of California Press, 1967.

Kantorowicz, Ernst H. *The King's Two Bodies: A Study in Medieval Political Theology*. Princeton: Princeton University Press, 1957.

Katzenellenbogen, Adolf. *Allegories of the Virtues and Vices in Medieval Art, from Early Christian Times to the Thirteenth Century*. 1939. Translated by Alan J. P. Crick. New York: Norton, 1964.

Koller, Kathrine. "Art, Rhetoric, and Holy Dying in the *Faerie Queene*. With Special Reference to the Despair Canto." *Studies in Philology* 61 (1964): 128–39.

———. "Falstaff and the Art of Dying." *MLN* (15 June 1945): 383–86.

Langston, Beach. "Marlowe's Faustus and the *Ars Moriendi* Tradition." In *A Tribute to George Coffin Taylor,* edited by Arnold Williams. Chapel Hill: University of North Carolina Press, 1952.

Lewalski, Barbara Kiefer. *Donne's Anniversaries and the Poetry of Praise: the Creation of A Symbolic Mode*. Princeton: Princeton University Press, 1973.

———. *Paradise Lost and the Rhetoric of Literary Forms*. Princeton: Princeton University Press, 1985.

———. *Protestant Poetics and the Seventeenth-Century Religious Lyric*. Princeton: Princeton University Press, 1979.

Lewis, C. S. *Preface to Paradise Lost*. New York: Oxford University Press, 1961.

Llewelleyn, Nigel. *The Art of Death: Visual Culture in the English Death Ritual ca. 1500–ca 1800*. London: Victoria and Albert Museum with Reaktion Books, 1991.

Lucas, D. W., ed. *The Poetics*. Oxford: Clarendon Press, 1968.

McClure, George W. "The Art of Mourning: Autobiographical Writing on the Loss of a Son in Italian Humanist Thought 1400–1461." *Renaissance Quarterly* 39, no. 3 (1983): 440–75.

McCutcheon, Elizabeth. "Denying the Contrary: More's Use of Litotes in the *Utopia*." *Essential Articles for the Study of Thomas More*. Edited by R. S. Sylvester and G. Marc'hadour. Hamden, Conn.: Creton Books, 1977.

Marcus, Leah S. *Childhood and Cultural Despair*. Pittsburgh: University of Pittsburgh Press, 1978.

Martz, Louis L. *The Poetry of Meditation*. New Haven: Yale University Press, 1954.

Mitchell, W. Frazier. *English Pulpit Oratory from Andrews to Tillotson: Study of Its Literary Aspects*. New York: Macmillan, 1932.

Morris, Harry. "Hamlet as a *Memento Mori* Poem." *PMLA* 85 (November 1970).

Muller, Janel, ed. *Donne's Prebend Sermons*. Cambridge, Mass.: Harvard University Press, 1971.

Myrick, Kenneth O. "The Theme of Damnation in Shakespearean Tragedy." *Studies in Philology* 38 (April 1941): 221–45.

Neale, John Ernest. *Queen Elizabeth I.* Garden City, N.Y.: Anchor, 1957.

Nichols, John, ed. *The Progresses and Public Processions of Queen Elizabeth.* 3 vols. London, 1823.

Nichols, Stephen G., Jr. "The Poetics of Historicism: Recent Trends in Medieval Literary Study." *Medievalia et Humanistica: Studies in Medieval and Renaissance Culture* 8 (1977): 77–101.

O'Connor, Sister Mary Catharine. *The Art of Dying Well: The Development of the Ars Moriendi.* Columbia University Studies in English and Comparative Literature. New York: Columbia University Press, 1942.

Orgel, Stephen. *The Illusion of Power: Political Theater in the English Renaissance.* Berkeley: University of California Press, 1975.

Panofsky, Erwin. *Early Netherlandish Painting: Its Origins and Character.* 2 vols. Cambridge, Mass.: Harvard University Press, 1953.

———. *Idea: A Concept in Art Theory.* Translated by Joseph J. S. Peake. Columbia: University of South Carolina Press, 1968.

Passavant, J. D. *Le Peintre-Graveur.* Leipzig: Rudolph Weigel, 1860.

Patterson, Annabel, ed. and intro. *John Milton.* London and New York: Longman, 1992.

Peterson, Douglas L. "John Donne's *Holy Sonnets* and the Anglican Doctrine of Contrition." In *Essential Articles for the Study of John Donne's Poetry,* edited by John R. Roberts. Hamden, Conn.: Archon Books, 1975.

———. *Time, Tide, and The Tempest.* San Marino, Calf.: The Huntington Library, 1973.

Pigman, G. W. III. *Grief and The English Renaissance Elegy.* Cambridge: Cambridge University Press, 1985.

Pollock, Linda A. *Forgotten Children: Parents-Child Relations from 1500 to 1900.* Cambridge: Cambridge University Press, 1983.

Puttenham, George. *The Arte of English Poesie.* Edited by Gladys Doidge Willcock and Alice Walker. Cambridge: Cambridge University Press, 1970.

Radzinowicz, Mary Ann. *Milton's Epic and the Book of Psalms.* Princeton: Princeton University Press, 1989.

———. "The Politics of *Paradise Lost.*" In *The Politics of Discourse,* edited by Kevin Sharpe and Stephen N. Zwicker. Berkeley and Los Angeles: University of California Press, 1987.

———. "Psalms and the Representations of Death in *Paradise Lost.*" *Milton Studies* 23 (1988): 133–44.

Reno, R. H. "Hamlet's Quintessence of Dust." *Shakespeare Quarterly* 7 (1961): 103–17.

Rèau, Louis. *Iconographie de l'art chrétien.* Paris: Presses Universitaires de France, 1957.

Ribner, Irving. *Patterns in Shakespearian Tragedy.* New York: Barnes and Noble, 1960.

Ribner, Rhoda M. "Chapman's *Ovids Banquet of Sence* and the Emblematic Tradition." *Studies in the Renaissance* 17 (1970): 233–58.

Rose, Mary Beth, ed. *Women in the Middle Ages and the Renaissance: Literary and Historical Perspectives.* Syracuse, N.Y.: Syracuse University Press, 1986.

Ross, L. J. "The Use of a 'Fit-Up' Booth in *Othello.*" *Shakespeare Quarterly* 7, no. 4 (1961): 359–70.

Rushforth, G. McN. *Medieval Christian Imagery.* Oxford: Oxford University Press, 1937.

Sacks, Peter M. *The English Elegy: Studies in the Genre from Spenser to Yeats.* Baltimore: Johns Hopkins University Press, 1985.

Schleiner, Winfried. *The Imagery of John Donne's Sermons.* Providence, R.I.: Brown University Press, 1970.

Schoenbaum, Samuel. *William Shakespeare: A Compact Documentary Life.* New York: Oxford University Press, 1977.

Shakespeare, William. "Othello." *The Variorum.* Edited by Horace Howard Furness.1886; Philadelphia: Lippincott, 1908.

———. *Macbeth.* Edited by Alfred Harbage. The Pelican Shakespeare. Baltimore: Penguin, 1956.

———. *The Variorum Shakespeare.* Edited by Howard Furness. Philadelphia and London: Lippincott, 1908.

Shrewsbury, John F. D. *A History of Bubonic Plague in the British Isles.* Cambridge: Cambridge University Press, 1970.

Smith, Jonathan Z. "Myth, Story, and History." Interpretation of Culture Lecture, Arizona State University, 1981.

———. *Map Is No Territory: Studies in the History of Religions.* Zurich: Brill, 1974.

Smith, Lacey Balwin. "English Treason Trials and Confessions in the Sixteenth-Century." *Journal of the History of Ideas* 15, no. 4 (1954): 471–98.

Snyder, Susan. "The Left-Hand of God: Despair in Medieval and Renaissance Tradition." *Studies in the Renaissance* 12 (1965): 18–59.

Spencer, Theodore. *Death in Elizabethan Tragedy.* Cambridge, Mass.: Harvard University Press, 1936.

Spinrad, Phoebe. *The Summons of Death on the Renaissance Stage.* Columbus: Ohio State University Press, 1987.

Spivak, Bernard. *Shakespeare and the Allegory of Evil: The History of a Metaphor in Relation to His Major Villains.* New York: Columbia University Press, 1958.

Stapleton, Lawrence. *The Elected Circle.* Princeton: Princeton University Press, 1973.

Steele, Robert and Oliver. "Introduction" to Edmund Spenser. *The Faerie Queene,* Books One and Two. New York: Odyssey, 1952.

Stein, Arnold. *The House of Death: Messages from the English Renaissance.* Baltimore: Johns Hopkins University Press, 1986.

Storer, Thomas. *The Life and Death of Thomas Wolsey Cardinall.* London, 1599.

Strachey, Lytton. *Elizabeth and Essex in Tragic History.* New York: Harcourt, 1928.

Strong, Roy C. *The Cult of Elizabeth: Elizabethan Portraiture and Pageantry.* London: Thames and Hudson, 1977.

———. *The English Icon, Eizabethan and Jacobean Portraiture.* London: Routledge, 1968.

———. *Portraits of Queen Elizabeth I*. Oxford: Clarendon, 1963.

Tawney, R. H. *Business and Politics under James I*. Cambridge: Cambridge University Press, 1958.

Thon, Peter. "Bruegel's *Triumph of Death Reconsidered*." *Renaissance Quarterly* 11, no. 3 (1968): 289–99.

Tillotson, Geoffrey. "Othello and the Alchemist at Oxford in 1610." *The Times Literary Supplement* 20 (July 1933): 494.

Tillyard, E. M. W. *The Elizabethan World-Picture*. London: Chatto and Windus, 1967.

Turner, Victor. *The Ritual Process: Structure and Anti-Structure*. Ithaca: Cornell University Press, 1977.

Tuve, Rosemund. *Allegorical Imagery: Some Books and Their Imagery*. Princeton: Princeton University Press, 1966.

———. *Elizabethan and Metaphysical Imagery: Renaissance Poetic and Twentieth-Century Critics*. Chicago: University of Chicago Press, 1947.

Wallerstein, Ruth. *Seventeenth-Century Poetics*. Madison: University of Wisconsin Press, 1950.

Warnicke, Retha M. *The Rise and Fall of Anne Boleyn*. Cambridge: Cambridge University Press, 1989.

Webber, Joan. *Contrary Music: The Prose Style of John Donne*. Madison: University of Wisconsin Press, 1963.

———. *The Eloquent I: Style and Self in Seventeenth-Century Prose*. Madison: University of Wisconsin Press, 1968.

White, Helen C. *English Devotional Literature 1600–1640*. University of Wisconsin Studies in Language and Literature, no. 29. Madison: University of Wisconsin Press, 1931.

———. *Tudor Books of Devotion*. Madison: University of Wisconsin Press, 1951.

Wilson, Frank Percy. *The Plague in Shakespeare's London*. Oxford: Clarendon Press, 1927.

Wittriech, Joseph A. *Visionary Poetics*. San Marino, Calif.: Huntington Library, 1979.

Wright, Louis B. *Middle-Class Culture in Elizabethan England*. Chapel Hill: University of North Carolina Press, 1935.

Wymer, Rowland. *Suicide and Despair in Jacobean Drama*. Brighton, Sussex: Harverster, 1986.

Yates, Frances. *Astraea: The Imperial Theme in the Sixteenth Century*. London: Routledge, 1975.

Zeigler, Philip. *The Black Death*. New York: John Day, 1969.

Index

291